Mafeking

A Victorian Legend

———

BRIAN GARDNER

Harcourt, Brace & World, Inc.

New York

First American edition 1967
Library of Congress Catalog Card Number: 67-19197
Printed in the United States of America

Contents

The choice therefore lies between an attempt at critical inquiry and thought, and the mere babble of blurred reminiscences and fanciful interpretations. The foremost task of honest history is to discredit and drive out its futile or dishonest varieties.

SIR LEWIS NAMIER

Illustrations

Between pages 182 *and* 183

One hundred days of siege
Baden-Powell sketching
Queuing for rations
Starving Africans
Trial
Death-warrant
Africans shooting dogs
The taking of Pretoria
Colonel Bryan Mahon
Sisters Craufurd and Buchan
The march-past
After Eloff's attack
Field-Marshal Lord Roberts
Leaving for a world tour
Baden-Powell posing for his photograph

Maps

Preface

My idea in writing this book was twofold: first, to tell the story of a famous military drama; second, to investigate why that event was so important to its generation—for the Relief of Mafeking brought a greater national communion than any similar occasion in British history till that time. The former had been done before, but without much attention being paid to the latter, the answer to which, as might have been expected, was found more in the final eddies of the Victorian Age in Britain than in Mafeking itself. As for the military drama, I discovered before I even began to write that the facts did not always support the legend.

On points of fact each of the biographies of the central character (some twenty works and booklets, all more or less eulogistic), and each of the books referring to the event at any length, have been contradictory at some point to one or more of the others. Thus I have tried when possible to rely on original sources—on diaries, reports, letters, and so on—and primary material now available in a number of books. Previous accounts have relied to a very great extent on the writings and official diary of Baden-Powell himself. I have drawn rather more on the papers of others. In particular, I owe a debt to the correspondent of *The Times* in Mafeking during the defence, Angus Hamilton; and to Benjamin Weil, the military contractor in the town.

Volume III of *The Official History of the South African War* is referred to throughout as 'the *Official History*'; Volume IV of *The Times History of the War in South Africa* as 'the *Times History*'; and William Hillcourt's biography of Baden-Powell as the 'official biography'. 'B.M.' refers to the British Museum, 'N.A.M.' to the National Army Museum, and 'P.R.O.' to the Public Record Office. Unless otherwise stated the extracts and quotes from newspaper correspondents are from their accounts and diaries listed in the Bibliography, and not from their dispatches. Details of books are given in the footnotes only for secondary sources not listed in the

Bibliography. Spelling of place-names is that in general use at the time. For constructive advice, comment and help at various stages I thank : Mrs C. S. Cassidy, Mr Willian Hillcourt, Mr Rayne Kruger, Mr Kenneth Parker and Wing Commander R. F. Pemberton. I am also grateful to various staff of the British Museum at Bloomsbury and Colindale, the Historical Manuscripts Commission, the London Library, the National Army Museum, the Public Record Office, the Rhodes House Library at Oxford, and the Rhodes University Library, Grahamstown. I am grateful to Lord Salisbury for permission to reproduce a personal letter by Lady Gwendoline Cecil; to the Controller of H.M. Stationery Office for Crown Copyright records, including Mafeking siege material, 1899–1900; and to the executors of Viscountess Milner and Messrs John Murray. I must stress that I alone am responsible for all expressions of fact and comment in the book.

B.G.

1. Prologue

It was the age of the Great Queen. People of all colours, religions and races, who lived on more than a quarter of the earth's surface, owed allegiance to the grumpy, Germanic monarch of the island off the coast of Europe. Britain was at the peak of her power. Her sons were administrators and merchants and lawyers and missionaries in every part of the globe. Her technical skill and her industrial might, dating from her early start in the industrial revolution, were acknowledged by all. Her Navy was the mightiest and most feared instrument of power in the world. Her people were proud.

In Britain, nationalism elsewhere was looked upon with suspicion, condescension, and occasionally with derision. British politicians harangued against nationalism abroad; British statesmen contrived to control it by a sophisticated system of balances; British expeditionary forces put it down with ruthlessness and efficiency; British battleships curbed it for a time, although seldom if ever entirely extinguishing it, by their mere appearance. The British themselves, however, swollen during a century by a vast new middle class which was steadily multiplying itself, were the most nationalistic and patriotic people in the world. They had won many great achievements and they enjoyed several fine qualities of character: they were modest about neither. In an age when millions lived in shabby streets, working in the warehouses and factories which produced the exports for which the world had an apparently unlimited demand, the Empire meant romance and colour. The bank-clerks, the shop-assistants, the works' managers, the small-time *rentiers*, the minor civil servants, who lived monotonous lives in the new suburbs that sprawled around the old cities, had developed a vast appetite for stories relating the mysteries of the East, music-hall songs of indomitable British soldiers, and all news of the Empire upon which, as it was frequently said, the sun never set. It was comforting to feel a part, however small, of something dramatic and important, and they were confident that it was right that the Union Jack should fly beside the Taj Mahal and the waters of the Nile; for were the British not 'natural rulers'; were they not the one race in the world who understood 'pluck' and 'grit', as the great Wellington had shown and as countless magazines and novels extolled?

It had been the 'British Century'. Now another century, the twentieth, had begun. It was not five months old. Was it a century that was to be dominated by Britain as the previous one had been? One could hardly imagine otherwise, but there was no escaping the fact that the Americans and the Germans did appear to be overtaking Britain in industrial power.

Since 1895 the supremacy of Conservative Governments had brought an aggressive and 'jingoistic' element into foreign affairs, not so much through arrogance as because Britain felt her superiority threatened; since that date Joseph Chamberlain had been Colonial Secretary, and he had made the office unusually important. His theme had been to strengthen the bonds between Britain and the self-governing colonies, to secure for the Empire its share of new lands, to develop the resources of the Empire, and to increase Empire trade. His insistence on the importance of the Empire suited the public mood, which was stimulated by the press, by writers like Rudyard Kipling, and by statesmen like Cecil Rhodes. The Prime Minister was Lord Salisbury, whose great work had been to divide up Africa with other powers without a resort to arms. But could one be absolutely certain about Britain's pre-eminent position and, above all, about her prestige? For something most extraordinary, most unexpected, and most unaccountable had occurred. British power had been flouted in a faraway area of Africa. Two 'absurd little republics', the South African Republic (commonly known as the Transvaal) and the Orange Free State, had gone to war with the greatest empire the world had ever seen. In itself there was nothing untoward in that. The Boers had given trouble before, and in a vast and scattered Empire such things were bound to happen from time to time. It had happened in New Zealand. It had happened in West Africa. It had happened in India. It had happened in the Sudan. This time, of course, it was white men, not natives, who had taken up arms against the *Pax Britannica*; but they were only poor farmers and had no troops worth noticing, or so it was said.

The extraordinary thing was that those irritating and arrogant nationalists in South Africa had not been firmly and thoroughly defeated in a few months as had been fully expected. On the contrary, they had actually invaded British territory and had caused a number of humiliating reverses. The lion's tail had been most painfully twisted. All this had been to the amusement of most of the rest of the world, and in some European countries it had been greeted with unconcealed joy. The question seemed to be : Is British power on the wane at last?

It was worrying.

In some odd way, for several months the whole question seemed to have revolved around the fate of the besieged garrison of a remote frontier town that had previously been among the most insignificant of the entire Empire : a place called Mafeking.

*

It was the third week in May, and the weather had been cool and the skies dark and overcast. As the clouds passed above, the English countryside, fresh after a fine spring, was bathed for brief moments in pools of sunlight and washed with gentle showers. In the cities, the great houses and the factory chimneys and the dark slums, with their rows upon rows of chimney-pots, all spouted forth columns of smoke into a dirty sky.

News from the war was frustrating. A considerable army had been shipped to South Africa, and the Boers as well as the British had suffered reverses, but for some reason the generals seemed unable to bring the war to a speedy conclusion. If Mafeking were to fall it would be an unbearable blow.

With remarkable frequency, messages from the beleaguered town reached the world outside. Only the previous morning one had appeared in the newspapers : 'One or two small field guns are shelling the town. Nobody cares.' It was typical, everyone was certain, of the nonchalant, British courage of the commander of the garrison— Colonel Robert Baden-Powell. Anyone who knew anything about the British would realize that the more gross Baden-Powell's understatement, the worse the conditions really were.

Baden-Powell's 'plucky', almost gay, messages had been printed throughout the world. They had created a great impression. The more they had insisted that all was well in Mafeking, the worse the world had been convinced it really was. No one considered it odd that a besieged township (before the widespread use of radio) had been able to communicate openly with the rest of the world. More believable reports had come from elsewhere. One, that same week, from the town of Lourenço Marques, in Portuguese territory, had said that the British in Mafeking had lost fifty men killed. A report from Reuters' correspondent in Pretoria, the capital of the Transvaal, had said: 'It is officially announced that the British relief column has been repulsed with great loss.' A report in the *Cape Argus*, to the effect that Mafeking had been entered by a Boer force, had been widely quoted around the world: 'The garrison then opened fire from the holes and burrows in which they live, killing and wounding seventeen and taking ninety prisoner.' Although such reports heightened tension, few could really bring themselves to believe now that Mafeking might actually fall to the enemy. Indeed, it seemed probable that it might—at long last—presently be relieved. There were thrilling reports that a relief column was at last on its way. And only just in time. A recent message from Mafeking had laid stress on a billiards tournament that was being held: a superb piece of British phlegm, it was thought, which only revealed how desperate matters had become.

On Friday evening in Britain, some clerical workers remained in the city centres after the day's work, as was the custom, to congregate over meals, beer and gin, or for a night out at the music-hall. They were joined by workers from the environs, anxious to spend some or all of their wages.

In London, the lamplighters had made their golden way through the streets. Gentlemen in silk hats had entered their clubs in St. James's. Long-skirted women had alighted from jingling hansom cabs at private houses and at hotels. In many of the great homes lavish dinners were being served. In the City, in the narrow streets around the Bank and the Stock Exchange, young men were chattering in those steamy eating-houses and bars that remained open. A major topic of discussion was the fascinating Parliamentary Committee on the Manchester and Liverpool Express Railway, under Sir John Kennaway. It was hearing evidence in support of the Bill for the construction of an express monorail system between the two northern cities. The promoter, a Mr Behr, had said that a Manchester–Liverpool monorail would be safer, cheaper and faster than the present system; he was prepared to invest nearly all his own capital in it, and he would guarantee a speed of one hundred and ten miles to the hour. It was widely accepted that such a hare-brained scheme would not get far. In London, however, a remarkable occurrence had taken place that very week: the first electric trains on the underground railway had run several times a day between Earls Court and High Street Kensington.

When the London money market, the greatest in the world, had closed that May evening in 1900, it had done so in a confident mood: '*Money*: still very abundant. *American Railroad Market*: final quotations were all higher than in the morning. *Foreign Market*: quiet but firm.'

It was a time when the middle class, apart from those members of it manning the outposts of Empire, stayed at home. Only the very rich and the very poor crossed the Atlantic: first-class transatlantic fares were from ten pounds.

In Washington that day an important meeting of the United States Cabinet had been held under President McKinley. The Cabinet had discussed the question of offering the good services of the United States in the South African War, with a view of instituting peace negotiations between Great Britain and the Boer republics. It had been decided 'not to mediate in any manner. The United States will continue to hold absolutely aloof.'

London itself provided a varied choice of entertainments that evening. There was the 'Women's Exhibition 1900', symptomatic of a growing awareness of women's place in society ('bicycle-shed free'), 'Women's Manufactures and Cottage Industries', 'Ladies' Military Concert'. There were Vesta Tilley, George Robey and Bransby Williams at the Tivoli. There was Mr Martin Harvey at the Prince of Wales. The most popular entertainments were those with a military flavour: at the Royal Military Tournament opening that night at the Agricultural Hall, there were 'Encounters on Horse and Foot with Lance and Sword and Bayonet, and a Balaclava Mêlée'; at the Polytechnic, 'A Patriotic Entertainment—latest animated pictures from the Front'; at Madame Tussaud's, 'Imposing and Realistic Tableau Representing Cronje Surrendering to Lord Roberts'; at the Crystal Palace, 'The National Horse Show, including military events'; at the Royal Aquarium, 'An Exhibition of the Kimberley War Relics'; and perhaps most popular of all, at the Alhambra Theatre there was the fabulously successful show *Soldiers of the Queen.*

Unknown to anybody in London that early evening, a telegraph message was on its way to the office of Reuters News Agency from its correspondent in the enemy capital, Pretoria. It had been dispatched at 11.35 a.m., local time. It arrived in the noisy, crowded news room in London, with jacketless reporters and editors in white shirts, their fob watches on the desks before them, at exactly 9.17 p.m., 18 May 1900. It read : 'It is officially announced that when the laagers and forts around Mafeking had been severely bombarded the siege was abandoned by the Boers. A British force advancing from the south then took possession of the town.' An excited copy-boy handed the piece of paper to the sub-editor. It was to be, perhaps, the most sensationally received telegraph message of history.

*

It had been arranged that if the news of the relief of Mafeking was received it should be telegraphed immediately to the Lord Mayor. Rumours had been spreading all day, as in the House of Commons the previous evening Sir E. Ashmead-Bartlett had asked the Under-Secretary for War about the possibility of an impending relief, and a small crowd had gathered outside the Mansion House in half-expectancy. As the doors of the balcony were flung open, the crowd rapidly grew. At 9.35 p.m. a placard was placed outside the entrance by an excited footman : MAFEKING IS RELIEVED. Drivers of trolleys and vans shouted out the news as they drove down Ludgate Hill and on to the Strand. At about the same time a notice was posted outside the offices of the *Daily Telegraph* announcing the relief. People stopped each other in the street to pass on the news, and 'total strangers shook each other heartily by the hand'.

The energy for what was about to happen seemed to generate at first from the square bounded by the Mansion House, the Royal Exchange and the Bank of England.

A huge coloured picture of Colonel Baden-Powell had been prepared, and now it was brought out and placed between the middle columns over the balcony of the Mansion House. The Lord Mayor appeared and read out a statement to the considerable crowd that had suddenly appeared from every street and restaurant and bar and building for a mile around. The whole area was packed with people. The Lord Mayor said: 'I wish the music of your cheers could reach Mafeking. British pluck and valour, when used in a right cause, must triumph.' When he had finished a great swell of singing rose from the crowd and drifted away across the massive grey buildings of the City, the financial heart and hub of the Empire. First they sang 'Rule, Britannia!', then 'God Save the Queen', and then 'Soldiers of the Queen'. Police, in their high-collared tunics and tall helmets, hurried from their stations, and already traffic was being directed away from the centre of London by way of side streets. The Lord Mayor returned to his office and composed a message to Mafeking, with a deafening noise of whistles, cornets, singing and shouting coming from outside the window. He took his pen and wrote: 'Your gallant defence will long live in British annals.'

By 9.50 the news had reached all parts of the West End. The speed at which it spread across the metropolis astonishes even today. By 10.00 the streets in the centre of London were in tumult. Crowds gathered in all the main thoroughfares, at Piccadilly, in Trafalgar Square, and in Leicester Square. They sang—groups endeavouring to drown the words of each other—and they embraced and they waved the Union Jacks that appeared in miraculous and unaccountable profusion. Parties of men marched together through the West End singing, waving flags, spreading the news, and answering calls and shouts from the tops of open omnibuses, from footpaths and from cabs. The sight of anyone wearing a uniform was the cause of uproar, and even humble postmen coming and going in the neighbourhood of St. Martin's-le-Grand were lifted from their feet. Cyclists with flags on long poles paraded the streets of outlying areas in procession. Groups of men chartered four-wheelers and hilariously shouted the news. In St. James's, where the diners had been rudely disturbed, women took refuge on the steps of the Junior Carlton and other clubs.

The news penetrated inside the theatres. At Wyndhams, where *Cyrano de Bergerac* was being performed, Mr Wyndham himself announced the tidings. The appropriateness of the fourth act, which represents a heroic siege and relief, was greeted with general uproar from the audience. At the Royalty, it was Mrs Patrick Campbell who announced the news from the stage: the orchestra played 'Rule, Britannia!' and the National Anthem, the audience joining in. At the Hippodrome, Miss Lilian Lea sang a special ballad eulogizing 'the gallant defenders'. It was encored eight times. At Covent Garden, the Prince and Princess of Wales were present for a performance of *Lohengrin*. 'After second act a voice, from somewhere, cried "Mafeking is relieved". Within another five minutes, House on its legs cheering! Royalties beaming! Then, without any talented assistance from band, choir or principals, the entire audience spontaneously sang, with one heart and voice, "God Save the Queen". Best operatic chorus ever heard!'[1]

Special late editions of the newspapers began to appear. Some excited newsboys gave them away; others, maintaining a better presence of mind, charged twopence for halfpenny papers and quickly sold out. A *Times* reporter wrote that night: 'From the Mansion House as far as the War Office [a distance of over two miles] there was a continuous roar of more or less articulate applause and an unbroken array of waving flags.'

The Queen herself was at Windsor. The Royal suite had been informed immediately by the Press Association. The news was received, predictably, in a different manner to that chosen by the vast majority of the Queen's subjects. There were no celebrations at Windsor Castle that night: the Queen herself had retired. The Press Association, which covered home affairs while Reuters dealt with those abroad, was not to be outdone: soon after Reuters' announcement it said that Baden-Powell's brother in London had received a telegram 'from a Dutch friend in Pretoria' informing him of the relief of Mafeking.

Elsewhere over the country church bells were ringing, maroons were being fired, and crowds were gathering that would not noticeably decrease, through the continuous arrival of reinforcements, for

[1] *Punch*, 23 May 1900.

8

three, four and even five days. The citizens of Liverpool were 'quite delirious with joy': flights of rockets pierced the sky, and an enormous crowd outside the Town Hall greeted the Lord Mayor, who had to abandon an attempt to speak 'and contented himself with leading the rendering of the National Anthem'. At Newcastle-upon-Tyne the rockets sent up from the *Chronicle* office were seen for miles around; every village knew what they signified and cheering and singing crowds instinctively gathered together. At Bradford the factory hooters sounded. At Brighton and Leicester processions grew to proportions never seen before. At Glasgow all church bells were rung, a vast crowd sang popular airs, and the vessels in the harbour sounded whistles and sirens. In Dublin there were unprecedented scenes when the news was announced in the Theatre Royal.

There had been great gatherings of the British people before: at the state funeral of the great Duke, at the Diamond Jubilee. There had been crowds and public rejoicing at the relief of Ladysmith. But already it was apparent that a spontaneous outbreak such as was now occurring, with no official sanction about it, had never before occurred on such a scale in the entire history of the country.

By eleven o'clock London seemed to have gone altogether mad. As the theatre crowds spilled out there was pandemonium. Lamp-posts were climbed. Hats and caps were thrown wildly away. Curtains were pulled back from shining windows and people in evening-dress called to the crowds below. 'They waved not only flags, but every sort of thing they could get hold of, including blankets, table cloths, towels and various feminine undergarments.' *The Times* continued:

At Piccadilly Circus matters culminated . . . as the stream of omnibuses and of cabs bringing people from the theatre thickened . . . [the traffic] grew slower and slower and then ceased. The Circus was jammed with people. And then a cornet or some such instrument struck up *God Save the Queen*. Immediately thousands of voices took it up and in a twinkling every hat was off. It was a wonderful sight under the glare of the Criterion lamps. The walls around the big space were alive with cheering and gesticulating figures. The pavements and the streets blocked with them, and motionless among them the streams of omnibuses and cabs, all crowded with persons waving hats, umbrellas, flags, anything . . .

I saw many cabs fairly blazing with Union Jacks; the people had obviously taken them to the theatre in anticipation. No one minded being stopped or crushed. Ladies in evening-dress were squeezed in the crowd, but only smiled happily. And over it all and throughout it all and through it all the cheers thundered on in a continuous roar like the sound of a heavy surf on a rocky shore.

At midnight crowds were still tramping across the bridges from the south bank in quest of confirmation of the news. Outside the War Office, all night, hung a small notice which read: 'No news.' And in the Commons, on the motion for the adjournment at twelve o'clock, Mr Henderwick asked the Leader of the House if he had any news to communicate to the House with reference to the reported relief of Mafeking. Mr Balfour replied: 'No, sir. The only news I have received is through the courtesy of the press. We have no official information at the War Office.' The House, in a gay and happy mood, adjourned. The news, if not convincing enough for the Government, was enough for everyone else.

The scenes in the centre of London showed no indications of ending, the crowds no inclination to disperse. It was alarming. The Victorian sense of propriety and orderliness was not happy about such behaviour. When would it all end? And where would it lead to? The city-dwellers of the new nation were not, it seemed, after all, the same men as the rural John Bulls who had peacefully lit their bonfires on the news of Waterloo. There was something frightening, something new, about such a vast concourse demonstrating, apparently unchecked and uncontrolled, with such fervour.

Express trains roaring through the countryside that night whistled loud and long at every halt and every village and every crossing. So the news was spread. Villages, long since abed, rose, and shops were opened well past midnight and bunting and cloth of red, white and blue was sold, and neighbours wakened, and toasts drunk.

Above all other emotions, even above the alarm felt by a few, one was paramount—a great and deep sense of relief. Everything would be all right, after all.

*

In New York, the news had been received first at the offices of the Associated Press at 4.21 p.m. local time—four minutes after the news had reached Reuters in London. Several newspapers had immediately published extra editions which were eagerly purchased, indicating the wide interest taken in the fate of the garrison. Crowds gathered around the newspaper offices for further information, and there was a great deal of excited comment from the passengers on the elevated railway and public transport.

American feelings about the war had been confused. There had been bitter disputes with Canada, not long before, in which Britain was believed to have played a controversial part. Only five years earlier there had been talk of an Anglo-American war over the Venezuela–British Guiana boundary; it was an age of swaggering, and it was not unusual for war to be mentioned over such minor issues. On the other hand, Britain, almost alone in Europe, had been generally pro-American in the Spanish-American war of 1898, a fact which had been widely appreciated in the United States. Although there was no sympathy for the British cause in the South African War, there was widespread interest in the sieges of Kimberley, Ladysmith and, since they had both been relieved, that of Mafeking. Baden-Powell had become one of the best-known Englishmen in America. Throughout the United States morning newspapers on Saturday gave unusual coverage to the story. The *New York World* said: 'Colonel Baden-Powell and his men have written a new page in the annals of human heroism.'

Reports of great celebration came from all cities of the Empire. Everywhere it was the same: public places seething with singing crowds, streets crowded with processions and bands, buildings festooned with banners and flags. In Canada 'every town and village went wild with patriotic fervour', reported the correspondent of *The Times*. At Montreal, 'a large quantity of powder is being exploded in salutes, while the British colours are flying in all parts of the city as well as over the shipping in the harbour.' In Melbourne guns were fired, church bells rung, and immense crowds thronged the streets; even the U.S. Consulate displayed flags. In Brisbane a public holiday was proclaimed. In Wellington, where preparations had been carefully laid, bonfires were lit on the surrounding hills; the Mayor said, 'Mafeking has been one of the noblest defences in the history of the

Empire'; a correspondent reported that 'seldom if ever have such rejoicings been witnessed in this city'. It was announced that Monday was to be a national holiday in New Zealand. In Singapore all business ceased: 'Europeans and Asians are equally jubilant.' In British South Africa the news was received with comparative serenity except in Cape Town, where a public collection had been made during May to prepare arrangements for official festivities on the relief of Mafeking. To most British people in South Africa it was merely a happy event in a distressing and bitter war that looked as if it might drag on a great deal longer than had been thought.

In the European capitals the news was received coolly, but not without interest. There was widespread hostility to Britain's part in the war.

In Britain, the party was just beginning.

A vast and apparently uncontrollable upsurge of joy, nationalism, and mended pride was on the move. It was to last for five days. As an outburst of patriotic emotion and immense relief at a timely proof of British superiority, and as the expression of a newly discovered freedom, they were to be the most remarkable five days of the Victorian era. The name of the remote little town near the Bechuanaland border was to be indelibly printed into British history for ever.

That Friday in May—'Mafeking Night'—was only the start of it. On Saturday, the British went wild . . .

*

In Mafeking itself, nearly 7,000 miles away from the capital of the Empire, it was hot and dusty.

As the relief column advanced, the final in the billiards tournament was taking place at the club, and it had continued undisturbed. On 16 May it had been a dull day, but towards evening friendly troops were seen in the distance. One who was present in the town remembered that people got on the roofs to have a look, 'but as they were not apparently coming in, people went to feed, and enthusiasm rather died away.'

At about 7 p.m. a patrol of the Imperial Light Horse, under Major W. D. Davies, rode unopposed into Mafeking. Major Davies presented Colonel Baden-Powell with a box of 'Queen's chocolates'. Thus ended the remarkable two-hundred-and-fifty mile ride of the relief column achieved in twelve days. After two hundred and seventeen days the siege of Mafeking was at and end. Major Davies, taken aback at the lack of interest shown at his arrival, told a passer-by in the street that his was the advance guard of the relief force. The man replied : 'Oh, yes, I heard you were knocking about,' and went about his business.[1]

---

[1] *Diary*, Baillie, 16 May 1900.

2. Preparations for War

*That an unpretentious settlement of tin-roofed dwellings had be-
come the most-mentioned place in the world was due to a train of
converging events and to the personalities of a number of people,
particularly that of an ambitious and remarkable soldier. It had all
begun some years before . . .*

For years war with the South African republics had seemed to some
people inevitable. The Transvaal, shut in on the west, south and
east by colonial and unsympathetic territories, had looked northwards for a hinterland and an area of expansion. But the British
South Africa Company, under Cecil Rhodes, had been developing
that area with some success: the Company's territory had been
named Rhodesia by proclamation on 3 May 1895. Rhodes envisaged
a united South Africa, including the British and Boer territories.
Paulus Kruger, President of the Transvaal, envisaged increased
Boer influence. He had just begun his fourth term as President, and
as an elder statesman had some influence over the other Boer republic also. The discovery of a large goldfield in the Witwatersrand
district of the Transvaal brought matters to a head. Kruger welcomed foreigners to develop and work the mines, but, determined to
keep the Boer element in the country predominant, he denied them
political rights. Rhodes took up the cause of the foreigners in the
Witwatersrand, many of them British; he was concerned with
the assembly of a force under Dr L. S. Jameson, an administrator of the
British South Africa Company, which was to ride to Johannesburg
and help the non-Boers there (the 'Outlanders') overthrow Kruger.
The force assembled near the Transvaal border close to Mafeking,
which Jameson made his headquarters and supply centre. The force
was easily surrounded and captured soon after it had invaded

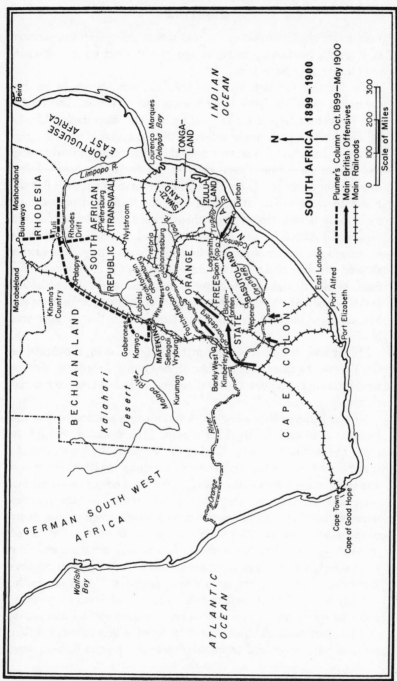

SOUTH AFRICA 1899–1900

Boer territory. The result of the raid was to strengthen the position of Kruger's reactionary party, and to gain support for his views in the Orange Free State also.

Rhodes and Jameson went to London: the former to see his dreams in ruins, the latter to serve a sentence in prison. The Kaiser sent Kruger a telegram congratulating him and encouraging him to believe that Germany might side with the Transvaal in war. Kruger, having in his own lifetime witnessed the Boers being pushed farther and farther away from the coast by British expansion, believed that there might never be a better time for confrontation with the British. Nineteen years before, at Majuba Hill, the Boers had proved they could beat British troops: and their reward had been diplomatic victory. Sir Alfred Milner, on the other hand, believed that the odds were 20 to 1 in favour of Kruger climbing down, so long as the British showed 'absolute downright determination'; but if there was to be a fight, he also thought it was better to fight then than later. Salisbury and Chamberlain, who were more uneasy at the prospect of war than Milner, were inclined to accept the latter's view that Kruger was bluffing.

Milner and President Kruger met at Bloemfontein, the capital of the Transvaal's sister Boer republic of the Orange Free State. Kruger was intransigent about the Outlanders and about his territorial claims.

Kruger believed that a few quick humiliating defeats, such as the Jameson Raid and the Battle of Majuba Hill, would be enough to make the British give way. During the summer of 1899 he concentrated his forces near the borders, ready for quick invasion. His troops were unlike any others in the world: apart from one or two commanders, and the artillery, they were barely trained in the military sciences: but they were frontiersmen with frontiersmen's skills, many of them expert riders, crack shots and masters of terrain. Organized into commandos—locally-raised detachments of mounted men—they wore slouch hats and well-worn bush-clothes, with double bandoliers slung over their shoulders and across their chests. They were, in the military sense, ill-disciplined, but they were proud. Each commando, followed by its train of ox-wagons bearing ammunition and stores, was self-contained. The Boer forces appeared to be a rabble, but they were mobile, tough and experienced over many years in bush warfare. They were, in open conditions, the most formidable military exponents in the world.

Few officers in the British Army had comparable experience of the art of bush warfare.

The British Army at the time was the opposite of the Boers. Hidebound as it was by tradition, conservatism, and outdated techniques, its recent reputation was based almost without exception on victories won by vastly superior fire-power over half-armed natives. Its two major figures were Field-Marshal Lord Wolseley and Field-Marshal Lord Roberts. Wolseley, son of an obscure Army Major, had spent much of his career in London, with occasional spectacular sorties into trouble-spots of the Empire. He had been closely associated with the considerable reform in the organization of the Army since 1882. He was the pride of all forward-looking and progressive soldiers. In 1899 he was Commander-in-Chief of the British Army. On 8 June 1899, he sent a secret memorandum to the Secretary of State for War, Lord Lansdowne, recommending that 'we should prepare for war' with the Transvaal. He outlined six measures which should be taken, including the accumulation of military stores and medical supplies in South Africa, and the dispatch of three companies of the Army Service Corps there.[1]

Roberts, a year older than Wolseley, had spent most of his service in India, much of it in the Quartermaster branch, and his great reputation was linked to that of the Indian Army, so highly thought of in Britain if not elsewhere in the world. He was the son of a General, and he had been awarded the Victoria Cross. He had made the famous march to Kandahar, resulting in the temporary 'pacification' of Afghanistan. He had come home in 1893 after forty-two years of almost continuous service in India, and in 1899 he was Commander-in-Chief in Ireland. He was the hero of all those who preferred 'fighting soldiers' to 'desk-wallahs'. He was universally known as 'Bobs'.

The Army was split between 'Wolseleyites' and 'Robertsites'. At the start of the South African War Wolseley had the greater power, and among his 'young men' was the commanding officer of the 5th Dragoon Guards, Colonel R. S. S. Baden-Powell.

---

[1] *War Office Papers*, P.R.O.

*

Baden-Powell at that time was a thoroughly unusual soldier. Without even seeming to try, he had met with remarkable success. Most
people put it down to sheer good luck. Others believed that beneath
the jolly exterior lay a dedicated and almost frenzied ambition.

Robert Stephenson Smyth Powell had been born in 1857. His father
had been a professor in geometry at Oxford University. Robert was
the eighth child of his third wife (the professor had fourteen children). The boy's mother was one of six children of an Admiral,
thought to be the descendant of Captain John Smith[1] who was saved
from death at the hands of American Indians by Pocahontas, and was
one of the founders of Virginia. Like her brothers and sisters, she was
an ambitious woman. All of the Admiral's children met with success,
and a strongly competitive element was introduced into the Powell
family by the marriage of the prolific professor with the Admiral's
daughter. Mrs Powell had high ambitions for all her children, and
she made this very clear to them. Many of the leading figures of the
day visited them at their home: Thackeray, Robert Browning, T. H.
Huxley and Ruskin were among them. In 1869 Mrs Powell changed
the family name 'by public notice' to Baden-Powell, Baden having
been a popular first name of her husband's family, farmers and
merchants, since the eighteenth century. So insistent was Mrs Powell
on the new name being observed that she became known in the
family as Old Mrs Hyphen.[2] Soon the new name became accepted,
and when Robert went to boarding-school he was already known as
'B-P.'[3] Through the persistent efforts of his mother he received a free
place at Charterhouse. There he was undistinguished in both work
and games, but he was a good shot and a mainstay of the school plays.
He loved dressing-up, perfecting make-up, and singing songs on the
stage. In 1876 he was turned down by Balliol College, Oxford, as
being 'not quite up to Balliol form'. He tried Christ Church, and was

[1] Smith was Baden-Powell's life-long hero. He did a sculpture of him which
was accepted by the Royal Academy. He was not, however, descended from him.
[2] A Royal licence for the additional name and arms of Baden was not received
until 1902 (*Baden-Powell*, E. E. Reynolds, p. 6).
[3] Baden-Powell said that the name should be pronounced to rhyme with 'maiden
and noël'.

also turned down there. Mrs Baden-Powell was outraged. The boy's father had enjoyed a fine reputation at the University; one of his brothers had just won a Chancellor's Prize and another had won a scholarship to Balliol. It seemed that young Robert was going to let his mother down. It was a most painful time for him.

Baden-Powell had given little, if any, thought to a career in the Army, but he took the entrance examination and did well in it. Instead of attending the Royal Military College at Sandhurst, Baden-Powell and several others were gazetted straight to regiments. Baden-Powell therefore did not have the advantages, or disadvantages, of a formal military education, a fact which never bothered him but which may not be irrelevant to later events.

Baden-Powell was considered a remarkable acquisition for his regiment, the 13th Hussars, which was in India. He was keen and efficient. He could draw clever caricatures and impressive-looking sketches with either right or left hand. He was good at the sport of pig-sticking (hunting wild boar while on horseback). He could, and did, attend a musketry course and pass out first-class. He could organize the most amusing entertainments that had been seen in Indian garrisons for years, and did not in the least object to taking a prominent part in them. By sending sketches to a London newspaper he was able to finance himself in polo, in which, it almost goes without saying, he also excelled. He had a fine singing voice, with an entertaining trick of suddenly breaking into a prima-donna falsetto. He could grip an audience with a dramatic character sketch, or have them in fits of laughter with a comic song at the piano. And he was reliable in his military duties; so much so that some maps he drew were sent to Wolseley himself for inspection. He was jolly, even frivolous it seemed, at any rate on the surface, but he was also abstemious : he neither drank nor smoked. He would do any task that was asked of him. Above all, he was the inevitable 'life and soul' of every party. He was an inveterate practical-joker. 'B.-P.' was a bit of a card.

In India, Baden-Powell met the man who was to be, perhaps, the closest friend of his life : Kenneth McLaren, who, when he joined the regiment, was mistaken for a fourteen-year-old youth, and hence was known always as 'The Boy' (Baden-Powell was known to 'The Boy' as 'The Bloater').

All this was very well, but Baden-Powell, as his official biography records, 'felt himself falling behind his brothers in the keen competition within the family'. His sketches in the *Graphic* were fair enough, but something more impressive was required. From the earliest days with his regiment Baden-Powell had taken the closest interest in reconnaissance, an activity which appealed to his sense of drama and adventure. He believed that success in modern war would depend on accurate knowledge of what the enemy was doing. It was not an original thought, but he was prepared to take the idea one step further than most of his contemporaries and say that this could best be done with self-reliant, independent, roving scouts who could live rough and act as the eyes and ears of the Army. It was probably no coincidence that a general order had been issued requiring garrison instructors to give N.C.O.s and men lectures on this very subject. The need for a short handbook on scouting for officers was thus obvious. Baden-Powell wrote *Reconnaissance and Scouting*, and sent it to his brother George in London, who had no trouble in finding a publisher for it.[1] In a letter to his brother, he said : 'Even if it did not sell more than twenty copies it would be a grand advertisement for me—because I could send copies to all the brass quartermaster-generals, Wolseleys, etc.'[2]

For getting on in the world the Baden-Powell family had a system they called 'grouping events' : one thing must lead to two others. To draw a series of sketches of pig-sticking was not enough; they should be sent to an art exhibition in Simla where they would be seen by the 'right' people. By breaking in successful horses Baden-Powell contrived to get his name in the newspapers. He got himself noticed by often being with the Duke of Connaught, Queen Victoria's third son, who was in the Army in India, and with Connaught's A.D.C., Lord Downe. Few social events occurred without Baden-Powell being prominently present. But he remained a bachelor. Jokingly, he

---

[1] Sir George Baden-Powell, Conservative M.P. for Kirkdale (Liverpool), 1885–98. Other brothers were F. S. Baden-Powell, a successful sculptor and painter; Baden F. S. Baden-Powell, an aviation pioneer and President of the Aeronautical Society; Baden H. Baden-Powell, a Judge in India; and W. Baden-Powell, a leading barrister. Owing to the many German manifestations of the Royal Family, German names had become fashionable in the late nineteenth century.
[2] *Baden-Powell: The Two Lives of a Hero,* W. Hillcourt with Olave, Lady Baden-Powell, p. 59.

wrote home to his mother : 'I'm going to wait until I'm a major and then it will be a £50,000 girl.' Encouraged by the success of his book on scouting, he followed it with one on pig-sticking. This he dedicated to the Duke of Connaught. In 1885 his *Manual of Cavalry Instruction,* a pocket-size booklet which was an exposition of his own training notes, was published. His two military booklets were gratefully consulted by young officers who had previously been in difficulties.

As for the Indians, he had forthright (and conventional) views. It was wrong, he wrote, for the natives to be treated as the equals of white men. The Indians had not learnt the value of obedience and discipline.

His steady rise in rank did not affect his style. A young subaltern who saw him at this time recalled him taking a leading part in a vaudeville show during the Cavalry Cup polo competition before a large and distinguished audience, dressed in the brilliant and exotic uniform of an officer in the Austrian Hussars. Said someone in the audience : 'Fancy a senior officer kicking his legs up like that before a lot of subalterns!' The young subaltern made the acquaintance of the 'Austrian Hussar' : his name was Winston Churchill, and some years later their paths were to cross again, by which time Baden-Powell was in the centre of a much vaster stage.

The regiment moved from India to South Africa, where Baden-Powell was able to put his scouting ideas into practice in an expedition to the passes of the Drakensberg Mountains. By 1887 Baden-Powell was well in the eye of Wolseley, at that time Adjutant-General. Wolseley sent the young Captain to Aldershot to inspect cavalry training, and to make suggestions for improvement. 'B.-P.' was beginning to be noticed.

A brother of Baden-Powell's mother, General Sir Henry Smyth, had become G.O.C. South Africa. A little influence was used and Baden-Powell was sent out as his A.D.C. Not content with his routine duties, he set up a tiny Intelligence Department at G.H.Q. and added to his knowledge of the techniques of scouting by studying the Zulu. ('Never forget to dig a hip-hole when you have to sleep on hard ground, if you wish to sleep well.') When General Smyth was appointed Commander-in-Chief at Malta, Baden-Powell accompanied him there. These postings, thanks to his mother and his uncle, brought him to wider notice in military circles. In 1893 Baden-Powell rejoined his regiment, the 13th Hussars, in Ireland, after many years on special duty. In the summer manœuvres of that year he again attracted the attention of Wolseley, who became Commander-in-Chief in 1895. Almost immediately after his appointment Wolseley had to send a force to West Africa to overthrow the Ashanti king, which was done successfully and without bloodshed. Baden-Powell was in the expedition. His most notable act was the burning of several of the largest and most ancient priestly houses in the capital of Kumasi. He produced articles and sketches for the newspapers the while (providing his paper with the greatest scoop to come out of the Ashanti expedition). On a Sunday after his return he was asked by a publishing house to do a book on the campaign, and he delivered the completed manuscript on the following Thursday. As a journalist he was reliable and conscientious; he wrote in a lively, anecdotal style much appreciated by the editors and readers of the two popular newspapers for whom he worked from time to time for a number of years. As an artist he was talented, and was able to work at remarkable speed: the gay but patriotic flavour of his illustrations, for ever pointing to the casual, devil-may-care approach of sporting Englishmen, made them the perfect accompaniment to his writings.

Within weeks of his return Wolseley sent him out to South Africa as Chief Staff Officer to Sir Frederick Carrington's force dealing with the revolt of the Matabele in the British South Africa Company territory north of the Transvaal. Bulawayo and other places were being harassed by howling mobs of fierce warrior natives. During the campaign Baden-Powell, as was expected of him, varied his staff work with a number of reconnaissance expeditions, which provided him not only with experience but also with copy for his occasional newspaper and magazine articles. He gained at least as much notoriety as the man who actually led the relief force from the south, and who, by prompt action, saved the settlers from possible extinction, Lieutenant-Colonel Herbert Plumer.[1] The following year *The Matabele Campaign* by Lieutenant-Colonel R. S. S. Baden-Powell was published—a highly personalized account of the campaign.

After the Matabele campaign Baden-Powell was a full Colonel.

---

[1] As it was, about ten per cent of the settler population in Rhodesia was killed or injured. The rising seriously delayed Rhodesian development and prosperity.

This caused some embarrassment on his return to his regiment, where his rank was senior to that of his commanding officer. Wolseley always enjoyed picking on young officers for special duties and promoting them out of turn, which was no doubt why he enjoyed such favour among some and why others were such ardent 'Roberts-ites'. In April 1897 Baden-Powell was given the command of the 5th Dragoon Guards in India.

It was on his first long leave from his regiment in India that Baden-Powell, on a fine July day in 1899, was summoned to the War Office while lunching at the Naval and Military Club at 94 Piccadilly. At the War Office he was taken to Lord Wolseley's room. The Commander-in-Chief said:

'I want you to go to South Africa.'

'Yes, sir.'

'Well, can you go on Saturday next?' (It was then Monday.)

'No, sir.'

'Why not?' snapped Wolseley.

'There's no ship on Saturday, but I can go on Friday.'

Baden-Powell could never resist telling a joke.[1]

He was then taken by Wolseley to the office of the War Minister, Lord Lansdowne. According to Baden-Powell, the Minister formally accorded him the title of 'Commander-in-Chief, North-West Frontier Forces'[2] and ordered him to raise two regiments from the white settlers in Bechuanaland and Rhodesia.

It was the most important assignment Wolseley had given him. His orders were verbal.[3] It was realized that the main Boer thrusts in a war would be eastwards from the Transvaal towards the Indian Ocean, with the object of eventually gaining access to the sea, and south-west from the Transvaal and the Orange Free State into the Cape, with the object of encouraging a rising of Boers in British

---

[1] This was 3 July 1899. The interview was recorded by Baden-Powell in *Lessons from the 'Varsity of Life,* and frequently reproduced elsewhere; but, according to Viscountess Milner, Cecil's instructions, which had already been dispatched (as he received them on 3 July 1899), stated that he was to depart with Baden-Powell on the following Monday.

[2] Probably a confusion between India and Africa (Hillcourt).

[3] The exact nature of the orders is discussed in the next chapter. The authority for raising Baden-Powell's force and for his command of it were written.

territory. The movement of their forces would probably be away from Rhodesia rather than towards it. Nevertheless, some protection would have to be accorded to that colony, and to Bechuanaland, and Baden-Powell was to provide it by means of two new regiments which he was to raise in the area.[1]

If there was to be a war, many an officer with Baden-Powell's instructions might have believed himself assigned to a certain 'sideshow'. But not the trim, tanned forty-two-year-old bachelor colonel with the immaculate clothes, the thinning fair hair under his felt hat, perfectly clipped moustache and twinkling eyes, who whistled as he swung across the Park to his mother's house at 8 St. George's Place, Hyde Park. He later wrote: 'I had by that evening formulated in my own mind my plan of campaign.' What this was must remain a source of speculation; as will be seen, it can hardly have been, at that time, being invested in Mafeking.

*

It was a story in which others were to play important roles, if none was to rival the leading player. The cast was beginning to assemble.

Not least among them was a beautiful and formidable young woman, Lady Sarah Wilson. She was the wife of Captain Gordon Wilson, Royal Horse Guards, the daughter of the Duke of Marlborough, and the sister of a brilliant politician, Lord Randolph Churchill, who had died at an early age four years previously. She had left for South Africa with her husband four weeks before Baden-Powell, intending to spend a few months in Rhodesia visiting friends. The Wilsons were staying at Bulawayo with Major Maurice Heaney, an American who had been one of the pioneers in the area. Lady Sarah, elegant, petite and very determined, was an adventuress in

---

[1] This plan was not mentioned in the measures recommended by Wolseley on 8 June 1899 (above), nor in his next memo on 7 July 1899 (the very week in which he saw Baden-Powell). Next month Wolseley wrote to Lansdowne: 'It is in Natal that the most serious danger threatens.' In the correspondence he did not mention the Bechuanaland and Rhodesia project. This would indicate that he did not attach as much importance to Baden-Powell's mission as many writers have claimed since. That Baden-Powell did not receive written orders was not unusual: neither did Lord Roberts when he went to South Africa, and Buller received no orders at all (except to take up his command).

the guise of a respectable Victorian lady. Her nephew, Winston Churchill, a dashing and ambitious former cavalry officer, was soon to follow her to South Africa, although he was as yet unaware of it. Churchill, obsessed with the idea that, like his father, he was to die prematurely, was determined to make his mark on posterity's glass without delay. That July he failed to enter Parliament in a by-election at Oldham. At his mother's house in London he was 'absorbed in the delightful occupation of playing with proofs'. He considered his latest book, an account of the Sudan campaign, his *'magnum opus'*. It was to be published in the middle of October, but, as Churchill later recalled, 'when the middle of October came, we all had other things to think about'.

While Lady Sarah discussed, with the settlers of Bulawayo, Kruger's latest moves, Baden-Powell, with two officers picked by Wolseley, was steaming for Cape Town. The two were Major Lord Edward Cecil, of the Grenadier Guards, designated Baden-Powell's Chief of Staff, and Lieutenant the Hon. Algernon Hanbury-Tracy, of the Royal Horse Guards, who was to be his intelligence officer. Cecil was the son of the Prime Minister, Hanbury-Tracy the son of Lord Sudeley. Cecil's father had suggested that he take his wife along with him, an idea which had been readily accepted. Before embarkation, at Southampton, the Cecils had been met by Mr Scott-Montagu,[1] a friend, who had taken them for a quick drive in his motor car— the first time they had ever been in one. It had been a most exciting start to their trip to South Africa.

On the R.N.S. *Norman*, departing on 15 July, just behind them, were more men hand-picked by Wolseley to join Baden-Powell: Colonel Plumer, an infantryman, unlike most of the others, who had passed through the Staff College and had been with Baden-Powell in the Matabele rising; Colonel C. O. Hore; Major Courtenay Vyvyan; Captain Charles Fitzclarence, son of the Earl of Munster and a descendant of William IV and an Irish actress; and Major Alexander Godley, who had been a last-minute addition to the party.[2] Fitz-

---

[1] Later the first Lord Montagu of Beaulieu.
[2] Later: Lord Edward Cecil, financial adviser to the Egyptian Government, 1912–18, died 1918; Field-Marshal Viscount Plumer, died 1932; Sir Courtenay Vyvyan, died 1941; Lieutenant-Colonel C. Fitzclarence, Irish Guards, died 1914; General Sir Alexander Godley, died 1957.

clarence was seen off by his wife, the former Lady Violet Spencer Churchill, who was a cousin of Lady Sarah Wilson and Winston Churchill. Plumer had first heard of his assignment while watching the 'Varsity match at Lords. He was at that time, according to his biographer, 'a rather small, delicate and retiring person, short-sighted and apparently more interested in novels than in his companions'. Godley had recently passed through Staff College, and was considered one of the most promising young officers of his generation. Godley, like Cecil, decided to take his wife with him. He also was a 'Wolseleyite' and had been picked out by the Commander-in-Chief for special service before.

Baden-Powell appears to have been dissatisfied with the choice of some of the officers assigned to him, and considered it would have been more 'fair' if he had been allowed to make his own choice.[1]

Far away from these affairs, and with as yet no thought of leaving for South Africa, was Colonel Bryan T. Mahon,[2] formerly of the 8th Hussars but now on special service with the Egyptian Army. Mahon, volatile, charming, and with a slight brogue, was a product of the minor West of Ireland squirearchy. He had been reported killed at the battle of Omdurman in the preceding year, and was now head of the intelligence branch of the flying column which was chasing the forces of the Khalifa into the Southern Sudan.

An insatiable demand for colourful news had made the task of the comparatively new position of war correspondent a daring and dangerous one (for this reason many newspapers employed former professional soldiers). At Omdurman *The Times* correspondent, Hubert Howard, had been killed. As war with the Boer republics was clearly coming, newspaper reporters were also converging on South Africa. They were the cream of their profession, which at the time was somewhat more vigorous than it is today; as well as writers, they needed to have something in them of the explorer, the scout, the marksman, and the rough-rider, as well as ability to mix freely with diplomats and cut-throats, and to have some genius with primitive communications. They were for the most part hard-drinking, hard-living, tough and extremely professional. Of those who were to play

---

[1] *Lessons from the 'Varsity of Life*, p. 200.
[2] Later General Sir Bryan Mahon; died 1930; Senator, Irish Free State, 1922–30.

a part in the Mafeking story, besides Churchill, Filson Young, who was to report the march of the relief column, was in Lancashire contemplating joining the Army as a reservist; Angus Hamilton was in *The Times* building at Printing House Square, in London; Neilly, a world traveller of the *Pall Mall Gazette*, was in South Africa cabling home that the Boers had made up their minds to declare war at the end of September or the beginning of October.

Late in July 1899 Baden-Powell and his two aides, passing through Mafeking in the train *en route,* arrived at the Grand Hotel, Bulawayo; the two principal railway towns of the area they were to protect were Bulawayo and Mafeking. At Bulawayo Baden-Powell had a happy reunion with his old friend 'The Boy' McLaren.

The party in the second boat arrived at Cape Town, were dined there by Cecil Rhodes, and proceeded to Mafeking, where Plumer left them, going on to join Baden-Powell.

Thus several young officers of the British Army had arrived in the area in the expectation of war with the Boers. They were to constitute the nucleus of two new regiments. Their mission was secret. They went about their business in civilian clothes, and travelled up and down the railway between Bulawayo and Mafeking under assumed names. It was the cool season and the vast blue sky was sunny, and the air and gentle winds invigorating, and the only talk was talk of war.

3. Preparations for Siege

While the industrious little colonel was making his first appreciation of the situation in Bulawayo, the white citizens of Mafeking were in an understandable state of confusion and fear. Unlike Bulawayo, Mafeking was on the very doorstep of the potential enemy. In the event of war, which seemed inevitable, what was to become of them? They were only eight miles from the Transvaal border, where it was thought Kruger would mass troops at the outbreak of war, and their vulnerability was obvious. No one could be sure how the Boers would treat them and their possessions. It was rumoured that the Boers would have no pity because Mafeking had been used as headquarters for Jameson's futile raid. The sensible thing seemed to be to get on the train and go south and wait until British troops were in sufficient strength to defend the area effectively. No preparations had been made to withstand a siege.

It was a lonely township in which to be: 650 miles from Cape Town, to which city the single track of the railway snaked down the continent mile after parched mile, but only 160 miles from the capital of the Transvaal, Pretoria. To the north, fifteen miles away, was the border of the Bechuanaland Protectorate, beyond which stretched the Kalahari Desert and over 1,000 miles of little-known and partly unexplored territory. To the west were the hundreds of miles of the mysterious, arid area of the Molopo, a wild bushland that ended across half a continent with the Namib Desert and the Atlantic shore. To the south, far away, were friends and British power and security. To the east, eight miles away, was the border of a hostile country. The vital railway itself ran for hundreds of miles close to the border.

It was, as Baden-Powell was himself to observe, 'a very ordinary-looking place . . . Just a small tin-roofed town of small houses plumped down upon the open veldt'. There had long been a native village at this place, and the modern settlement had arrived for no other reason than that it was a convenient centre at which to trade with the natives and there was a good supply of water from a natural spring; in other respects it would have been difficult to find a less hospitable place in all South Africa. The white man's settlement had been first laid out in 1885. The railway had arrived as recently as 1894; the rail connection with Bulawayo had been in operation for only two years. Mafeking was a frontier town.

In appearance it did not differ in any noticeable degree from countless other minor trading settlements in South Africa. It was a scattered, modest, unattractive place that had no pretensions at all; if there was civic pride at Mafeking, it had been lost, like so many other noble aspirations, in the torrid, sweltering heat and in the remorseless downpours of the rainy season. For about a mile from east to west, and south to north, stores, dwellings and shacks, many with a hen-run and outbuildings behind, were scattered in what seemed to be the skeleton of some future grid system of streets. Built of earthy sand and mud, the walls of the houses could be powdered in the hand. The roofs were of corrugated iron. Only one building was more than a storey high and few had any pretensions at all— the railway station, Dixon's Hotel and a law office beside it, the Mafeking Hotel, the new hospital with seventy beds and its accompanying convent of hardy Irish nuns, the circular Town Office, the little fort and barracks of the British South Africa Police, over which fluttered the Union Jack, and at the very edge of the settlement the racecourse with its tin-roofed grandstand. Beyond the racecourse was the water spring, channelled to the town in both pipes and open ditches. In what could be discerned after a while as the centre of the place were two 'squares'—the grandly named Market Square and Government Square. Here and there pepper trees had been planted down the sides of the streets; in season they came out in bright red berries. All around stretched the veld, like a barren, stony prairie, dipping a little where the town ended and then, a little later, rising again here and there to gentle slopes. Mafeking lay like some insignificant scrap of toast in an enormous, shallow, brown-and-green plate.

The ground was rough and ungenerous; only tufts of grass and stunted shrubs had burst through. Here and there a scraggy tree stood in isolation, so rare that each was known by a name. Mafeking, in the native language of the place, meant 'Place of Stones'.

Half a mile to the south-west, on both banks of the muddy stream called the Molopo River, which was half-hidden by its own bushy banks, was the dun-coloured native village, from a distance almost indistinguishable, except to the trained eye, from the veld itself. In the cluster of thatched, beehive-shaped mud huts lived Africans still in the process of emerging from savage into semi-civilized native. South of the river was a third settlement, the half-breeds' 'location', carefully and neatly separated from both white man's town and native village so as to upset the sensibilities of none.

In normal times the white population of Mafeking was about 2,000 souls, but as war approached barely 1,200 remained. In the native section there lived normally some 6,000 Africans, swollen now by over 1,000 refugees from the Transvaal. From the village came the vegetables for the town, grown by the banks of the river; meat and dairy produce came from nearby farms.

It was not a grand place, but it was the only one of any size at all in British Africa for some hundreds of miles. Bulawayo was 420 miles to the north-east, and Kimberley 200 miles to the south. Mafeking was, therefore, an administrative centre for a large area, as well as a trading centre for the Africans and the few hundred white settlers living in vast isolation on the open veld. There were a commissioner for native affairs, a magistrate, a court-house and a jail; two schools; a number of ramshackle chapels, and a masonic hall; a modest lending library; a branch of the Standard Bank; and such services as a chemist's, a barber's shop, a photographer's, a bicycle shop and a printer's. As well as Dixon's, the centre of town life, there were two other guest-houses, with saloons, pool-rooms and shaded verandas.

Mafeking seemed a place that had a tenuous hold on the outside world: just the thin line of the railway across the wilderness, with the telegraph poles beside it striding away as far as the eye could see.

In the early summer, from November to February, it was so hot that the plain itself seemed to be baked in the cruel sun; all sensible things kept in the shade. After Christmas came the bright, deafening electric storms, and then the torrential rains clattering on the tin roofs like a thousand kettledrums; and then, from April, cool, refreshing weather, with fine, crisp air, sunshine and cool nights.

*

To raise two regiments in a desolate part of Africa was no easy task. But once the news spread that volunteers were required men began to come in : some from the Rhodesian farms and from Bulawayo and Salisbury, some—mostly ne'er-do-wells and adventurers—from the Bechuanaland border country; many from the Cape and the coast. They signed on 'for not less than five shillings a day, in addition to rations, clothing and equipment'.

The authorities in the Cape were anxious that as little fuss as possible should accompany the recruiting for fear of alarming the Boers and precipitating war. They also mentioned constitutional difficulties about recruiting in Cape Colony. Already Baden-Powell was aware of a singular lack of enthusiasm for his activities from Cape Town.

Baden-Powell split his efforts into two : one regiment, the Rhodesia Regiment, was to be centred on Bulawayo and commanded by Plumer; the other, the Protectorate Regiment, was to be centred on the village of Ramathlabama, inside Bechuanaland and under twenty miles from Mafeking, under Colonel C. O. Hore. The Cape authorities were adamant that Baden-Powell should not concentrate one of his forces on Mafeking. They felt that in the event of war such a concentration would serve to attract a large enemy force to the town, with the consequent cutting of the railway and the probability of a siege—which would have to be relieved by troops better employed elsewhere. It was expected in the Cape that Baden-Powell would use his two regiments to patrol the railway, harass the enemy, threaten his rear and flank, and provide protection, particularly for Rhodesia; Bechuanaland, it was felt, had no strategic value and, indeed, little potential value to the enemy of any other kind. At first Baden-Powell seems to have had no wish to enter Mafeking. He kept Colonel Hore's force out of the town. This, however, was not to the liking of some of the citizens and merchants of the place, who started early on to exert pressure on him to move into the town. But Baden-Powell protested against going into Mafeking, as will be seen. It was at about this time that he applied for a transfer to his own regiment; his request was turned down. Although Baden-Powell had received his command from the War Office, because he was in Bechuanaland he came under the control of the Colonial Office, which was a most unsatisfactory arrangement. For if the Cape authorities and the Army were not prepared to send up guns and authorize the establishment of a garrison at Mafeking, who was going to defend the place?

In September a few of the citizens of Mafeking, fearing a Boer raid on the town, appealed to Sir Alfred Milner, the High Commissioner, for military protection. They received a vague reply, through the Resident Commissioner of Bechuanaland, based in Mafeking, saying that 'everything that is possible is being done'. More encouraging was a postscript added by the Resident Commissioner, Hamilton Goold-Adams:[1] 'I can personally assure you that the military armament of this place is about to be materially increased, and this increase, in the opinion of the senior military officers, will render the town safe from any probable attack that will be made upon it.'[2] For 'senior military officers' most people of Mafeking read Baden-Powell, who had been closeted in long private discussions with the Resident Commissioner.

The Commander-in-Chief, Cape Colony, was General Sir William Francis Butler, the senior British officer in South Africa. General Butler was not only an able military commander, he was also the most unpopular man in South Africa. Of all those in authority on either side, he was almost alone in believing that war between the British and the Boers was not only undesirable but also preventable. It was for this reason that he had insisted on Baden-Powell and his aides going through Cape Colony in civilian clothes, that he had discouraged recruiting for the two regiments in Cape Colony, and that he had made sure they kept out of his 'territory'—for Butler's military authority did not extend into Rhodesia and Bechuanaland. But there was no doubt that Mafeking was among his responsibilities; in 1895 Bechuanaland territory south of the Molopo, including Mafeking, had been annexed to Cape Colony. Butler had no desire at all to turn Mafeking into a vulnerable military base.

---

[1] Later Sir Hamilton Goold-Adams, Governor of Queensland: died 1920.
[2] *Besieged With B.-P.,* J. E. Neilly, p. 8.

Butler was a sixty-one-year-old product of a famous Anglo-Irish family, born in Tipperary. He had served some years in Canada, and had written two books about his experiences there, as well as a biography of Gordon and other books. He had married a well-known artist. More recently he had served on the Nile, in the expedition for the relief of Gordon at Khartoum, the failure of which had embittered him; he described the expedition as 'the very first war during the Victorian era in which the object was entirely noble and worthy'. He was a tall, strong, active, genial man, with a striking force of character. In 1898, Wolseley, who thought highly of him, had sent him to command in South Africa. Butler had immediately been depressed at the widespread acceptance of the inevitability of war. He considered that the grievances of the British 'Outlanders' in Johannesburg were being deliberately used to excite indignation, and that there existed 'a colossal syndicate for the spread of systematic misrepresentation' with the object of bringing relations between the two races to a climax, forcing war on the Boers, and establishing British rule in southern Africa once and for all. He believed in fact that there was 'a plot to force war on the Transvaal'. He had already made his view plain in his secret dispatches home : '[Present] policy, in my opinion, can only end, if persisted in, in producing a war of races—a conflict the ultimate consequences of which no one could adequately estimate . . . I believe war between white races would be greatest calamity that ever occurred in South Africa.'[1] When Sir Alfred Milner got to hear of this, he 'severely censured' Butler.

Like one man trying to divert a flood, Butler had set himself the task of doing everything he could to lessen the tension. For he believed South Africa was best left the way it was at present, with both Boer and British territories, and that every assistance should be given the Boers to maintain their two states. He said that South Africa did not need 'a surgical operation'. At a time when his career might have been about to end in glory, he was on the brink of personal disaster.

Meanwhile the training at Bulawayo and at Ramathlabama continued. Baden-Powell's recruits were not only British, but of many nationalities : farmers, butchers, printers, tailors, jockeys, clerks,

---

[1] *Report of the Royal Commission on the War in South Africa.*

soldiers of fortune, and adventurers. As Butler had already explained to Lansdowne: 'There is always in South Africa a floating population of loafers, mostly men who have made Europe too hot for them, who are ready to join any corps raised for any service.' Nearly all the horses provided were unbroken, and many of the men could not ride; it was a tough and rigorous business; they were clothed and equipped and underwent a minimum of drill and a maximum of rifle practice.

Plumer's regiment trained on the racecourse outside Bulawayo. Lady Sarah Wilson, still in Bulawayo, could not conceal her delight at the way events were shaping: 'The drilling and exercising of the newly recruited troops were the excitements of the day . . . To while away the time, I took a course of ambulance lessons, learning how to bandage by experiments on the lanky arms and legs of a little black boy.' Her husband, having nothing better to do, offered himself to Baden-Powell and was appointed A.D.C.

It was considered essential to take twelve months to train a soldier. Plumer and Hore did it in less than two.

During September, Baden-Powell, unknown to Cape Town, sent Major Courtenay Vyvyan into Mafeking to organize secretly a further force, this time from the town itself. Entirely unknown to G.H.Q., this force, known as the Town Guard, was raised, armed and partly trained. With the local police, its strength included twenty-seven Dutchmen, fifteen Arabs and Indians, six Russians, five Norwegians, four Americans, four Germans, and two Swedes. Among them were at least three veterans of the Crimea—a survivor of the Siege of Plevna in 1877, a man who had fought in the American Civil War, another who had served with the Prussians before Paris, and a veteran of the Turkish Army.

Baden-Powell was already making arrangements to defend the town, knowing full well that it would entail a siege and that, in the words of his official biography, 'he had not been sent to South Africa for the purpose of defending Mafeking'. In letters to Cape Town, he had done all he could to get out of the responsibility of defending the place at all.

*

According to the *Official History* Wolseley's instructions to Baden-Powell were three :

> To raise two regiments of mounted infantry; to organize the defence of the Rhodesia and Bechuanaland frontiers; as far as possible to keep forces of the enemy occupied in this direction away from their own main forces.[1]

These are exactly the same as in Baden-Powell's version of his orders, given in his report to Roberts after the relief : the report therefore is no doubt the source used by the *Official History*. The exact terms of the last instruction are important : they do not suggest that one of Baden-Powell's tasks was to draw Boer forces from other sectors—only to detain those Boer forces already engaged in operations on the border. To attract large numbers of the enemy to his own small force, and to have successfully defended the border, would have been a contradiction of orders, which Wolseley would have well appreciated; for the former would clearly have endangered the success of the latter. In the event, Baden-Powell's efforts to fulfil the third of these orders—in any interpretation of it—met with failure, although this point also has not been brought out.

Baden-Powell himself was contradictory on the subject of his orders. On different occasions he varied them both in content and in stress. His attitude during the summer of 1899, in particular, was different from that which he and his admirers expressed later, after the enormous fame and prestige which the defence of Mafeking brought him. After the war, he told the Royal Commission : 'I was sent out to South Africa on Special Service in July 1899 with instructions to raise two regiments of Mounted Rifles for the defence of the Rhodesian and Bechuanaland frontier. In the event of war to raise the local armed forces of the countries; to keep the natives in order, and, especially, to draw as large a force of Boers as possible from opposing the British on their southern borders.' These are not the same orders he had described earlier to Roberts. But in later years the orders were to change still further. The chief exposition of his orders after Wolseley's death was in his main autobiographical work :

---

[1] *Official History*, p. 140; *Report* to Roberts, 18 May 1900.

very similar versions were repeated by him when writing on the subject in the later years. These orders were as follows:

(i) to attract Boer forces away from the coast so that they should not interfere with the landing of British troops

(ii) to protect British possessions in 'Rhodesia, Mafeking, etc.'

(iii) to maintain British prestige among the native tribes in the area.[1]

These differ still further from the original version of the orders, and have progressed from that given to the Royal Commission. The third section of the original version has been changed to keeping the Boers from the ports—in the version to the Royal Commission it was to keep them away from the southern borders of the Boer republics, which is quite a different thing: moreover this has become the first rather than the last of the orders. In the original version it was 'to keep forces of the enemy occupied', to the Royal Commission this became 'to draw' the enemy, in the versions of later years it has become 'to attract' the enemy. Such a role, gallant and self-sacrificing, would certainly have fitted in with the conception the public were to come to have of Baden-Powell. In fact, however, by accentuating this version of his orders Baden-Powell made his own position weaker, if more dramatic, for if the object of his force was to attract the enemy, it was not successful. It detained the enemy in steadily decreasing numbers. On Baden-Powell's own figures, the enemy he managed to detain at Mafeking from start to finish decreased by seventy-five per cent. After the start of the investment no enemy were attracted to his force at all. And at the start of the war Baden-Powell wrote in orders, 'It is only necessary for us to inflict a good blow on them and send them back again.'[2] Unusual advice to troops who were apparently expected to detain an enemy.[3]

The conduct of the defence was to be governed for most of the time by the principle of 'sit tight and let them go away', which also is not the way to attract an enemy. The reference to aiding the landing of British troops further weakens Baden-Powell's position

---

[1] *Lessons from the 'Varsity of Life,* p. 200.

[2] *Weil Papers,* B.M., 11 October 1899.

[3] Godley wrote that these 'appeared to be' Baden-Powell's orders.

(Mafeking itself was over 500 miles from the nearest port): the period of the most landings was the period when Mafeking detained the least enemy.

In the second of the orders 'Bechuanaland' has of later years become 'Mafeking'. But in September 1899 Baden-Powell wrote to G.H.Q. Cape Town that the defence of Mafeking was not his task at all. 'The Protectorate Regiment was raised under War Office instructions to protect the border and to make diversions later when necessary. But under present circumstances, owing to there being no efficient garrison at Mafeking, it is tied there to protect its stores.'[1] In this message he described his presence in Mafeking as 'a departure from instructions'. He went on to recommend the reinforcing of the local detachment of police. In the Standing Orders of the Protectorate Regiment, Baden-Powell wrote before the war: 'The force has been raised for the duty of defending the border.'

Then there is the third of Baden-Powell's later versions of the orders: the question of the natives. This is not in his official version at all: he cites it in the report to Roberts as a reason for defence, not as an order. The native question was certainly of importance. It was imperative to both British and Boers that the warlike tribes, which had been pushed westwards and northwards beyond the railway and the Limpopo, should remain quiescent in the event of there being 'a white man's war'. There was some fear among the British that the capture of places like Mafeking would so lower British prestige that there would be uprisings of the Africans; there is little reason to suppose, however, that the Africans would have been less impressed by a mobile British force than by the sight of one impotent and bottled-up in Mafeking.[2] That Baden-Powell was well aware of this at the time is shown in a message to G.H.Q. Cape Town in which he appealed for cavalry, which would be 'infinitely better for our prestige than sitting down to be invested'.[3]

After his original version of his orders to Roberts, Baden-Powell listed six reasons for holding Mafeking in particular: because it was 'the outpost' for Kimberley and Cape Colony; also for Bechuanaland

[1] *Staff Diary*, 29 September 1899.
[2] In fact, many Africans rebelled anyway, including most of one tribe, the Rapulanas.
[3] Hillcourt, p. 162.

and Rhodesia; it threatened the Transvaal; it was the centre of the native districts of the whole area; it contained important railway stocks and works; and also contained large food and forage supplies.[1] But Mafeking was too far removed and vulnerable to be 'an outpost' worth holding on behalf of any of the places mentioned. It was no threat to the Transvaal while it was invested by Transvaal forces. The railway stocks were useless unless the railway were kept open, a responsibility which an invitation to siege would automatically abdicate. But Mafeking did hold large supplies . . .

A point which Baden-Powell never mentioned at the time, but which was mentioned later by himself and his admirers, was that an agreement existed between the Cape Dutch and the Transvaal Boers that on the capture of certain towns, among them Mafeking, the former were to rise in rebellion. No impressive evidence has ever been brought forward from Boer sources to substantiate this claim. When this point was put forward after the war in a book by Creswicke, Baden-Powell claimed it as the major justification for the defence, thus weakening his earlier reasons.[2]

It had also been claimed that it was essential to prevent the Boers from acquiring a base 'for any designs they might have on Kimberley or Cape Colony'. Those who knew the Boer well, including Baden-Powell, would have realized that the fast-moving Boers would have had no use at all for such a base, particularly so far from all conceivable objectives. Kruger's directives reveal that he was not at all interested in holding Mafeking for long, an act which would only have put the Boers in a vulnerable defensive position—a move against all their known customs and intuitions; their intention was probably to leave a small garrison of local burghers in the place, as they did elsewhere, which could leave the moment it was threatened. From time to time other reasons and versions of the orders have been put forward concerning the defence of Mafeking. It is doubtful if any such simple military move has ever had so many reasons. Baden-Powell changed the emphasis of his orders and the reasons for holding Mafeking almost every time he wrote of them. Historians and

---

[1] *Report* to Roberts.
[2] Many Cape Dutch rebelled during the defence of Mafeking, and several commandos were raised in the area between it and Kimberley.

biographers seem to have taken their choice. Many of the reasons are couched as justifications.

The evidence of his writings at the time, however, suggest—despite what he said later—that Baden-Powell had no wish or obligation to defend Mafeking at all until it was clear that the authorities were not going to support him with further forces; that Wolseley's orders were to protect the far northern frontiers of the Transvaal, and that the force he had been given was all he could have for the time being; that Baden-Powell was extremely agitated about the problems of supply; and that he did not think he could protect both the frontier and Mafeking with the force available.

Baden-Powell decided to get into Mafeking as quickly as he could. As war drew nearer, his requests to Cape Town were increasingly for permission to get into the town rather than to stay out of it. Cecil, who had been quietly purchasing supplies for the Protectorate Regiment, approached Benjamin Weil, of Julius Weil & Co., a firm of Cape Town and Mafeking merchants who had large storage space available in Mafeking; Cecil talked in terms of very large sums of money and of stocks so vast that they could not have been entirely for military use.

The only military importance of Mafeking was as a base for supplying Baden-Powell's frontier force. It was also its weakness : for bases have to be protected. Baden-Powell's wildly exaggerated fears for his supply lines (in contrast to the attitude of Plumer, who was to face the same problem), and his eventual somewhat timid acceptance of investment, are oddly at variance with the great reputation for daring, initiative and open warfare that was to come his way.

*

On 23 August General Butler handed over his command, having resigned in protest at what he believed was a calculated policy to wage an unnecessary war against the Transvaal. With his departure, arrangements were made for supplies enough for a small army, let alone one modest regiment, to be poured into Mafeking.

Butler's successor was Lieutenant-General Sir Frederick Forestier-Walker, who had been rushed to Cape Town at very short notice. From him Baden-Powell received no encouragement about the safety of the Protectorate Regiment's stores. In answer to Baden-Powell's observation that in the lack of adequate support in Mafeking he was having to secure the town himself, Forrestier-Walker said that he would 'have to make the best of the situation'.[1]

Meanwhile Baden-Powell's chief staff officer, Major Lord Edward Cecil, was still in Cape Town demanding supplies. At length the Major, using his influence as son of the Prime Minister, raised the necessary cash for supplies from civilian sources by signing a 'note of hand' for £500,000, a great deal of money at any time, but in 1899 a princely figure indeed.[2]

According to Benjamin Weil, Cecil said : 'I place this order with you without the authority of my superiors. I may have to pay for it myself, but I will take the responsibility on my own shoulders.' Cecil had asked the authorities for a grant of £500,000, but they had turned it down.[3] Cecil's wife wrote: 'After several frustrated days, and after consulting Sir Alfred Milner, Lord Edward gave Messrs. Weil, the big Mafeking contractors, his note of hand for half a million pounds' worth of stores. It was very sporting and very shrewd of the Weils to take this risk; they must have known that he himself had not a tenth of this money. But they banked on Lord Edward's personality and on his father's position, and the deal saved Mafeking.'[4]

Cecil left Cape Town for Mafeking, but had to leave his wife at Kimberley; she had stepped out of bed there 'on to a not very well-swept floor' and trodden on a pin, which had to be extracted from her toe by an 'unshaven and collarless' local doctor. She returned to Cape Town on 30 August.

Goods wagons puffed up the line from Cape Town and Kimberley loaded with supplies and stores of all kinds. Already there were many cattle in the area immediately surrounding the town, principally belonging to the Africans. It had been expected that a customs duty on goods entering Rhodesia would be introduced that year, and many supplies had been going up the railway to beat it; but owing to the threat of war the duty had been postponed indefinitely and these goods were now in the railway sidings and sheds of Mafeking.

---

[1] Hillcourt, p. 162.
[2] About a tenth of this credit was used.
[3] *Weil Papers.*
[4] *My Picture Gallery,* Viscountess Milner, pp. 125–6.

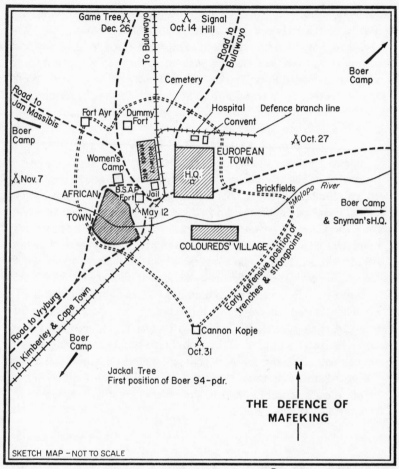

Game Tree ✗
Dec. 26

Oct. 14 ✗ Signal
Hill

To Bulawayo

Road to Bulawayo

Cemetery

Boer
Camp

Road to
Jan Massibis

Fort Ayr

Dummy
Fort

Hospital

Defence branch line

Convent

✗ Oct. 27

Boer
Camp

Women's
Camp

Railway
Works

EUROPEAN
TOWN

✗ Nov. 7

AFRICAN

B.S.A.P.
Fort

Jail

H.Q.

Brickfields

Molopo River

Boer Camp
& Snyman's H.Q.

TOWN

✗ May 12

COLOUREDS' VILLAGE

Early defensive position of
trenches & strongpoints

Road to Vryburg

To Kimberley & Cape Town

Boer
Camp

Cannon Kopje

✗ Oct. 31

Jackal Tree
First position of Boer 94-pdr.

N

THE DEFENCE OF
MAFEKING

SKETCH MAP – NOT TO SCALE

© CASSELL & CO. LTD 1966

Much of these belonged to Weil and to the Mayor of Mafeking, Mr Whiteley. Baden-Powell was aware of this, and approaches by Captain Ryan, of the Army Service Corps, were made to Whiteley and to Benjamin Weil, who was in Mafeking; they agreed to put these supplies at Baden-Powell's disposal in the event of a siege. Weil, convinced that there was going to be a siege, and sensing a business opportunity, glutted his stores with as many foodstuffs and supplies as transport could bring.

By half-way through September, Baden-Powell considered his two regiments reasonably prepared. But defences in Mafeking were primitive: a few stockades and upturned wagons where the streets ended. Desperate to get his force into the town, Baden-Powell thought up one of his well-known pieces of bluff. 'I got permission from the Cape Government to place an armed guard in Mafeking to protect these stores, but as the strength of that guard was not stipulated I moved the whole regiment into the place without delay.'[1] One can detect his sense of relief as he hurried his force into the town.

Baden-Powell had entangled himself by his own busy preparations. He had defeated most of the usefulness of half of his force before the war had even started. By having to protect his unnecessarily vast stores he had committed a classic military blunder, the dangers of which were stressed at military colleges around the world: to allow the guardianship of stores to dictate the immobility of all those for whom the stores were intended, the stores being only a means to an end and not the end itself.

*

Equipment and men arrived in town by train from over the Bechuanaland border. The new soldiers, in their baggy khaki uniforms, yellow puttees and 'smasher' hats, rode into the town, tents were erected, camps laid out, and Dixon's Hotel taken over as headquarters, with Minchin's Law Office next door.

There was much to be done; soon everyone, under the direction of the lively little Colonel, was hard at work. There was a new sense of purpose, of growing confidence, in the town.

---

[1] *Lessons from the 'Varsity of Life,* p. 202. Telegram from Cape: 15 September 1899.

Despite his busy schedule, Baden-Powell found time to tend to his literary career. For his most recent pocket booklet, *Aids to Scouting*, he had been unable to find a publisher in London. He had left the manuscript with his brother Frank, who had now placed it with Messrs. Gale & Polden. It was his seventh publication. Baden-Powell had heard of this in August, and had asked to see the proofs. These were sent to him in September, were corrected, and one chapter was revised. It was an unusual military textbook, including anecdotes, games, examples and contests; its relentlessly jolly style suggested that it might appeal as much to boys as to professional military men. It was dedicated, diplomatically, to Major-General Locke-Eliot, Inspector-General of Cavalry in India, where Baden-Powell's regiment still was. The first chapter was concerned with that admirable quality, by which the Victorians were so obsessed, Pluck : 'the main key to success in scouting is to have pluck and self-reliance.' The proofs left, rewrapped in the same paper in which they had arrived, on one of the last trains to leave Mafeking before the war. In due course the book was published, but it was unprepossessing in appearance and apparently slight in content; the military hierarchy took little notice of its underlying theme—that scouting (or the individual use of the infantryman) should be an integral part of training, a neglect which later it had good cause to rue.

Meanwhile the other half of the force, that under Colonel Plumer, Baden-Powell ordered to Tuli, near the junction of the Bechuanaland, Rhodesian and Transvaal borders : a good choice for the enormous task of covering the borders, which it would now be expected to undertake on its own.[1] It seems to have been Baden-Powell's intention all along to stay with the Mafeking force, and he therefore now lost sight of half his force for six months, although of course he was not to know of this at the time. According to Godley, most people expected the siege, considered inevitable, to last not more than six weeks.

On 4 October Baden-Powell assumed command of all forces in Mafeking and of the defences of the town. Permission had been granted in answer to yet another of his requests, and at last Cape Town had capitulated.[2] Preparations for defence, which had

---

[1] See Map, p. 15.
[2] *Staff Diary.*

previously been conducted in semi-secret (a fort had been constructed as a 'rifle-range') could now continue rapidly and in earnest.

The force that was assembled under Baden-Powell was as follows :

	Officers	Men
Protectorate Regiment (*Lieut.-Colonel Hore*)	21	448
B.S.A. Police (*Lieut.-Colonel Walford*)	10	81
Cape Police (*Inspectors Marsh and Browne*)	4	99
Bechuanaland Rifles (*Captain Cowan*)	5	77
The Town Guard (*Major, local Lieut.-Colonel, Vyvyan*)	6	296
Railway Detachment (*Captain Moore*)	1	115
Cape Boy Contingent	1	67
	48	1,183[1]

The last three sections were, at best, only half-trained.

The Cape Police were the local police, and the British South Africa Police was the Rhodesian police force, which had a base in Mafeking. The Bechuanaland Rifles were almost entirely Mafeking men. The Town Guard has already been described. The Railway Contingent was raised in a few days from the railway staff, and other employees, in the town, the Cape Boy Contingent from the coloured half-breeds' village. Of the total, 576 were equipped with magazine rifles, the remainder with Martini-Henry single-loaders. About a third of the force were citizens of the town and consisted of practically all the able-bodied men who had not already left. Although there was little doubt that the Boers would have no inclination to hold Mafeking, should it be left undefended, there was no telling what damage they would do should they raid it, so that on the whole the citizens were relieved at first by Baden-Powell's decision and glad to have the opportunity of defending their homes under a professional soldier. As well as these nearly 1,200 assorted troops, ranging from officers of the Grenadier Guards to coloured house-servants, railway labourers and ex-convicts, Baden-Powell decided to enrol a force from the African village, whom he

---

[1] *Official History*, p. 145. Baden-Powell gave a smaller figure for Captain Moore's Railway Detachment, which seems to have fluctuated considerably in strength.

armed with elephant guns and obsolete rifles, to serve as cattle guards, watchmen and scouts; these amounted to about 300. In the event, they covered the south-western approach to the town, around their own village, with only a small force of police in support. They were known as the 'Black Watch'. This was one of the few instances in the South African War of the unwritten rules of a 'white man's war' being broken. The native village was not provided with shelters for women and children, it being held that the Boers would not shell the Africans.

The most serious shortage was that of artillery. It was hardly adequate to mount an expedition against natives, let alone to keep off the canny Boer. There were two muzzle-loading seven-pounders with a range variously described as between 1,800 and 2,500 yards. They were out-dated, and were so worn that the fuses had to be wedged into the shells with paper. After repeated pleas to Kimberley, two more antiquated seven-pounders, in little better condition, arrived from that town, itself making preparations for a siege. Also available in the way of light pieces were a one-pounder Hotchkiss, a two-inch Nordenfeldt, and seven Maxim machine-guns.

On 5 October a Boer force began concentrating in a number of camps near the south-west border of the Transvaal.

Because he expected an artillery barrage on the town, Baden-Powell wisely decided to push out the defensive perimeter as far as possible, thus reversing the few arrangements already made by the Town Guard. At first this perimeter was five and three-quarter miles in extent.[1] Baden-Powell considered the northern section of the town the most vulnerable to attack. Sending out men to collect all the spare pieces of track lying beside the line for some miles, he ordered the construction of a spur to the railway of about a mile in length, at right-angles to the main line. Two armoured engines were sent up from Kimberley and wagons were armoured with steel plates and rails so that riflemen could fire standing up inside them. It seemed an excellent ploy—a movable defence to cover at a moment's notice that entire approach to the town. Lady Sarah, who had come down with her husband from Bulawayo, and who was an observer at all these preparations, was no military expert, but she was not impressed: '. . . this train proved to be absolutely useless.'

---

[1] *Staff Diary.*

Baden-Powell, Godley and Vyvyan drew up an elaborate plan for the defence of the town, and during the early days of October there was feverish digging of trenches and construction of dug-outs and shelters. Said Lady Sarah: 'We were, indeed, as jolly as the proverbial sandboys during these few days in Mafeking before the war commenced.' Frequent alarms were sounded to practise the garrison and populace in the defence of the town. At the convent, the six Irish Sisters set about organizing a casualty ward. At the hospital, the Matron, Miss Hill, prepared for the reception of wounded, under two medical officers, Major Anderson and Lieutenant Holmden, helped by a number of lady volunteers. Several civilian doctors were also available. As it was doubtful whether the water supply could be defended, old wells were renewed before the siege began, thus ensuring the most vital of all necessities for the town's defence. A number of notices appeared in the town:

> The Inhabitants are warned that mines are being laid at various points outside the town in connection with the defences. Their position will be marked, in order to avoid accidents, by small red flags. Cattle herds and others should be warned accordingly. Mafeking: Dated this 7th day of October, 1899.

SPIES

> There are in town today nine known spies. They are hereby warned to leave before 12 noon tomorrow or they will be apprehended.

> It is possible the Boers might attempt to shell the town, and although every endeavour will be made to provide shelter for the women and children, yet arrangements could be made with the railway to move any of them to a place of safety if they desire to go away from Mafeking, and it is suggested that some place on the Transvaal border, such as Palapye, Siding, or Francistown, might be more suitable and less expensive places than the already crowded towns of the Colony. The men would, of course, remain to defend Mafeking, which,

with its present garrison and defences, will be easy to hold. Those desirous of leaving should inform the Stationmaster, Mafeking, their number of adults and children, class of accommodation required, and destination.

COLONEL BADEN-POWELL, *Colonel Commanding Frontier Forces.*

On 8 October Kruger issued an ultimatum to the British Government demanding, among other things, the withdrawal of British forces from the border areas.

Each contingent at Mafeking was given a section of the perimeter to hold: to the west, the Protectorate Regiment under Colonel Hore lined the trenches, the Baralong tribesmen of the village holding the north-west corner, with a detachment of Cape Police under Inspector C. S. Marsh in support. Godley, although junior in rank to Hore, had command of the entire western approaches. Cannon Kopje was assigned to the British South Africa Police under Walford, with parties of 'Black Watch' natives manning the line at either side. At the south-east corner of the defence system were the remainder of the Cape Police, under Inspector J. W. Browne. Then came the Bechuanaland Rifles in the east, with the Railway Detachment, and an armoured train, to the north. The motley Town Guard held the inner perimeter around the town itself. A system of telephone communication was constructed to the command points of the various sectors from Baden-Powell and Cecil at Dixon's Hotel and Minchin's office next door so that reserves could immediately be thrown in to any position. The defensive arrangements were good in conception; whether they were good in detail, and whether they had been properly carried out, remained to be seen.

The news had quickly spread south that Baden-Powell had moved into Mafeking, and was preparing for a siege. Among the correspondents now converging on the town were Angus Hamilton of *The Times*, Emerson Neilly of the *Pall Mall Gazette*, F. D. Baillie of the *Morning Post*, Vere Stent of Reuters, E. G. Parslow of the *Daily Chronicle*. Hamilton wrote: '. . . a crowd of journalists drifts about smothered beneath a variety of secret reports.'

When not in the dugout they were at Reisle's Mafeking

Hotel : 'Over twenty bedrooms, sale rooms, ladies' drawing-rooms, lounge and private bar, shower baths, and stabling.' The most intrepid of the reporters was Neilly, who arrived at the town on 4 October. He wrote : 'I reconnoitred the outskirts of the town, and several times rode over to the wire fence that formed the line of demarcation between the Colony and the Republic . . . I was warned back by Boer guards . . . "I do not wish to spy on your laagers," I said. "I am a newspaper war correspondent, and wish to have a talk with your commandant. Our countries are not at war, and I hope they will not be." A strapping young fellow in the uniform of the Staats Artillery brought my note up to the commandant, and I waited over an hour for a reply. He regretted that he could not find time to grant me an interview as he was very busy.' Baden-Powell also went out, 'in the dark of night', and estimated the Boer strength by the number of camp fires and wagons.

Far away in London, on 8 October, within an hour of the receipt of President Kruger's ultimatum in the capital, young Winston Churchill was approached by the *Morning Post*. As Churchill said : 'The terms were higher, I think, than any previously paid in British journalism to war correspondents.' To a young man of twenty-four they were extraordinary : £250 a month, all expenses paid, entire discretion as to movements, and four months' minimum guarantee of employment. Before departing, Churchill had an interview with Joseph Chamberlain, having recently made the Colonial Secretary's acquaintance : it took place in a hansom cab jogging between Chamberlain's home and the Colonial Office. Chamberlain was optimistic about the probable course of the war in the major area of combat, Natal. Churchill said :

'What about Mafeking?'

'Ah, Mafeking, that may be besieged. But if they cannot hold out for a few weeks, what is one to expect?'

Churchill was depressed at the attitude of the War Office. The Intelligence Branch had informed the War Minister that 200,000 men would be required to beat the Boers, and had prepared two volumes of information about the difficulties that would be encountered; these had been rejected. Churchill, with a *Times* correspondent, A. W. A. Pollock, boarded the *Dunottar Castle* for Cape Town in the second week of October. Also on board was General Sir Redvers Buller, v.c., burly and supremely confident, with his staff, on the way to take over the South African Command from Forestier-Walker. Buller, a sixty-year-old Devonian, was perhaps the most prominent of all the Wolseleyites. He had received no instructions as to what he was to do when he got to South Africa; but, according to the Milner Papers, he was already 'much under the influence of Butler'.

In the Sudan, Colonel Bryan Mahon had other things on his mind apart from Mafeking—of which, indeed, he may well have never heard: he was now deep into the desert, chasing the defeated Dervishes.

In Mafeking the trenches and shelters were nearly completed, although work had been hindered by a sudden plague of locusts. Hamilton of *The Times* wrote: 'There is lacking but one thing— war. The troops want it to prove their efficiency, the journalists demand it to justify their existence, and the countryside approves since it has sent the price of food-stuffs and of native labour to a premium, [and] the Boers want it.'

The jolting old black mail-coach from Mafeking to Johannesburg made its last journey, baggage strapped on top, clattering out of the town in a cloud of dust. It did not return.

Jameson himself had arrived in the town, anxious to remain for the siege. Lady Sarah wrote, 'he was hustled away with more haste than courtesy by General [*sic*] Baden-Powell, who bluntly told him that if he meant to stay in the town a battery of artillery would be required to defend it.' 'Doctor Jim' disappeared up the line in one of the last trains out of Mafeking.[1] He was soon to be heading for the town of Ladysmith. As for Lady Sarah Wilson herself, Baden-Powell 'did not look on my presence with great favour . . . We had taken a tiny cottage in the town, and we had all our meals at Dixon's Hotel, where the food was weird, but where certainly no depression of spirits reigned . . . I even bought a white pony, one of the best I have ever ridden . . . Then I was allotted comparatively safe quarters at the residence of Mr Benjamin Weil, of the firm of well-known South African merchants. His residence stood in the centre of the little town, adjacent to the railway station . . . On all sides one heard

---

[1] Jameson had earlier revealed in a letter that he had no intention of staying in Mafeking, and wanted to go to Natal for the 'real fighting'. *Life of Jameson,* Sir I. Colvin (Arnold, 1922), Vol. II, p. 187.

reproaches levelled at the Cape Government, and especially at General Sir William Butler, until lately commanding the troops in the Colony.'

On 11 October, at five o'clock in the afternoon, Kruger's declaration of war became effective.

That morning a train steamed out of the town, and away across the distant veld, with a hundred and seventy women and children on board. The Cape authorities, still uneasy about the preparations for a siege, refused to pay their fares. With it went one of the armoured trains. Those who remained sat on the verandas and waited. There were 1,074 white men, 229 white women, 405 children, and about 7,500 Africans.

Later that day scouts cantered into the square and reined up at Dixon's. They reported Boer troops crossing the frontier fence.[1] A notice, signed by Baden-Powell, was posted outside headquarters:

> In consequence of the armed forces of the South African Republic having committed an act of war, by invading British territory, I give notice that a state of war exists, and that the civil law is for the time being suspended.

Baden-Powell was now in supreme command, virtually with powers of life and death, in Mafeking.

In the evening a staff officer, apparently alarmed by the numbers of the Boer force now converging around the town, told Lady Sarah, and Godley's wife who was also in the town, to leave immediately. He expected the town to be rushed the following day, and the garrison would be obliged to fight its way out. Mrs Godley rode north for Bulawayo. Lady Sarah left for a settlement fifty miles down the road to Kimberley.[2] Having got there in an exhausted condition, she heard the following night 'a dull booming noise [which] almost froze the blood in my veins. There was no mistaking the firing of guns at no very great distance.' She fled to another settlement, twenty-five miles

---

[1] Neilly had already been out that morning and had casually watched the Boers crossing the border.

[2] It was reported in the London newspapers that she had trekked 200 miles. One paper said: 'It was all very well for Lady Sarah, who doubtless was accustomed to violent exercise, but we commiserate her poor maid.'

west, far from the road and not far from the Kalahari itself. There she stayed with the lone British inhabitant, a Mrs Keeley, wife of a farmer who was in Mafeking; she awaited events.

On 12 October the telegraph line south from Mafeking went dead: somewhere down the track it had been cut.

That evening, towards sundown, lookouts at Jackal Tree reported Boers tearing up rails to the south. A train-load of women and children which had just left for the south returned and confirmed that the line was up. If it was part of Baden-Powell's mission to protect the railway link with Rhodesia, he had failed—inevitably, against a force far stronger than his own—within twenty-four hours of the start of the war. One of the armoured trains had been sent south to meet the second armoured train returning from Kimberley, but the latter was south of the break in the track made by the Boers. It was the firing at the capture of this train, probably the first shots of the Boer War, that had been heard by Lady Sarah Wilson. The Boer commander who took the train, after a brisk engagement, was J. H. de la Rey—'dark, with shaggy eyebrows, great aquiline nose, deeply lined face, and a vast burly beard', he was fifty years old, a rich and courteous farmer who had an English governess for his children, was a member of the Volksraad (or Parliament) who had opposed Kruger's policies, and still had a military reputation to forge. Tearing up the rails to the south of the town, de la Rey took the first action of the investment of Mafeking; fate was to arrange that it would be he also who would take the last. For the present he appears to have moved south with his commandos, towards Kimberley.[1]

The following day, 13 October, a great quantity of superfluous dynamite which had been found in the town, and which Baden-Powell considered highly undesirable in view of the fact that the station-master was an Irish nationalist,[2] was taken seven miles up the line in two old trucks. It was eventually fired on by some suspicious Boer scouts; the resulting explosion alarmed friend and foe alike for many miles. The line was broken to the north, and Mafeking was thus cut off by rail. In both the morning and afternoon the remain-

---

[1] *Good-bye Dolly Gray,* Rayne Kruger, p. 69.
[2] Churchill interview, the *Morning Post,* 27 June 1900.

ing armoured train trundled out of the town a short way to reconnoitre; on the first occasion, greeted by fire, it briskly returned.

That afternoon the telegraph line north also went dead.

The advance of the enemy was being made without haste: it was
uncanny, slow, sinister. The reports of scouts said that the enemy had
been seen to all sides.[1]

Baden-Powell waited.

The Transvaal forces in the west were led by Commandant-
General Cronje, 'Honest Piet', a stolid, ponderous, bearded leader
in his sixtieth year. In a previous war with the British he had been in
command of the unsuccessful investment of the British garrison at
Potchefstroom in 1881; he had been unable to force their surrender
before the armistice. Latterly he had commanded the force which
had taken the surrender of the Jameson raiders. Among the Boers
he had a great military reputation. Now he was in over-all command
of all Transvaal forces in the western area, not just those near Mafeking. His eyes were cast south, towards the more valuable prize of
Kimberley. Cronje intended brushing aside Mafeking. He was
described as a man of 'truculent and stubborn energy'. With
him were the Potchefstroom, Lichtenburg, Marico, Rustenburg
and Wolmaransstaad commandos, with the Bloemhof commando
farther south. With this force he intended—after joining with
Orange Free Staters under Commandant J. Prinsloo—to sweep
west and then south, past Kimberley, and on to the Orange River,
threatening the Cape.[2] But first there was Mafeking. And then there
was Kimberley. Whether, in the eighteen years since the siege of
Potchefstroom, 'Honest Piet' had learned what, if anything, to do,
about an isolated enemy garrison, remained to be seen.

The size of the force that now set up temporary camp around
Mafeking varies remarkably between sources. The highest figure was

---

[1] Baden-Powell, on at least one occasion—*Adventures and Accidents*—put the
start of the siege a day earlier: 12 October. The *Official History* and other
accounts agree on the evening of the 13th. Thus Baden-Powell sometimes referred to a siege of 218 days instead of the customary 217.

[2] According to most sources, but one Rhodesian source (*Milner Papers:* 11
November 1899) claims Cronje intended going north to take Bulawayo, and
Baden-Powell once made the same claim in a letter to Colonel N. F. F. Chamber-
lain, Private Secretary to Roberts (*Roberts Papers*, P.R.O., 30 June 1900).

that given by Baden-Powell long after the war: 12,000. The lowest was that given by Goold-Adams in an official report to Cape Town: 4,000. At the time, Baden-Powell himself gave an estimate of '5,000 to 6,000'.[1] The main non-official Boer account of the investment gives the Boer force as 6,000, but most Boer figures include the commando to the south, and also the forces around Vryburg (a day's journey away by train).[2] Baillie of the *Morning Post* said the figure of 6,000 was 'undoubtedly correct'. Hamilton of *The Times* also gave 6,000. The *Official History* gave 6,750, although Baden-Powell, in his report to Roberts, had by then put his figure up to 8,000 (an estimate which became the most popular among later writers on the defence, although 9,000 and 11,000 were also stated).

The War Departments of the two Boer Republics kept no records of the number of serving burghers, but it is probable that not more than 32,000 Boer troops crossed the frontier in October, about a quarter of them in the projected thrust into the Cape in the Mafeking-Kimberley area, and most of the remainder in the Ladysmith area in the thrust to the Natal coast.[3] With them, at this stage, they had Krupp and Vickers-Maxim machine-guns. They were bringing up high-velocity, breech-loading artillery, as up to date as Baden-Powell's pieces were ancient. The Boer artillery was manned by professional gunners, who served for three-year terms even in time of peace. Baden-Powell's fear was that if the Boer commanders knew how to use their artillery—concentrating it on one point in support of a rush—his defences might be breached. If they knew . . . But Baden-Powell, with his knowledge of the Boers, must have been confident that the threat of a rush of well-prepared defences by the Boers was so unlikely that it could almost be dismissed. What he had to do was to protect his force from bombardment and wait . . . about six

---

[1] Baden-Powell's figures are given in fuller detail in Chapter 15. Goold-Adams's figure from *Roberts Papers*, 29 October 1899.

[2] *Met Cronje Aan Die Wesfront*, F. D. Conradie (Bloemfontein, 1943).

[3] British Intelligence's figure of the entire Transvaal Army (P.R.O.). The combined forces of the two republics at the start of the war were said to be 40,000 by Kruger in his *Memoirs*, and 45,000 by de Wet, *Three Years' War* (Constable, 1902). The *Cambridge History* gives 48,000, of which 20,000 were on the whole West Front of more than 300 miles. The German official history, *The War in South Africa*, gives 40,000. Over 50,000 Boers in the two republics were liable for military service; there were 1,000 regulars, plus armed police.

weeks probably, until relief came; but if it were longer, then he was very well prepared indeed.

And so the two sides had come together, almost as if hypnotized: the one timidly sacrificing its freedom and inviting investment; the other bewildered, unsure, surrounding a bait of the desirability of which it was not even certain. On one side one of the most ambitious officers in the British Army, but also one of the least 'educated' in a military sense, was in command; a good man at a party, with a quick mind and a sense of fun, excellent at social games, the indefatigable 'life and soul'. To him the chance of a lifetime to display his gifts had occurred. On the opposing side were investing troops who were by nature cautious and by instinct unwilling to take part in a clash of arms, preferring to outflank their foe by hard riding and superior manœuvrability, and enforce surrenders.

The stage was set; the actors were assembled. Whatever the justifications, the military value or lack of it in the context of the war now beginning, it was to be perhaps the most casually conducted and jauntily withstood siege in modern history—so much so that at times it hardly took on the characteristics of a siege at all.

4. Battle and Bombardment

The siege of Mafeking began, as it was to end, with blood, death and confusion. On Saturday, 14 October, the first full day of the investment, was fought the action of Signal Hill and Five-Mile Bank. It was a sharp, bitter conflict; it smelled and sounded like war.

Early that morning, when it was still dark, Lord Charles Cavendish-Bentinck, who commanded one of the four squadrons of the Protectorate Regiment, was returning to town with a patrol. He was approaching the railway line when he and his men heard voices nearby. With a low 'Halt!' he brought up the patrol. 'Dismount' was whispered from man to man, and each swung from his saddle, rifle in hand. A party of Boers was observed in a hollow, talking and brewing coffee; a pleasant smell of cooking pervaded the air. The African dawn was lighting the horizon. Magazines and breeches were loaded and, at Cavendish-Bentinck's orders, a volley was loosed off, followed by another. Within seconds the patrol was mounted and careering away across the veld to heavy rifle fire from the disturbed Boers, few if any of whom appeared to have suffered injury. Cavendish-Bentinck made one of the few sound decisions that morning and, having completed his patrol, returned to Mafeking to make his report.

The alarm was raised in the Boer camps in that area, to the north of the town and some seven miles from it. In Mafeking the armoured train was soon steaming out into the plain, which was half-lit by the morning light. Both sides drew towards battle.

The train, manned by fifteen troopers of the British South Africa Police, passed the patrol of Cavendish-Bentinck as the latter was riding up the line near the town.

'Go along and engage them, and when you find them, give them beans,' shouted Lord Charles.

However, it was not the restricted and clumsy train which found the enemy, but the quick and mobile enemy which found the train. Cautiously it proceeded up the line, puffing hard and clicking over the metals. About four and a half miles out, at a bend near Signal Hill, a well-placed ambush opened heavy fire.

There was a tremendous din. The wheels of the train stopped and it slid to a halt. The Mauser bullets of the Boers spattered over the armoured sides of the two wagons, and the bullets of two machine-guns rained onto the metal and whined away, flattened, into the bush. In the train itself, a machine-gun in each wagon firing wildly out of the firing holes, the racket was deafening. Driver Waine and Fireman Moffat, in the heavily protected cabin of the engine, waited while steam hissed from the engine and wondered, in some desperation, whether their own side was winning or whether they were shortly to be slaughtered by 'merciless Boers'.

For twenty minutes or more heavy and fairly ineffective fire continued from both sides. Inside the train the men, most of them under fire for the first time, were safe. Outside, the Boers charged about brandishing rifles and firing, with occasionally one falling to the ground.

In order that both wagons could more effectively use their firepower, efforts were made to get the train in a more practicable position. This was difficult because the noise was so great that Waine was unable to hear the order on the speaking-tube. At length a ceasefire was called so that this instruction could be conveyed. As the train moved off, the Boers cheered, believing it was leaving the field and that they had won the day.

As soon as the train halted again, the Boers, exposed to greater fire, scurried away for cover, leaving several bodies strewn across the grass. The firing died down.

By now the newspaper correspondents had arrived. Baillie had narrowly escaped capture when his horse had been shot beneath him. Neilly surveyed the situation from a hill, through his binoculars. As the firing ceased, he reached the train. He reported: 'The experience of Waine and his mate Moffat was not one to be borne by men of weak nerve. Closed in their cab, they were almost deafened by the noise of action and the hammering of the enemy's bullets against the steel armour . . . Like men in the closed stokehold of a warship, they were imprisoned where they were, and all the time were in suspense.'

The noise of battle could be faintly heard in the town, and a group of alarmed citizens gathered in the Market Square. It seemed as if the Boers were about to storm the place. The tension was considerable and there were ugly scenes when some Boer women (about two hundred Boers were living in Mafeking) taunted and jeered the alarmed British. Baden-Powell sent out a squadron of the Protectorate Regiment to secure the train, which he now feared would be cut off, and to discourage the Boers from launching a full-scale attack. They were under the command of Captain Fitzclarence, and with them went *The Times* correspondent, Angus Hamilton, the most perceptive and experienced of the reporters in Mafeking. Hamilton said: 'This movement began the more serious and certainly the more determined portion of the engagement.'

On the arrival of Fitzclarence's force, the Boers fell back still farther; by then there were about 400 of them, according to British accounts. As they had at that time no intention of trying to storm the town, they were no doubt puzzled by the increasing British activity.

Hamilton described the situation thus: 'The two forces were both in extended order, the one falling back upon the lines of a position which had been carefully selected and which was admirably adapted to their methods of fighting, the other pursuing . . . Had Captain Fitzclarence but realized it, and had this young officer not been so intrepid, he would have recognized in this Boer movement the ruse by which they hoped to entice [his force] within range of a position from which it could be more effectually surrounded.' When they had settled in their new position, the Boers opened a heavy fire, and Fitzclarence and his men were obliged to seek the shelter of three native huts. They were now about a mile from the armoured train and the railway, and had lost its supporting fire.[1] Hamilton wrote: 'The action of Captain Fitzclarence in endeavouring to meet the Boer commando was one of those inopportune acts of gallantry where loss, should the fight be successful, is overlooked. Technically speaking, of course [it] was all at fault, and it soon was seen how serious the

---

[1] The *Official History* describes 'Fitzclarence, manœuvring brilliantly, and well-supported by the armoured train'.

situation had become . . . From the ridge of the Boer position our complete formation and the situation of each unit could be seen. It merely required a little sharp-shooting, keen sight and sufficient energy to cause a disaster. Our men lay upon the ground seeking cover where they could find it, but they had neither the trees nor the low-lying shrubs nor the rocks . . . which had lent themselves to the Boers' shelter.' Soon Fitzclarence's men were falling dead and wounded, even the rather wild shooting of the Boers having to take its inevitable effect. Major Anderson, the Army doctor, had come up and had taken over one of the huts as a dressing-station. He had not received any orders, and had come on his own initiative. Angus Hamilton was in the dressing-station. 'It was the first time that any-one had seen the effect upon human beings of the Mauser bullets. One man, as he came back, was advised not to sit down; another man, with extraordinary coolness in seeing the nature of his wounds, which were seven, exclaimed that it still might be possible for him to enjoy the functions of a married man.'

Neilly, meanwhile, had ridden back to his hotel in the town to have his breakfast. His horse having hit a thorn fence on the way, he returned to the scene of fighting on a borrowed bicycle. On arrival at the three native huts, he was greeted by a voice from the ground saying, 'For 'eaven's sake, sir, dismount. Your 'andle-bar's drawing fire.' It seemed that the sun reflecting on the nickelled bar had attracted the enemy, and Neilly flung himself from the saddle as bullets flew around him.

Owing to the persistence and rapidity of the fire, ammunition soon ran short; one section had none left at all, and a volunteer who went to get a supply received fatal wounds. Still Fitzclarence would not withdraw. Throughout he acted with personal bravery, if not with military intelligence.[1] Everyone was praying for artillery support, which was a long time coming as the force was holding a position which it had never been intended to occupy. At length a gun appeared about a mile off and, as Hamilton put it, 'each for a brief moment stopped to congratulate his fellow upon the succour at hand . . . Suddenly a cloud of smoke hung over the gun and a shell

---

[1] He was again to show great gallantry at Gheluwe, Flanders, fifteen years later almost to the day.

shrieked through the air. We rapidly speculated upon the amount of damage it would make, when, with noisy force, it burst among us.' The second seven-pounder shell fell on one of the huts which was sheltering the wounded; fortunately it was too ineffective to do more than cause dismay and extreme anger.

By now Baden-Powell had become aware of the general situation by field-telephone. It was clear that not only his armoured train, with its two precious guns, was in danger of being cut off; nearly a quarter of his only fully-trained regiment, heavily engaged, was now in the same peril. He sent a message to Fitzclarence advising retirement; it did not get through. From his H.Q. in the centre of the town, he had telephoned Colonel Hore and had ordered out yet another troop of the Protectorate Regiment. As Godley pointed out: 'Had the Boers pushed home their attack in the first instance, nothing could have stopped them from riding straight into the town.' Baden-Powell, however, was more familiar with the Boer. He had already told the garrison: 'The Boers will never come on and storm a position. They cannot possibly get in or even near the place if everyone sticks to his post and shoots straight.'[1]

At Five-Mile Bank the skirmish appeared to be at a decisive stage. Neilly wrote that evening: 'Our position was an open one, with little cover. Here and there was a khaki dot that represented a fighting man, and yellow-putteed legs and spurred heels peeped from this tuft of scrub and that. Now the fire slackened to a mere crack, crack; again it blazed out anew into almost deafening sound, and thousands of bullets fairly screamed overhead and knocked spurts of dust from the dry veldt like the splashing of raindrops in a placid pool.'

With ammunition almost gone, Fitzclarence's men stopped firing soon after eight o'clock. The Boers were in command, but, as so often in war, the position was no more clear to them than it was to those who were on the brink of annihilation. The Boers ceased firing also. The fresh detachment of the Protectorate Regiment arrived. The British force got up, mounted their horses and left the field unmolested. The train, which all this while had been able to offer little support owing to Fitzclarence having been drawn by the Boers, collected the wounded and steamed back to town. It then immediately

---

[1] *General Orders*, 13 October 1899.

returned to the scene of battle to collect the bodies of the two British dead. The stretcher-bearers, although accompanied by a Red Cross flag, were fired on by the Boers on their walk from the railway to the scene of the fighting.

It was four hours since the fighting had begun with Cavendish-Bentinck's first shots, and in that time there had been a very heavy expenditure of rifle and machine-gun ammunition.

The return of the troops was witnessed with some relief by Baden-Powell, the garrison and the townspeople, although not by the sharp-tongued Boer women, who shortly found themselves in jail, as much for their own safety as for any other reasons.

British casualties were two killed and sixteen wounded. British estimates of the Boer losses vary widely. In his official report after the siege, Baden-Powell put Boer losses definitely at fifty-five killed and many wounded, but in his report at the time he said this figure was 'probably an exaggerated estimate'.[1] The *Times History* gives the official Boer figure of casualties at this engagement as three.

There is no doubt that the fortitude of the Protectorate Regiment throughout the morning had considerably impressed the Boers, and the fact that Baden-Powell apparently had an offensive notion of defence should have provided them with thought also. The reckless-ness of Fitzclarence thus had an adverse effect on Boer morale, although if it were typical of the military expertise of the garrison it should have filled them with joy.

This haphazard and ill-conducted affair was proudly described by Baden-Powell in his official report as, 'This smartly fought little engagement.'[2] Lord Edward Cecil described Fitzclarence's move-ment as brilliant. Commented Hamilton: 'It is a question whether this movement was not, at least, characterized by an equal amount of foolhardiness.'

*

---

[1] Baden-Powell dispatch as reported in *The Times*, 23 October 1899.
[2] According to one of the biographers, however, Baden-Powell 'warned them against disregarding his injunction not to allow the Boers to draw them into a position from which they would have to be extricated by others': *Baden-Powell*, R. H. Kiernan.

That afternoon, messages arrived in Mafeking from scouts to the effect that Boer forces were concentrating in two areas. After a while they could be seen, through glasses, gathering at points of assembly and making their traditional fortified encampments or laagers. Alarm arrangements had already been made, and that day a red flag flew from Baden-Powell's headquarters all day, and a red lantern at the same place was shown throughout the night. A Union Jack at the flagpole, or a green light at night, signified 'All Clear'. A night attack was fully expected and few people slept in Mafeking as they waited for the dawn; but not one shot was heard, only the barking of distant dogs and the occasional crisp orders of the watch.

The following day, being a Sunday, was expected to afford some respite. No one thought the devout Boers would fight on a Sunday, and they were correct. The townspeople crowded their places of worship—Catholic, Anglican, Wesleyan—to an unaccustomed extent, and sang the National Anthem and prayed for the Queen; the Boers, across the veld, sang their fervent hymns and prayed for strength and justice.

Baden-Powell had sent a messenger to Cronje to complain of the firing on the Red Cross flag the previous day. Even he must have been surprised by the response. A Boer doctor drove into the town in an open carriage surmounted by an enormous Red Cross flag. He was entertained to lunch. He apologized to Baden-Powell and said that Cronje had not been responsible; the shots had been fired by young men who had not realized the significance of the flag. Cronje was willing to execute those in command of the party which had fired if Baden-Powell could show that any of his men had been killed or wounded by the act. It was clear that the Boers were determined not to take second place to the British in the matter of how to conduct a civilized war. Baden-Powell replied with a polite note, and the doctor returned to Cronje with a present of a bottle of whisky and some beer. Soon another note arrived, this time from Assistant Commandant-General J. P. Snyman, who had been in local command, and who had probably been reprimanded by Cronje. He said that a ceasefire would be observed that evening for the purpose of collecting the dead.

Next morning, at 9.50 a.m., the bombardment of Mafeking began. Baden-Powell had advised everyone to take cover during the day.

Shells were fired into the town for several hours at one period, but then gradually ceased till they finally stopped altogether after mid-day, most of them dropping into the ground with vapid explosions, throwing up little puffs of earth and smoke. Only two buildings were hit, one of them being the hospital. The total casualties of this entire bombardment were one hen killed and one dog wounded (it later died). Said Neilly: 'It was simply amazing. At that rate it would take the enemy the best part of a century to batter down the place.' Said Hamilton: 'It is perhaps no exaggeration to say that nothing so ludicrous in the history of modern warfare has been propagated . . . The shells were of such poor quality as to be incapable of any explosive force whatever.'

Said the *Official History*:

It will be seen how Britons' historic genius for triumphing in such situations was to be maintained at Mafeking; how, unshackled by the cautious laws of war, they were once more to make good their own peculiar law, that numbers count for little against endurance, or heavy guns against enthusiasm. The British soldier is not versed in the history which his predecessors have made; yet, though Lucknow or Jellalabad are but names to him, he may be trusted to reassert always the spirit of such, apparently, hopeless defences.

Not only were the shells ineffective because of the powdery walls of Mafeking, of the wide dispersion of buildings in the generously spaced town, of the lowness of the buildings and defensive works, and of their own high proportion of defectiveness, but also the aiming of the Boer gunners—despite their training and the smart uniforms which they alone in their Army wore—was eccentric in the extreme. Moreover, the shells which they mostly used were shrapnel which could cause but little damage so long as the garrison was under cover.

The Boers, anxious to discover the effect of the barrage which had seemed and sounded impressive enough from where it was launched, sent a messenger with a white flag. He turned out to be an Englishman, named Everitt, who was fighting for the Boers—his white flag being four very soiled handkerchiefs tied together. His message was that Cronje suggested the unconditional surrender of the town to avoid further bloodshed. When news of this got around Mafeking, the defenders, already lightheaded at the ridiculous bombardment, gave vent to understandable mirth. Mr Everitt was 'asked to lunch at Dixon's, and there provided with ham, cool whiskeys and sodas, besides various other delicacies'.[1]

During the days that followed more dugouts were constructed. For the enemy was observed at work on Jackal Tree Hill, two miles south of Mafeking, building an emplacement for a much larger gun than hitherto; more serious danger was expected if and when this gun arrived.

Sergeant Moffat, in charge of the Signallers, with the aid of a Mr Walker, the agent for the South African Acetylene Gas Company, had constructed a searchlight out of two biscuit-tins pressed into a cone and an acetylene burner; it vastly impressed the Boers when trained towards, if not on, them at night. Unfortunately it was short-lived as the carbide escaped after a hit on the store. But this was just the kind of thing that appealed to Baden-Powell, whose particular gifts, theatrical and unconventional, were finding themselves in a perfect setting. Already he was proving himself a resourceful if (as will be seen) sometimes careless defensive commander, one who might be an unpredictable adversary so long as the fighting remained static. He had not, however, brought in a system of rationing.

For a week little happened. There were many false alarms, and at length the nerves of the townspeople became so frayed that the ringing of bells as an alarm signal—they had rung frequently and always needlessly—was revised. During the week the water supply, as expected, was cut off; but the old wells, already renewed and prepared, were immediately brought into use and there was 'an abundance of water', with the Molopo flowing through the lines and the house rain-tanks well supplied.

Then a message arrived from Cronje, addressing Baden-Powell as 'Honoured Sir' and warning him of a further bombardment with which he intended to conquer the town. Baden-Powell replied:

'To His Honour, Piet Cronje . . . I would remind you that the

---

[1] *Diary*, G. H. Bell, 17 October 1900.

present war is of one government against another—not of people against people. Now you propose to inflict damage upon private property in a peaceful town, and possibly to injure women and children under the excuse of war. If you do this it will justify us (although such method of retaliation is repugnant to me) in ordering similar methods to be taken in a wholesale manner when the time comes for our forces to enter the Transvaal . . . I have the honour to be, sir, Yours most obediently, R. S. S. BADEN-POWELL, *Commanding H.M. Forces, Mafeking.*

This was clear enough, but whether it would have much effect on the phlegmatic Cronje was doubtful. In the same letter, Baden-Powell pointed out that three Red Cross flags which he asked to be respected were at the convent (converted to an auxiliary hospital), the hospital and the women's camp which had been prepared on the outskirts of the town. A yellow flag would fly over the jail when certain Boers were being held in custody.

Final preparations took place in expectation of a more powerful barrage which Cronje had thoughtfully intimated would begin sometime after 6.0 a.m. on Monday, 23 October. (Shelters and fortifications continued to be changed, added to and improved throughout the defence.) Trenches were dug in the town itself—through the streets, across backyards and the Market Square—primarily to protect the inhabitants against shells. Most householders constructed their own shelters beside their dwellings, and a more elaborate one was made for H.Q. beside Dixon's Hotel. Dugouts, containing fifteen to twenty men, were provided with food and water for two days. The most obtrusive of them were dummies, and a very pretentious dummy H.Q. was built at a far distance from the real H.Q., with Union Flag, protective earthworks and sandbags.

The farthest point south in the defensive line was an old fort known as Cannon Kopje, built on rising ground beyond the river, which commanded the entire town; from it the defences went round the east of the town, skirting some brickfields, round the hospital and adjacent convent, then to Fort Ayr, built on rising ground two miles to the west, behind which was the women and children's camp of tents with its underground shelters connected by covered ways, constructed in a slight depression, then round the native village, across the river and back to Cannon Kopje.[1] Inside this perimeter of trenches and dugouts, zarebas of thorns, which had previously been used successfully by the British in wars against African spearmen, were constructed at some points. A number of small mud forts were built at intervals along the line of trenches. Wisely concentrating on the mobility of their limited armour, Baden-Powell and Vyvyan had emplacements ready for the reception of a gun on every side of the defence perimeter, which now stretched for nearly seven miles. Some of the defensive arrangements were inspired by Godley, who, although he was only concerned with the western approaches, was the source of many ideas and much advice. At H.Q. a lookout was made on the roof, and there Baden-Powell and Cecil could sit at a writing table, observing all sides, with a speaking-tube to the telephone exchange below. It was Cecil, oddly enough, not Baden-Powell, who eventually had the idea of forming a Cadet Corps for Mafeking boys. Uniforms were provided for a group of boys over nine years of age, and Cecil drilled them and organized them in competitions and games until they could be trusted to act as orderlies and messengers.

Mines had been laid around the town, but for every one mine three dummies were laid. Of all his ruses, Baden-Powell was perhaps most proud of the 'mine ruse'. He went to great trouble to alarm the Boers about the strength of the minefields, warning Cronje in his letter to him and himself going out to blow up a stick of dynamite in order to convince the enemy that mines really existed there. In the event, few of the real mines ever exploded, and the Boers were able to observe cattle contentedly strolling about over the 'minefields'.

While waiting for artillery reinforcements, Cronje sent his son—well known among the Boers for his dash and daring—down the railway line to take the village of Vryburg.

Mafeking waited. What was happening elsewhere in the war no one knew : Mafeking was far away and it was alone. But, certainly, there was a feeling that if this was war matters could be a great deal worse.

Hamilton summed it up when he wrote : 'Our wires are still cut to north and south. Our line is up, and all around us the Boers are sup-

---

[1] See Map, p. 41.

posed to be encamped, yet as the days go on it is becoming harder and harder to realize that we are seriously engaged in war, and we are more inclined to believe in the cheery optimism of Colonel Baden-Powell. It is very like some gigantic picnic . . . On the whole it is quite impossible to believe that we are engaged in repelling an enemy who already are investing us. To get away from the hotels, to get more into contact with the spirit of the siege, I have been camping out for some days at the most outlying position upon the west facing of the town, but even by such means it is infinitely difficult to find much that is instinctive with active and actual campaigning . . . As the time passes we receive messages daily from different units in the Boer commando to friends in Mafeking, which are sometimes amicable, sometimes impudent in character; but to increase the irony of the situation, if we be engaged in the press of battle at dawn, it is certain that at dusk we shall be dining with no small degree of luxury at the hotel.'

And they waited.

On 21 October the local weekly newspaper appeared as usual. Among the advertisements in the personal column were: 'Expert Shorthand Writer and Typist Requires Evening Work, large or small quantities; Apprentice or Junior Wanted; Wanted—a Cook, male or female.' An official notice in the newspaper declared that: 'Outposts have orders in future to detain all strangers trying to pass through who are not in possession of passes.'[1] Passes were obtainable from the Chief Staff Officer.

Early in the investment Baden-Powell called all the correspondents together and told them that he would not permit criticism of the conduct of the siege or of the officers, because the correspondents could not be conversant with all the facts on which to base their opinions.[2] Reports were to be handed in daily between 3.0 and 4.0 p.m.

News of the siege was already appearing in the press at home, messengers riding out of the town at night. A message from Weil to his brother in Cape Town was one of the first to be published. It was Weil, not the military, who kept the town in contact with the out-

[1] The *Mafeking Mail*, Vol. 1, No. 23.
[2] Reynolds, p. 100.

side. He organized the runners, and later the dispatch-riders; he did it so well that not a single week passed throughout the investment of Mafeking without at least one messenger departing or arriving. At first, however, the flow was nearly all one way—out of Mafeking. Newspaper dispatches and official dispatches were passed to him, and also mail from the post office. He kept copies of nearly everything, and many official letters within the perimeter mysteriously found their way into his own private papers, where they were carefully filed away. It was Weil who provided interpreters for the staff. It was Weil's lookout who was asked to warn the headquarters trumpeter (an early system of warning) that enemy artillery was getting range on the town. And it was Weil who was humiliated for being a Jew, by Neilly among others, and who constantly gave gifts from his stocks (on one occasion some hundreds of blankets).[1]

By 21 October the *Cape Times* was publishing reports, and these, and Reuters' reports, were published all over the world. On 25 October *The Times* published more than a column from Hamilton, written less than two weeks before. Hamilton insisted on the smallness of operations at Mafeking, but his report received almost as much space as the sanguinary battle of Elandslaagte, which had just occurred. He finished his report of the Five-Mile Bank skirmish, 'Colonel Baden-Powell directed the operations with consummate coolness.' Baden-Powell himself sent a message to G.H.Q., which Weil sent via the nearest post office, fifty miles away in Bechuanaland, through where the Boer lines were said to be. From there it was wired to Plumer's base at Bulawayo. Plumer, always meticulous in such matters, decided that his staff in Bulawayo should send it on to G.H.Q. at Cape Town, via the British Consul at Beira in Portuguese East Africa. From Cape Town someone sent it back to London. The message read: 'All well. Four hours' bombardment. One dog killed. BADEN-POWELL.' The public at home loved it. It was indomitable. It was pluck. It was British.

Who was this man Baden-Powell? That started it all.

---

[1] All from *Weil Papers*.

5.   A Few Affrays

Alarming reports had reached Mafeking of the nature of the gun that was being brought from the Transvaal. Natives were going in and out of the town at will, and many reported having seen an enormous gun being hauled across the border. Some said its barrel was big enough to swallow an ox. It appeared on Jackal Tree Hill on 23 October, and was seen through telescopes to be not so fearsome after all. It was, in fact, a French Creusot, a ninety-four-pounder, one of four which had recently been bought by the Transvaal. A big piece, but not the giant siege gun that had been expected. With it came a party of Scandinavians who, before long, succeeded in discovering and dismantling a large number of the mines so proudly and carefully laid by Baden-Powell's men. (About fifty to sixty Germans were also with the Boers at various times, as well as a party of Frenchmen.)

That morning everyone waited in the shelters that had been dug beside houses and at the women's camp. The barrage that they first heard, however, was from their own guns : a typically cheeky move ordered by Baden-Powell.

It was not until the next day that the big gun began its work.

In the afternoon of the 24th the lookouts reported that the gun was being prepared for firing. The alarm was given and all waited in some suspense. The few who, through the nature of their duties, were not underground, watched the distant gun position with apprehension. On the skyline a cloud of smoke rose into the air, there was the sound of the whooshing of air, and then the ground and air quivered with the impact of an explosion far greater than anything hitherto. The first shell had fallen harmlessly into the veld. The next shell fell near the railway yards. Inquisitiveness getting the better of caution, people ran into the streets to collect bits of the shell as souvenirs and to examine the damage, which was very little. Experts pronounced on the size of the shell and calibre of the gun. The Boers also maintained the barrage with their smaller guns; the general view was that the opening shots had been range-finders. The big gun was used for two and a half hours firing twenty-three rounds, a shell falling on the Mafeking Hotel within a few feet of E. G. Parslow, the correspondent of the *Daily Chronicle*; the force of the explosion hurled him unharmed onto a pile of wood. Neilly was in the beer-cellar of the hotel; the staff and guests, mostly newspapermen, had been provided with mattresses, food, fire-buckets and sandbags. A group of men was playing nap when the shell struck the hotel. 'The ladies wept and the men's faces blanched.' Two of them went upstairs. Neilly wrote: 'The place was full of the white smoke of the bursting charge of the shell . . . But there was no fire. The tables were laid for luncheon, and the only thing disturbed was a dessert spoon, which was swept from its place. It needed no trained military eye to see what had saved the wall. Had it been composed of honest bricks it must have been badly smashed, but it was built of a species of mud in squares and, offering no opposition worth speaking of, the shell merely made a hole to get through. The rottenness of the wall saved it, and if all Mafeking were built of the same absurd stuff the town would be safe.'

All Mafeking was built of the same absurd stuff.

That was the end of the serious bombardment of the day. 'With the curious inconsequence that has marked the Boer proceedings in their investment of Mafeking,' wrote Angus Hamilton, 'the enemy threw no more of these heavier shells during the afternoon, contenting themselves with discharging at odd moments those of lesser calibre . . . Up to the present it has been impossible to consider very seriously the attempt of the Boers to besiege Mafeking.'

On the following day shelling began early, with a gun detachment under Lieutenant Murchison answering the Boer fire. By nightfall over two hundred shells had fallen into the perimeter of the Mafeking defences since the defence had begun; damage and casualties were still trivial. One shell landed in a gun emplacement among the crew, but buried its nose in the earth and did not explode. During the day the Boers staged an ill-conducted and futile demonstration on most sides of the town, with 3,000 horsemen charging about, most of them apparently aimlessly. A feint was made towards the African village, which the Boers fully expected to find undefended. But the Police were waiting for them, to say nothing of the Baralong tribesmen who let off an enthusiastic fusillade with their Snyder rifles and shotguns. The startled Boers made off without further ado. At news of the meek collapse of this feint, the main Boer attack, on the east side of the town, never got under way. The only British casualty was one man mortally wounded.

The defenders were surprised at the remarkable hesitance and reluctance of the Boers; while it was recognized that the Boer, by nature, did not care for frontal attack, no one had expected such lack of vigour from the investors. Did they really want to take Mafeking at all?

No one in Mafeking knew at that time—although they were to discover it soon—that Cronje had received orders about Mafeking from President Kruger himself. Whenever anyone in Pretoria mentioned an assault on Mafeking, the old man flew into a violent rage. He said that the place was not worth fighting for. Cronje should either take the place in the next few days, or, if he could not do so without heavy fighting, he should leave it to itself, with only sufficient guard to keep its troops out of the war, and proceed to the south. On no account were more than fifty casualties to be expended in taking the place.[1] Cronje assembled his burghers and told them this, thus diminishing his chances of taking the town.

As it happened, all this was much to Cronje's liking. He believed he could take the place because of his overwhelming superiority in numbers, and had asked whether he should do so. Kruger was adamant that he should not. Of all the Boer commanders, Cronje had the least taste for the facts of war. He had a dread of causing useless loss of life, and suffered to an unusual extent, for a man experienced in war, at death in battle. His son, however, took a very different view. And his son, impatient at the delay in taking Mafeking, anxious to strike at the infinitely more important prize of Kimberley, was on his way back from Vryburg; for that place had already been secured by a party from Commandant de la Rey's force on its way to the Kimberley area. The officer in charge at Vryburg,

---

[1] MS. of H. P. de Montmorency, P.R.O.; from the 'unimpeachable authority' of an American in Pretoria. Also Hillcourt.

Mafeking Night at Piccadilly Circus

The Hero of Mafeking—
*Radio Times Hulton
Picture Library*
◀

The Colonel at work
◤

Baden-Powell in his
scouting outfit
*Radio Times Hulton
Picture Library*
◤

Major-General Sir
William Butler in 1898,
just before he took up
the South African
Command

Sir Alfred Milner
in 1897

The last coaches to leave
Mafeking for the Transvaal
before the war

Commandant-General
Cronje with his wife

The investors—Snyman and
Botha ▶

Major Lord Edward Cecil

The defender—Baden-Powell
at Mafeking

The war correspondents
around their shelter—from
left, Neilly, Vere Stent,
Baillie and Hamilton

The armoured train with its
crew

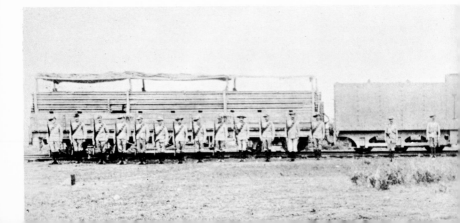

Creaky

The damaged convent, the
only two-storey building in
Mafeking

Baden-Powell and his staff. Top row, from left: Major
Panzera, Captain Ryan, Captain Greener, Lord Edward Cecil,
Captain Wilson, Major Hanbury-Tracy, Captain Cowan.
Seated: Major Godley, Lieut-Col. Vyvyan, C. G. H. Bell,
Baden-Powell, F. Whitely (Mayor), Colonel Hore, Dr Hayes.
On the ground: Captain Moncreiffe

Assistant-Commissioner Scott, had shot himself, 'being broken-hearted at his inability to defend the place in consequence of the duplicity and the treachery of the inhabitants.' The Transvaal flag had been raised in the town, to the accompaniment of psalm-singing.[1]

Young Cronje, on his way back to Mafeking, was a very forcible man.

*

On the next day, 26 October 1899, the Boers once again assembled *en masse*, as if to assault the town. But while they were making their prolonged preparations, and taking up positions, a heavy downpour of rain occurred. Within minutes men, beasts and terrain were soaked and soggy. Dispirited and drenched, the attackers moved off without a shot being fired. In Pretoria it was officially reported that the ground had been 'too slippery for military operations'.

Only on the eastern approaches of the town had the Boers been making ground. Stealthily they had been advancing, apparently unobserved despite the many lookouts in the defences. On 27 October a Boer trench was observed within 2,000 yards of the perimeter—not an untoward distance, it might be thought, but during the day bullets began whistling into the town. Baden-Powell, quite rightly, was determined to allow the enemy no footholds suitable for launching attacks anywhere near his defences. He immediately devised a plan to raid the trench that night. It was a good plan. Under cover of darkness a squadron of fifty-three men of the Protectorate Regiment would approach the trench from a flank. A small party of Cape Police was to provide covering fire. Who better to lead the expedition than the intrepid Fitzclarence himself? Thus was arranged the most bloody conflict of the defence of Mafeking.

The raiding party assembled on foot between 8.0 and 9.0 p.m. At 9.30 they moved off in silence, wearing white arm-bands. The moon was low and the only light was the dim one from the stars. Fitz-

---

[1] A Boer commando was formed from the many rebels in Vryburg; with forces from the Orange Free State it repeatedly attacked the township of Kuruman, where 50 Europeans, supported by 30 coloureds, gallantly held out against more than 1,000 Boers till 1 January; the Vryburg commando then went south towards Kimberley.

clarence gained the flank of the enemy trench undetected, guided by two lights in the town which, when in line, beamed on the Boer position.

The Boers had placed a roof of corrugated iron, torn from the stand of the racecourse, over a section of the trench as a shelter. They were below. All Fitzclarence's men were armed with the bayonet; rifles were not loaded, to prevent the men accidentally raising the alarm and shooting each other in the mêlée.

With a great crash that could be heard in the town, Fitzclarence and his men jumped onto the roof and charged into the trench below. The Boers had no time to offer any resistance. They were mostly slaughtered where they lay or sat, some while on their knees begging for mercy, some knocked senseless first with the rifle butt. There was a great deal of screaming, cursing and commotion. Fitzclarence was armed with a sword, with which he accounted for four of the enemy, one of whom he decapitated. It was all over in minutes. Soon the party were tearing back independently to the British defences with heavy firing on all sides—not only from the diversionary and covering parties, but also from a supporting trench of the Boers, who fired into their own trench believing the British to be holding it, and thus killed many of their friends who remained alive.

As the realization of what had happened spread among the Boers, at first panic, and then horror, overcame them. A machine-gun was brought up and fired into the trench, and for long after the British party had returned, all fire having ceased from the Mafeking defenders, the night sky was lit up by the random shots of parties of Boers, often firing at each other. The Boers did not use bayonets themselves; they were not equipped with it. Many of them believed it was not a white man's weapon at all, but like something which the Africans would use and, therefore, degrading. It was the first time most of them had ever come across its work.[1]

The Boer casualty figures for this engagement are even more contradictory than usual. Baden-Powell gave them as 100, forty of which were killed or wounded with the bayonet. The *Times History*,

---

[1] From time to time the garrison hoisted the same lights at night as had guided Fitzclarence, and this always resulted in wild firing and alarm in the Boer lines.

culled partly from Transvaal sources, gave them as three. The latter is certainly too low, the former probably too high. It is the custom of military commanders to exaggerate or belittle uncertain casualties, according to the light in which they see the engagement. In Baden-Powell's case there was throughout the siege an obvious advantage to morale to make propaganda out of enemy casualties. It was not unnatural that these same figures of Boer losses should later find their way into his Report. However, it would not be impossible for fifty-three men armed with steel to kill or injure forty of the enemy if the latter were totally unprepared, as the Boers seem to have been. The *Official History* found it embarrassing to accept the figure of a further sixty killed or wounded by rifle fire : 'Of the sixty burghers reported to have been shot, many must have fallen to the rifles of their own side, for the Protectorate men had not discharged a round.'

Fitzclarence's losses were six killed, nine wounded and two missing, almost all of which were incurred in the run to the town after the raid.

The raiding party, returning out of the confusion and the darkness, arrived back in the town. They went at once, in an excited condition, to Baden-Powell's headquarters. Their bayonets revealed the work that had been done. Fitzclarence made his report to Baden-Powell, and the men were all given a much-needed glass of whisky. Then they dispersed.

It had been a daring and successful operation; for his work on this and two later occasions in the siege, Captain Fitzclarence was awarded the Victoria Cross, on Baden-Powell's recommendation to Lord Roberts.

Neilly, mingling with the men of the Protectorate Regiment, and a close observer of all that went on, gave the only one of the many accounts, official and unofficial, of this episode which mentioned one unpalatable fact. 'The work was largely held by boys who, of course, had to take their chance with the men in the massacre. It is not too much to the taste of your soldier to bayonet a lad of thirteen or fourteen; but if any shame attaches to the killing of the youngsters, it must rest on the shoulders of those fathers who brought them there.'[1]

---

[1] Neilly, p. 91.

*

Cronje's son had by then returned from his easy task at Vryburg. He taunted his father into making one last serious attempt to take Mafeking. Cronje *père* agreed; but Kruger's ruling that no attack was worth more than fifty casualties would still apply. His son's plan revolved around the strongpoint of Cannon Kopje, which he had rightly seen to be the clue to breaking the defence of the town.

Cannon Kopje was a cluster of stones and rocks on a slight hillock which commanded Mafeking. It was the nearest prominence of any kind to the town itself, and from it an enemy had definite command over the place. Owing to the barren and unyielding nature of the ground, it was not easy to build defence-works there, and no serious attempt had been made to do so. Some fortifications had been built there years before, and these had been allowed to fall into total disrepair. On the site of the old fort a simple breastwork of stones had been constructed by the defenders, and there was a trench eighty yards to the rear. Of all the shelters from bombardment that had been constructed at Mafeking, this was the weakest and least carefully prepared. And yet Cannon Kopje was so exposed as to be an easy and obvious target for any artillery which the Boers might wish to bring against it. What made it an even easier target was a tall lookout construction that had been placed on the summit. Unfortunately the commander of the garrison, Baden-Powell, had not been as quick to appreciate its importance as had the young Cronje.[1]

An attack at this place was expected, an enemy telegraph message having been intercepted.

The sector was held by forty-four men of the British South Africa Police, under Colonel Walford, Captain the Hon. Douglas Marsham and Captain Charles Pechell, with a machine-gun section from the Protectorate Regiment: fifty men in all.

At daylight on 31 October heavy and concentrated artillery fire was brought to bear on the position. In contrast to previous shelling, it was extremely accurate. Fire came from several quarters, including an enemy gun emplacement at the racecourse, to the rear of Cannon

---

[1] On this point the *Official History* is obliged to find fault with Baden-Powell.

Kopje. Walford's force took cover in the trench and was unharmed.

The bombardment on Cannon Kopje continued, and as it did so the enemy gradually moved forward into attacking positions, the defenders—huddled in their trench—being unable to hinder them. A strong force was also assembled in the river bed of the Molopo in readiness to assault the town should Cannon Kopje fall.

The only man not in the shelter of the trench was the unfortunate lookout on his tower, who happened to be an elderly German soldier of fortune named Baron von Dankberg, serving in the ranks of the British South Africa Police. He kept up his observations and reports as the slender tower swayed and tottered to the explosions below. A chunk of metal tore a slice out of his greatcoat. His telescope was smashed by a bullet. Miraculously, he survived.

By 6.0 a.m. the enemy had drawn so near that Walford, on news from von Dankberg, ordered his men out to the breastwork, as it was in danger of being overrun. At this the Boers increased their barrage. The men of the British South Africa Police were fearfully exposed, and immediately they began to be hit by flying fragments of shell, causing dreadful wounds. Nevertheless, they kept up a desperate fire against the horde of Boers—there were probably nearly 1,000 of them —who were now advancing towards the splintering barricade.

Trooper Lloyd was kneeling down attending to a wounded man when he was struck and received a fatal wound. Marsham, son of the Earl of Romney, was hit by a Mauser bullet in the chest; as he swung round another went through his Sam Browne belt and pierced his heart. The other captain, Pechell, was also hit.

Despite their losses, the defenders kept up a furious fire and the advancing Boers came to a halt. Here and there a man among them was beginning to fall; even the humblest Boer had heard of Kruger's limit of fifty casualties, knowledge which placed their leaders in an almost impossible position from the start in any engagement.

Baden-Powell had observed all this from his lookout on the roof at headquarters; he found time to draw, from what he could see through his glasses, a dramatic sketch of 'the proceedings' at the table which was always kept there. An attempt, on his orders, to provide relief for Walford by attacking the enemy in flank failed from the start; the relevant contingent of the defence forces 'could not be got to move'. However, a seven-pounder was moved into position on the enemy's flank by Lieutenant Murchison, and it fired into the Boers to good effect. In his official report, Baden-Powell said that 'every shell went in among them and effectually stopped the further advance of the Boers'. This was hardly fair to Walford's detachment, who had kept up steady rifle fire at the worst of the bombardment. The Boers began to draw off and disperse, a further heavy bombardment covering their withdrawal.

Out of Walford's fifty men, eight were killed and three severely wounded. The Boer losses were not heavy. It had been a carefully worked-out and well-conducted assault by the Boers, with a more sophisticated use of artillery than they had shown hitherto. Had the spirit of their men been of the same quality as the planning and organization of their young commander, then they must have taken the position, and probably the town. The *Official History* puts it well: 'The achievement of the Police was as notable for its good fortune as its valour; for nothing could have saved them from an enemy but half as resolute as themselves.'

There was a certain amount of discontent among the survivors of the Police. It was felt that they had not received any support until it was too late. It was felt that it was time Baden-Powell should be observed, sometimes at least, at places where the fighting was going on. It was felt that this would be more in keeping with his reputation as a man who was said to have undertaken daring scouting exploits in the past. But Baden-Powell, very sensibly, had a different notion of the place and task of a military commander; nevertheless, he had made secret arrangements for the command to pass to Goold-Adams in the event of his being killed or disabled. At 3.0 p.m. that afternoon he visited Cannon Kopje and congratulated Walford and his men. He also profusely congratulated them in General Orders. This did something to soothe matters. Hamilton wrote in his diary of 'the folly of which Colonel Baden-Powell was guilty in leaving the [fort] unprotected. It is too late to say much now, but we have paid a heavy price for our neglect and carelessness.'

Thus ended one of the two really determined attempts of the Boers to take Mafeking during the investment.

After Baden-Powell's visit, work was quickly begun on improving the position. The following day another barrage was put down on Cannon Kopje, but the expected assault did not materialize.

Two wagons which trundled to Cannon Kopje with sandbags, equipment and digging utensils returned with the dead stretched out upon them. After the funeral service, the bodies were lifted off, still in their blood-stained uniforms, and interred in sacking to the strains of the Last Post. As the solemn notes died away, the congregation dispersed to the trenches, shelters and earthworks, in which garrison and townsfolk were waiting for the Boer to go.

*

Baden-Powell's advice to the townspeople was: 'Sit tight and wait for them to go.'[1] In General Orders he had given the following encouragement: 'We only have to sit it out.'[2]

Baden-Powell certainly was not preparing anyone for a long wait. He had already told the garrison: 'It is possible that a few days of this will sicken them and they will give up the idea of capturing Mafeking, and will draw off—and we will follow with them. Already they are complaining that they must get away to their crops . . . so that if we were to sit down and do nothing they would probably in the end draw off, but they may in the meantime give us opportunities of hitting them hard, which we must be ready to seize and utilize.'[3] On the next day he had provided further encouragement: '[Their] food supplies are failing, so they will not be able to spend many days with us.'[4] But they did not go—not yet. A week later Baden-Powell told the garrison that the Boers 'will have to go away within the next few days'.

If, as Baden-Powell later told Roberts, and often repeated, his orders were to detain, even attract, Boer forces to him, then his attitude at this time is not easy to understand.

*

Meanwhile, on the western side, opposite Godley's defences, the

---

[1] Neilly, p. 94.
[2] *General Orders*, 14 October 1899.
[3] *General Orders*, 12 October 1899.
[4] *General Orders*, 13 October 1899.

Boers had been observed dismantling mines, and there were all the signs that they were about to bring their artillery closer up. To forestall this Godley advanced his line, his men going forward by twos and threes. He had a strong position built, the parapet showing only one foot above the surface, and Boer activity ceased.

On the night of 4 November the Boers attempted to run a railway truck into the town loaded with fused dynamite. Another extraordinary lapse in the defensive arrangements was that no obstacle had been placed across the line. The truck began to roll down the gentle incline towards the town, but fortunately for the defenders it exploded long before it reached them. Hamilton wrote : 'It was night, and the town was just about to rest, when it was shaken to its foundations by a most deafening roar; sand and stones, fragments of trees came down as hail from the skies, the whole place being lighted with a livid glow of blood-red flame. To the north of Mafeking, and so close to the cemetery that it might have been a pillar of fire coming to earth to claim its own, an immense arc of fire and smoke was ejected out of the ground. After it there came silence, broken here and there by the rattle of debris upon the roofs of the houses, and by the shouts and shrieks of a town in the confusion of a panic.' Neilly had been relaxing at his hotel : 'While I was enjoying my after-dinner cigar, there was a stunning explosion that knocked my gas-globe over in splinters, moved small items of nick-nacks in my apartment, and seemed to make me jump in my chair. I went out and found the townspeople in a state of fright.' But all was well : none was hurt. After this Baden-Powell had sandbags placed across the line. It was yet another example of the British being saved by the remarkable inability of the Boers to press home their various measures.

On 6 November the big gun, now known variously as 'Creaky', 'Big Ben' and other friendly names, was moved from its position on Jackal Tree Hill and installed at a new emplacement nearly two miles east of Cannon Kopje. The Boer command, disappointed and surprised at the ineffectiveness of the weapon of which it was most proud, was determined that a more deadly barrage should be made on Mafeking. The gun proved to be as ineffective in its new position as in its old one. The defenders now took a blasé view of its performance, the more nimble of them having discovered that after the first sight of its puff of smoke on the horizon they still had time to take cover.

On the following day Baden-Powell and Godley organized an attack on the nearest Boer camp to the town, a camp which held between 200 and 250 of the enemy. Baden-Powell, unlike many of his contemporaries, was never frightened of launching operations at night, and this one began at 2.30 a.m. Ninety men, with three guns, moved out about three-quarters of a mile in front of Godley's lines. When dawn broke they were on a ridge above the Boer encampment, from which they were about a mile distant. At 4.15 a.m. they opened fire, and surprise was complete. The Boers ran in all directions to find cover. But the reaction of the Boers when they found themselves in such apparently hopeless situations was quick. Within a few minutes they were responding with machine-gun and light-artillery fire; reinforcements—disordered, without commands, but rapid—began pouring in from a much larger camp nearby. Godley (who had a bullet through his hat) therefore ordered a retirement, and this was very neatly conducted by his troops, all of whom were, of course, irregulars. By that time perhaps over 800 Boers were on the scene. The party of Bechuanaland Rifles, which covered the retirement, held steady when attacked by a posse of mounted Boers who were attempting to surround Godley's force. In the rush of the retirement one of the guns broke its limber hook, and with feverish haste the crew repaired the break with rope under heavy fire and got the gun moving again just in time.

Five men were wounded in this operation, which once again had an adverse effect on Boer morale if nothing else. It was extremely hazardous, and the squadron of the Protectorate Regiment had the Bechuanaland Rifles to thank for their survival. The instinctive tactic of the Boer was always to cut his enemy from his base, but fortunately for his enemies he was not always very good at it.

Four days later Baden-Powell sent out a message to the Chief Staff Officer at G.H.Q., Cape Town: 'Enemy have closed round us therefore communication difficult. Our casualties slight. Supplies available for next three months.' Thanks to Weil's runners, in previous reports he had been able to give not only his own situation, but those of Plumer and of a force from Bulawayo patrolling the railway to

the north of Mafeking.[1] Until then the Boers had been concentrated
to the east of the town.

*

From that day no action took place for seven weeks. Baden-Powell
waited for Cronje to go. Cronje waited for Baden-Powell to give in.
They communicated ceaselessly, usually concerning themselves with
the Africans or with long arguments about the placing and observance of Red Cross flags[2]: always formal, always addressed 'Sir' and
always signing themselves the 'obedient servant' of the other. Cronje's
letters were stiff and indignant: Baden-Powell's mocking and
indignant.

One day a letter came from John E. Dyer, an American who was
Surgeon-General to Cronje. He said:

It is understood that you have armed bastards, Fingoes and Baralongs against us. In this you have committed an enormous act, the
wickedness of which is certain, and the end of which no man can
foresee. You have created a new departure in South African history. It has hitherto been a cardinal point in South African ethics,
both English and Dutch, to view with horror the idea of arming
black against white, and I would ask you to pause and even now,
at the eleventh hour, reconsider the matter, and even if it caused
you the loss of Mafeking to disarm your blacks and thereby act the
part of a white man in a white man's war.[3]

The camps of the Boers could be seen far away, like brown mole-
hills rising on the slope of the plain. They were seldom less than three
miles away, observing what was jokingly described in the town as

---

[1] Baden-Powell to C.S.O. Cape Town, 10 November 1899, and dates in October
1899. *Weil Papers.*
[2] Such arguments occurred on all fronts. President Kruger made a number of
indignant remarks about the British use and 'abuse' of the flag in his speeches
in Pretoria, and eventually protested to the neutral powers.
[3] Neilly, p. 98. Another American, Dr. R. D. Long, was in charge of the Boers'
field-hospital.

'the three-mile limit'. From Cannon Kopje the Boer camps were seen spread about like mining camps; the daily life of the enemy could be observed. Somehow it was difficult to think of a foe so human, quietly going about the routine of his business, as an enemy who brought with him death. Hamilton scribbled in his diary:

In the early morning the smoke of many fires swings in its spirals to the sky, and the silence of the plain is broken by the echoes which echo back the noises of the camp. It would seem that they are as regular in the ordering of their camp life as we are. When the sun has warmed the air, and evaporated the morning dew from the grass, we can see them out-pinning their horses, driving their cattle to fresh pastures . . . So far as our own outposts are concerned, along this line there are many days in which nothing whatever happens.

The main irritants for the defenders were the fleas, the flies, the mosquitoes and the insidious ants, which were taking full advantage of the opportunities offered them by the unprecedented digging of trench and shelter; and the whine and crash of shells, at least a few of which could be expected each day. That the latter were no more than an irritant may be gauged from the assertion that the alarm now brought everyone, not to cover, but out in the open to watch the bursting of the projectile in soft and deadening wall or earth in order to gather the fragments, which were much sought after. An auction was set up from time to time in order that the market in these souvenirs could be conducted to the best advantage. Sometimes, when the barrel of 'Creaky' appeared from behind its emplacement, pointing at the town, a bell was rung; when the smoke appeared, another bell rang. Frequently its shells did not burst. More serious were twelve-pounders which appeared in the Boer lines; they were smokeless, and gave no advance warning.

To their surprise the defenders discovered that letters could be dispatched to friends and relations in Rhodesia (stamp: one shilling), the Cape or England with every expectation of their reaching their destination. They were posted at the post office in the normal way, the only difference to peacetime being the slightly more expensive stamps, the postmaster—who paid Weil's runners out of public funds

—having had to increase the postal rates. Not only was the Boer invest-ment of the place far from complete, but large parts of the areas be-tween their camps were not even patrolled; Africans had therefore begun to go to and from the town, bearing messages for the north, with regularity and impunity. The nearest telegraph office free from the Boers was in Bechuanaland, fifty miles away. As the *Official History* says: 'The Boer dispositions seemed marked by a peculiar dullness, and Mafeking was never ringed entirely.'[1] This was in total contrast to the idea of a siege, in the classic sense of a Lucknow, that had formed in the minds of the public at home. They nevertheless read the reports from the town which were appearing in the press, with little curiosity as to how those reports had been delivered.

On Guy Fawkes' Day there was the traditional fireworks display. Before it began, however, Baden-Powell had the pleasant thought of warning Cronje 'not to be alarmed'[2]; it was a Sunday, and he did not wish the enemy to think he was breaking the customary Sunday truce. This latter was particularly valued by the women of the town, as on that day—there being no shelling—they did their washing.

Sunday was the day when Baden-Powell was most seen about the town: spruced up, cheery, usually whistling. He looked like a man having the time of his life, and, indeed, there is every indication that he was. He had always enjoyed organizing games and sporting events; now he did so continually, handing out the prizes at pony-racing (not, of course, on the outlying race track), gymkhanas, foot-ball matches and cricket. All this was invaluable in lifting the minds of the populace from depression and fear. The first polo game of the siege was held on 26 November; it was followed by a concert. Baillie found the polo ground 'very fair, and the ponies surprisingly good'. Baden-Powell himself captained one of the teams.

First thing on Sunday morning the women and children came streaming across from their camp, in which they had been confined all week. A large Union Jack fluttered bravely above Baden-Powell's headquarters (on other days, a 'tiny' flag flew there). On Sunday mornings a band played in the recreation ground; in the evenings there was often a concert, and, needless to say, the star performer was

---

[1] *Official History*, p. 149.
[2] Baillie, 5 November 1899.

the camp commandant himself. He acted in sketches, fooled on a
variety of musical instruments, recited, and sang songs. He even tried
out a few songs of his own composition on the captive audience. He
was widely popular among the women, wildly so among the children,
and liked by many of the men and some of the officers. Others, however, thought less of him and they did not entirely hide their feelings.
Some even suggested that a cavalry regiment like the Protectorate had
no business shutting itself up in the town; that it should, like the
Boers, be mobile, providing its own stores on sortie, and join up with
Plumer. One of those who got on least well with Baden-Powell was
Colonel Hore, commanding officer of the Protectorate Regiment; a
heavy, blimpish-looking man, he was as thick-set as Baden-Powell
was trim.

Meanwhile Baden-Powell had been perfecting many ingenious
ideas and devices to aid the defence; they were indeed his main personal contribution. For a time he employed men to walk about
the perimeter, every now and again bending down as if they were
getting through a wire fence; knowing that wire was invisible at a
distance, he hoped by this means to deter the Boers from charging
the defences. With a makeshift megaphone he conducted bogus con-
versations and orders about attacks he was going to make on the
Boer lines. ('A joyous little dodge of my own.') It is difficult to say if
these and other ideas in which Baden-Powell took an obvious and
more than merely professional delight had much effect on the Boer,
himself a fairly wily opponent; like so many of their originator's
ploys, they smacked more of the practical joke than of military de-
ception. Indeed, the megaphone ploy was considered 'a joke of the
Colonel's' in Mafeking at the time.[1]

Defence works were improved; shelters made stronger; fruit and
vegetable gardens cultivated where there had been none before;
dummy defences constructed; the armoured train, making its occasional sorties down the specially constructed spur, was camouflaged
mottled green and yellow, with bits of bushes, so that it could not be
so nearly and so easily sacrificed again; and the native chief,
Wessels, was deposed by Baden-Powell 'for want of energy'—a more
amenable chief taking his place.

---

[1] *Diary*, A. M. Craufurd, 21 December 1899.

The lack of mail from the outside world, and the absence of newspapers, had been perhaps the most depressing effect of the siege to date. Far more letters went out than ever came in. The editor of the local newspaper, the *Mafeking Mail*, had been encouraged by the newspapermen in the town to bring out a daily edition. This he managed to do almost without a break, despite his office receiving three shells during the course of the defence. Censorship was a problem, but the editor left large blank spaces to show where the blue pencil had been at work. There were sports results (in which Fitzclarence and Baillie featured prominently), Freemasonry news, and notices of events; but mostly the paper contained editorials about the investment, decrying or mocking the Boers and arousing indignation about the shelling of the women's camp.[1]

The editor was G. H. N. Whales, and his assistant was E. G. Parslow of the *Daily Chronicle*. It was printed by Mr Townsend, the local printer. The amount of news from outside was remarkable in quantity and accuracy, if out of date; reports from Reuters (at Durban), Beira, and the *Bulawayo Chronicle* appeared fairly frequently, even in November, when the town has often been reported as being totally cut off.

On 9 November the newspaper declared that there would be 'probably another fortnight of siege'.

The paper suffered a serious loss on its second day of publication. At 10.0 p.m., 2 November, Parslow was shot dead in the bar of Dixon's Hotel by Lieutenant Murchison, who had done some useful work with the garrison's meagre artillery. After an argument, Parslow had said to Murchison: 'You're no gentleman.' Murchison was ordered to be tried for murder by Field General Court Martial. He was locked up in the jail to await Lord Roberts's pleasure. In the evening Parslow's funeral took place; his coffin was carried, in moonlight, by the other newspapermen in the town.

On 9 November reliable news of the Natal campaign arrived—via a messenger sent by Lady Sarah Wilson from the farm where she was then staying; and six days later an American correspondent of Reuters News Agency, named Pearson, arrived in the town, having ridden up from Kimberley. He had stayed with Lady Sarah Wilson

---

[1] The *Mafeking Mail* did not cease publication after the relief, and continues as a weekly newspaper to this day.

on the way up. He was able to give a great deal of news; and, having examined the defences and spoken to many in the town, he went off to Cape Town with his report, which was soon going out to many capitals. A correspondent of the *Daily Mail* made two trips to the area in order to send reports to London.

Because of the news which he was now receiving from outside, Baden-Powell had to revise his ideas on how long the investment was likely to last. He came to the conclusion that the Boers were unlikely to depart altogether, and that there was little likelihood of relief 'for many weeks, if not months', owing to the commitments of British forces elsewhere. The food stocks in the town were still 'ample', but as no firm date for relief could be foreseen it was thought best to conserve all such stocks until further notice. Enough fresh vegetables were grown within the perimeter to provide normal supplies for the entire garrison and townspeople without too much difficulty. Livestock seemed to be plentiful, although sufficient grazing ground was not easy to find. All merchant stocks were taken over by the military and an inventory made by the very capable Army Service Corps officer, Captain Ryan. A scale of rationing was worked out. At first this was so generous, and supplies obviously so fulsome, that very little notice was taken of the new regulations. They came into force on 17 November. The allowance per person per day was as follows:

> Meat 1 lb.
> Bread 1 lb.
> Vegetables 1 lb.
> Coffee 1/3 oz.
> Salt 1/2 oz.
> Sugar 2 oz.
> Tea 1/2 oz.

It was hardly rigorous, and at that time nothing else was rationed; thus milk, eggs and poultry were unrestricted, although they were hard to find. Fortunately there was a very plentiful stock of tinned milk in Weil's store. And at the stores everything from pickles to *pâté de foie gras* could be obtained.

Prices of rationed foodstuffs were to be controlled : civilians to pay two shillings for their entire daily ration (women in the women's

and children's camp paying a reduced price of nearly half that figure);
free rations were distributed to many of the refugees from the Transvaal.

And so the people of Mafeking settled down for a siege.

A month after it had begun Baillie of the *Morning Post* wrote in
his diary: 'One thing only is certain, that from 4.30 to 5.0 a.m.
'Creaky' will fire a round or two, and probably stop till after breakfast; and that from 8.30 to 9.0 p.m. she has never missed her fare-
well shot.'

*

What were the Boers going to do? For some weeks the newspapers
in the Transvaal had been embarrassed by the fact that Mafeking had
not already fallen, and a number of stories had been concocted to
explain the situation to the impatient. Early in November Cronje had
reported to Pretoria: 'I think the enemy cannot hold out much
longer.'[1] On one occasion a reporter who had visited the Boer camps
had anticipated the fall of the town on his return to Pretoria: a report
which had to be denied. Boer forces had been kept from taking the
place by the fears of President Kruger that heavy casualties for so
inconsiderable a prize would dent his popularity, and by the equal
reluctance of the Boer commander, Cronje. The Boers never felt safe
at night; their guns, in which they had placed so much hope, had
failed them; and frontal attacks were likely to be too costly. They had
allowed Baden-Powell and their political command at home to dictate to them the terms of the engagement.

In the town, Hamilton was becoming further depressed at the lack
of exciting copy. 'There has been no battle round Mafeking,' he
wrote. 'A few slight skirmishes upon our part, much proud boasting
upon the part of the Boers, is the limit of mutual operations which
have centred around Mafeking. We are waiting and, in the interval,
preparing. That is all which can be said.' And on 15 November he
wrote: 'When we come to consider the siege of Mafeking in its more
elemental details, the picture is not unlike those presented by the
farcical melodrama. It is now nearly six weeks since Mafeking was

---

[1] *Official Transvaal Dispatches*, N.A.M., 5 November 1899.

proclaimed as being in a state of siege and, although there has been no single opportunity of any commercial reciprocity between ourselves and the outside world, the ruling prices are at present but very little above normal, distress is wholly absent, danger is purely incidental, and indeed it would seem, as Colonel Baden-Powell said in a recent order, that "Everything in the garden is lovely".'

On 18 November unusual activity in the Boer lines was observed from lookouts from Cannon Kopje and by scouts. Suddenly the news spread. The Boers were breaking camp.

Cronje, urged on by messages from President Kruger, had decided to move on. He had at last decided to bestir himself. As the *Times History* put it : 'At last, after he had been sitting in front of Mafeking for five weeks, the absurdity of wasting nearly a third of the two Republics' available forces on the capture of one small town became obvious.' According to another authority, Cronje had 'come to the conclusion he was wasting his time and expending the energies of a large force needed elsewhere'.[1] Moreover, President Kruger was anxious for an advance into a more populated part of the Cape in order to encourage a rising of Boers there. In a great cloud of dust the Potchefstroom and Wolmaransstaad commandos, with their hundreds of wagons and their vast herds of cattle, moved away south. Cronje was to take over Prinsloo's command near Kimberley.

Baden-Powell ordered all squadrons to be ready to start moving at once, but it was felt that Cronje might well be making a ruse to draw Baden-Powell's forces into the open. Baden-Powell cautiously watched events from the roof-top of his H.Q.

In case there was any misunderstanding, 'Creaky' was more active than usual. Although Cronje had taken several of his best guns, 'Creaky' was to remain; and so were Boer forces, variously estimated between 2,000 and 4,000 strong, with six other guns. In his Report, Baden-Powell said up to 4,000 Boers remained, but in a message to Nicholson, soon after Cronje's departure, he gave their number as 'around 2,000'.[2] The new commander was Assistant Commandant-

---

[1] Hillcourt, p. 183.
[2] Baden-Powell to Nicholson, 6 December 1899, *Weil Papers*. Guns according to Baden-Powell's report; Hillcourt says ten guns remained. From 2,000 men according to *The Times* (Boer sources). Snyman's command included also the investment of Kuruman.

General J. P. Snyman, who, like Cronje, also had a reputation from past conflicts. The Boer system was that the commandants of commandos should elect their own local commanders, but Snyman's election must have been based on a regard for deeds of the past rather than hopes for the future; he was not an energetic man and he was known to be over-fond of the bottle. He also happened to be a man of great and quiet patience—so much so that the volatile Baden-Powell detested the memory of him for the rest of his life. It was soon clear that Snyman intended to mount a straightforward blockade. His attitude was that if he could starve the defenders into submission, well and good; if he could not, then at least he held the entire area for the Republics by safeguarding any danger on Boer communications and flanks from Baden-Powell. Under Snyman was Commandant J. D. L. Botha.[1] Whether Snyman's intention was equal to the vigour with which he was prepared to mount such a blockade, of a force perhaps less than half the strength of his own, was far from certain.

In the town, some officers wondered whether Baden-Powell—now not containing so great an enemy force—might not make a daring break-out at night, open up the war in the north and make a dash through the almost unprotected northern Transvaal, to combine in an operation with Plumer that would not only embarrass the Boers and threaten the Rand, but would also bring all Cronje's forces back again.

---

[1] Not to be confused with his relative, the very much abler General Louis Botha, the investor of Ladysmith and victor of Spion Kop.

6. Patrolling the Frontier

The tubby little man with the monocle, now organizing the defence of the British territories north of the Transvaal, did not seem a likely saviour of the hardy, pioneering Rhodesians. Far more than the people of Mafeking, the people of Bulawayo were accustomed to living with danger; they lived close to the very brink of civilization; ever since the place had been settled they had been threatened with extinction by a vast uprising of the unsettled and unreliable African populations all around them. Herbert Plumer was unimposing, small and retiring. He was the opposite of Baden-Powell in character; he preferred to keep himself to himself, and made little if any effort to popularize himself among his rough volunteer troops. He suffered from very short sight and was inclined to stumble into things. All in all, he did not, in Bulawayo, cut a very impressive figure. One of his officers wrote: 'We, who served under him, suffered from his taciturnity: sometimes for hours he seemed as if he were struck dumb, incapable of issuing an order: he appeared to be awaiting some revelation or inspiration which never came.'[1] But it was the same officer who wrote, at the end of the campaign: 'Plumer undoubtedly had more of the science and art of war than Baden-Powell.' And Plumer's Matabele efforts had not gone unnoticed.

At the start of war Plumer found himself with what was to be the most intimidating task presented to any British commander throughout the entire war. From Mafeking to the north-eastern edge of the Transvaal was approximately 500 miles. To protect this with the forces available now that Baden-Powell's column, 'courting investment deliberately', was not available, must have seemed an impossible task; even to prevent the Africans in this vast area from rising,

[1] Montmorency.

89

once they saw half their 'protectors' under investment, might not be considered easy, but to mount a threat to the Transvaal itself must have seemed out of the question. Nevertheless it was the last of these projects, on instructions from Baden-Powell, that Plumer was soon to attempt, by concentrating his force at Tuli, near the Transvaal border.

The risk involved in taking his main force away from the area of native settlement was great. Only three years before there had been the terrifying native rising of 1896. Far to the north there was trouble with a tribe about the hut tax. Even the four great chiefs who ruled Bechuanaland with British protection could not be relied upon, especially since their respected adviser, the District Commissioner, Goold-Adams, was cut off from them in Mafeking. The most pro-British of these kings was Khama, Chief of the Bamangwatos, with his capital at the huge settlement of Palapye; but Sebele, chief of a tribe around Gaberones, a settlement on the railway, was of uncertain loyalty.[1]

The total force which Plumer was able to call on for these various responsibilities was puny, and at first not even all of this was immediately available to him. It was to consist of : the Rhodesia Regiment, raised by him that summer—420 men; British South Africa Police—nearly 1,000 men, spread across a vast area; and South Rhodesian Volunteers and volunteers from Mashonaland, whose numbers were inclined to fluctuate wildly according to the needs of their farms. The most Plumer's force ever reached, spread across an area twice the size of England and Wales, was about 1,760. For his move to Tuli, however, Plumer only had available the Rhodesia Regiment and eighty men of the British South Africa Police. The total artillery was six guns, and there were eight machine-guns.

Plumer was fortunate in having the support of Colonel J. S. Nicholson, the Commander of the British South Africa Police, who was based at Bulawayo. He was an able and efficient man, and organized Plumer's lines of communication and supplies with skill. Even before the war he had arranged for sufficient supplies to be brought into Rhodesia to last the white population for eight months, partly by purchasing far greater stores for the police than he knew could

---

[1] *Khama*, J. Mockford (Cape, 1931).

possibly be needed. He also had a great deal to do with Plumer's regiment being equipped and trained within two months of its formation. When Rhodesians began enlisting in larger numbers he was concerned with the raising of the South Rhodesian Volunteers, which included the unusual feature—for that time—of a cyclist corps. In the railway workshops at Bulawayo three armoured trains were fitted up; these were probably more effective than any others in the campaign.

On 14 October, a few hours after the siege of Mafeking had begun, Plumer and his small force of 500 men rode into the remote bush outpost of Tuli.

*

On his arrival Plumer was given a letter from Baden-Powell which had been awaiting him. Inside were his orders. They were:

(i) To defend the border as far as it can be carried out from the neighbourhood of Tuli as a centre.
(ii) By display of strength to induce the Boers to detail a strong force to protect their northern district.
(iii) To create diversions in the north of the Transvaal, co-operating with the invasion of the south by our main force, if necessary advancing into the Transvaal for the purpose.
No portion of your force is to cross the frontier till you receive orders. Instructions will be sent to you as to the date for co-operation with the other column.[1]

These orders were a bit of a puzzle for Plumer. It was soon obvious that there was no question of a British force advancing just then into the Transvaal from the south, with which he could co-operate. There was also the added problem of what to do about Mafeking. Should he make an attempt to relieve it? It had been decided that Nicholson should send a small force from Bulawayo, with the armoured trains, to probe down the railway, to gauge the strength of the Boers in the area, and to impress the Bechuanaland tribes. This force was to be commanded by Major (acting Colonel) G. L. Holdsworth, with the

---

[1] *Official History*, p. 187.

armoured trains under the command of Captain H. Llewellyn. It was through Llewellyn that Nicholson and Plumer were able to communicate with Baden-Powell. Meanwhile Plumer decided to concentrate on Baden-Powell's first two instructions. As the *Official History* put it: 'To "defend a border" as long as the railway from London to Aberdeen, to "display strength", and to "create diversions" with one weak regiment composed of novices, these were orders which nothing but success could justify.'

The instructions had been written by Baden-Powell before the Boers had appeared around Mafeking. A few weeks later he sent another message, via Nicholson: 'Tell Plumer act for best according to what news he has from Natal, etc., and not await my orders. I will endorse his action.'[1] With these words Baden-Powell gave up effective command of the northern section of his force; but, although he could not know it then, he was to be in frequent communication with Plumer almost throughout.

The common frontier of Rhodesia and the Transvaal was the Limpopo River; that great waterway also marked about half of the Bechuanaland–Transvaal frontier. It was a most inhospitable valley. Except during the short season of flood, the river represented more a muddy stream, and only then was it passable for most of its length. Its banks were lined with woods and thickets of thorn; north of the river this developed into dense bush, from which jutted rocky and craggy hills. It was a place where reconnaissance was difficult, and where surprise was easy. Here and there the river disappeared into treacherous swamps. Few white people lived near, and those that did were mostly wasting with disease.

Six weeks' supplies had gone to Tuli in advance of Plumer. But since the start of the defence of Mafeking no further supplies could come up to Bulawayo on the normal rail route from the Cape. It was decided that Plumer's force should not live entirely off the stores which had accumulated in Rhodesia, these being necessary for the civilian population as well; it had to be supplied by ships from Durban to Beira, then by rail, then by wagon to Bulawayo, and then on to Tuli, a distance of over 1,500 miles. This supply line seemed—and

---

[1] *Weil Papers*, 20 October 1899. This has not been revealed in official or unofficial accounts.

was—quite extraordinary in 1900. The *Official History* described it as 'almost unique in its complexity'. Plumer, relying a great deal on the administrative ability of the admirable Nicholson in Bulawayo, was not intimidated by the difficulties of supply. He managed to maintain considerable mobility in his enormous area, making much use of a shuttle service of wagons, taking wagon-loads with him and, like the Boers, replenishing stocks locally.

The Boers, too, were not in an enviable position. The area between the south bank of the river and the mountain ranges some sixty miles further south was an area of salt flats and gigantic trees bearing acrid fruit; in the winter, which was now just over, it was virtually waterless; in the summer it was permeated by the almost suffocating smells from the saline pools which dotted the landscape. Through this wilderness a Boer force advanced northwards on the outbreak of war. About 1,300 strong, it took up a position thirty miles south of the Limpopo. Its commander was Commandant van Rensburg, and among the officers were Field-Cornet Sarel Eloff, who was Kruger's grandson, and von Dalwig, a German artillery expert. Patrols were sent up to the river and posts established on its banks, first reaching the Limpopo on 16 October. Apart from skirmishing and shouting taunts across the river, the Boers seemed content to wait.

It became evident to Plumer that the enemy was expecting an invasion across the Limpopo. Sending his patrols between fords and crossings, he had brought about a great deal of activity on his own side. His plan was to deceive the Boers as to his numbers, and the plan worked well. However, his movements to and from a vulnerable crossing known as Rhodes Drift seem to have been inspired as much by a certain lack of determination as by a desire to elaborate his ruse. The Boers believed his strength to be 1,400 men, whereas it was, in fact, only 500.[1] Boer supply difficulties were also great, their line of communications ('fearful' as their commander described it) being across 150 miles of almost uninhabited wilderness. They detested the place they were at, and were haunted by fears of drought, fever and a native invasion from Bechuanaland.

Another Boer force, nearly 600 strong, under Assistant Commandant-General Grobelaar, moved south-west, opposite the Bechuanaland border, threatening the railway and the tribes.

[1] *Times History.*

On 2 November, van Rensburg, urged on by Grobelaar, tired of waiting. He sent 400 men, with two guns, across the river at Rhodes Drift. They cantered into Rhodesia, easily avoided Plumer's outpost, and rode for Tuli.

*

After four miles the posse reached an isolated building known as Bryce's Store. A convoy of eight wagons, escorted by twenty-six men, had just arrived there on the way to the outpost at Rhodes Drift. Overwhelmingly outnumbered, nearly half the escort were wounded or taken prisoner; the remainder dispersed into the bush.

Instead of pressing home their success, the Boers now entrenched themselves at Bryce's Store. Ill-supplied, apprehensive of their position and handicapped by divided counsels, they knew not whether to continue or to go back.

Plumer, meanwhile, brought some of his outposts in from their distant positions down the river and waited in daily expectation of a full-scale assault on Tuli. But no more activity came from the Boers until Grobelaar, with 400 more men, arrived on the scene. Thoroughly roused at their inaction, he spurred on the men from van Rensburg's commando. His intention was to defeat or surround Plumer, to raid Rhodesia and destroy the Bulawayo railway. Weary of inaction, he sent his vigorous and aggressive plan back to Pretoria for approval.

Grobelaar's plan was promptly rejected, and for similar reasons to those which had already moved Cronje's force away from the north. The State Secretary replied from Pretoria that the danger to the Republics lay not in the north but in Natal and Cape Colony, where British forces were assembling. He was not to attack Tuli, and was to remain in a passive role. He was to split the force into three detachments of 400 men each; each detachment was to take up a strategic position from the nearby Portuguese border to Mafeking. The remaining 500 men were to leave at once for Pretoria.[1]

A few weeks later the Boer forces were further reduced. It seemed

---

[1] Correspondence between Grobelaar and State Secretary, Pretoria, 13 November 1899: described in *Official History*, pp. 192–3.

to Plumer that there was no opposition facing him at all apart from a few widely dispersed outposts. He himself led a reconnaissance of British South Africa Police over the Limpopo, thereby disobeying Baden-Powell's first instructions. They covered fifty-four miles in eighteen hours, with no watering place on the way and in extreme heat: a remarkable feat. His men began to revise their opinions of the delicate-looking, silent Englishman with the monocle.

*

This strenuous probe into Transvaal territory confirmed Plumer's suspicion that the enemy had left the vicinity. It was information very much to his liking and relief. He had never relished his position at Tuli. He had now to reconsider his task.

His orders from Baden-Powell required him to remain at Tuli, which Baden-Powell considered 'a desirable point to hold'. Plumer, however, thought differently. He decided he must act independently. The matter which concerned him most was the state of the natives in Bechuanaland. As a man who had already seen the results of an African rising in the area, he was always inclined to consider the threat from that quarter as at least as serious as, if not more so than, any threat from the Boers.

During the Tuli operations Llewellyn had been patrolling the railway with his armoured trains. These sorties had stretched nearly 350 miles from Bulawayo. South of this, however, the Boers had crossed the frontier and the railway, on a number of occasions, and had negotiated with the tribes. The latter were in a state of increasing excitement, and suspicions as to everyone's intentions were keen. The Bechuanaland Africans believed they were about to be invaded by the Boers; the Boers believed the Africans were on the brink either of invading the Transvaal or of joining them in force; the British believed the Africans were about to support the Boers. Cronje had, in fact, written to President Kruger saying that there was a possibility of 30,000 Africans joining him;[1] most Boers would have found assistance from that quarter unwelcome, having as they did a perpetual and reasonable fear of hordes of Africans advancing on whites.

---

[1] Kruger's speech to the two Volksraads, 7 May 1900.

Tribesmen massed to the west of the railway and faced Boer detachments a few miles away to the east. Incidents occurred about water supply, prisoners and horse-thieving. Tension was high.

On 25 November 1899 a part of Holdsworth's force detrained from an armoured train and attacked a Boer camp. Holdsworth was supported, against his will, by a mass of Africans. There was a great deal of chaos, looting and burning. The Boers were astounded at what they considered an unspeakable outrage : the use by the British of savage Africans against white men.[1] Friction between Boers and Africans increased. In the interests of keeping the Africans under control, the British found themselves in the strange position of policing the border to keep Boer and African apart.

At Tuli, Plumer considered the Limpopo to have risen high enough to prevent the Boers getting a large force across for the time being. He therefore decided to move south-west, towards the railway. On 13 December he sent a telegram to Baden-Powell, via Nicholson in Bulawayo, about this. Late in the month Baden-Powell replied, approving of the move.[2] But Plumer had already left Tuli two days before, making use of the authority which he had already received from Baden-Powell to 'act for the best'. Anxious to play a more constructive role in the war, he had taken the initiative and, with his force of hardy Rhodesians and South Africans, was making his way across 175 miles of sparsely populated country to the long, exposed railway line which snaked across the map from Bulawayo to Mafeking.

---

[1] This incident caused something of a scandal, and in 1901 the Colonial Office demanded an explanation (P.R.O., Col. 634). Baden-Powell, who was well informed about everything that was going on to the north, informed Nicholson that he was 'not satisfied' at the incident (*Staff Diary:* 4 December 1899). Kruger, however, was still hopeful that the Africans would soon join with the Boers. A great deal of humbug was aired over the question of African support on both sides.

[2] *Weil Papers* and *Staff Diary*. The *Official History* gives the erroneous impression that Plumer received no advice or instructions at all from Baden-Powell at this time. Baden-Powell told G.H.Q. that he had 'ordered' Plumer south (*Roberts Papers*, 25 December 1899).

7. A Merry Christmas

Eddies of hot wind swept across from the Kalahari to the little township on the edge of the desert. The Union Jack fluttered idly at each new gust. The flies buzzed and swarmed. Occasionally a stronger wind sent sand and dust whirring across the trenches, clogging men's mouths and nostrils. The sun beat down, disinterested and pitiless, on all creatures below.

Women yawned. Men dozed beside their rifles. Children were listless. It was the hot season.

Would the Boer ever come? And if he did not, what was there to do? How long would it last?

Baden-Powell wrote to Nicholson in December: 'Enemy now enclosing to invest us . . . they are today destroying railway two miles north.'[1]

The trench system was developed. The Boers had closed in here and there; their trenches were more extensive, but very few, even yet, were within a mile of the British lines. These latter were further linked and joined nearly round the entire circumference. 'We kept on extending our lines,' Baden-Powell said, 'pushing out our trenches and capturing their forts. We had to do this to secure grazing and breathing space.'[2] At night those on duty slept in these trenches, on sacks or skins, or just on the bare earth; open boxes of ammunition, with rifles and cartridge-belts, were always within reach. Occasionally, at daybreak, there was the whine and thud of a shell; perhaps the stutter of machine-gun fire once or twice later in the day. Between 8.30 p.m. and 9.0 p.m. 'Creaky' always sent over a shell, almost as

---

[1] *Weil Papers,* 30 December 1899. The previous break in the railway had been six miles north.
[2] Churchill interview, the *Morning Post,* 28 June 1900.

if to mark the ending of yet another day. But for hour after basking hour nothing happened at all . . .

Across the dry veld carrion-crows circled and swooped above the great expanse of worn grass where Cronje's camp had been. There was nothing there but the glistening white skeletons of horses and cattle, broken-down wagons, empty crates, and the ashes of a hundred fires.

The Boers remaining around Mafeking did not find the investment unenjoyable. Boers never liked to stray too far from their homesteads, as many commando leaders knew well enough. By law the Boer was only liable to military service and not to unconditional obedience; discipline therefore depended to some extent on good will. Most of those at Mafeking came from the western Transvaal and few were far from home; although there were some who complained at the inactivity, most of them appear to have been at this time very satisfied with their role, and were all in favour of investing Mafeking indefinitely. Snyman, having disregarded all ideas of taking an initiative, allowed his men even more liberty than was customary in Boer units. So long as the British were deterred from making a break-out, he was satisfied; and as the British had themselves prepared for and invited a siege, a break-out seemed unlikely. One report, based on Boer sources, declares that to them the siege was 'little else than a pleasant picnic', marred only by the extremely rare occasions when Baden-Powell made one of his rushed little sorties.[1] A regular and frequent service of stage-coaches was organized from Johannesburg to the main Boer camp. It brought various comforts and luxuries, newspapers and sightseers. Men departed on each coach for short visits to the city or their homes. They were visited by their womenfolk, for whom a common treat was to fire off a shot from one of the guns in the direction of Mafeking.

On 3 December Baden-Powell wrote with confidence : 'The Boers do not intend to attack Mafeking, but mean to starve us out.'[2]

On Sundays the Boers walked over to the British lines, chatted and engaged in trade; for bundles of newspapers they would accept a little whisky. It was strange for the defenders to read advertisements

[1] *Times History*, p. 586.
[2] *Staff Diary*, 3 December 1899.

in the Pretoria newspapers stating that the advertisers were manufacturers to Her Majesty the Queen, and to read in the London Letter about social chit-chat from the British capital.

No attempt was made to enclose Mafeking; Snyman did not have enough men, and, indeed, the Boers never considered their operation as one of besieging Mafeking in the classic sense of the word.[1] There were few obstacles for those who wished to get in or out of the town individually, unless they actually went right into the Boer lines. From the early days of haphazard dispatches, a system of communication was being perfected. Baden-Powell was by now communicating regularly with Cape Town (via Bulawayo and Beira). Ordinary individuals and officers alike found that communications with the outside world was scarcely interrupted. Messengers left for Bechuanaland two or three nights a week; from the postal stations in Bechuanaland, letters and telegrams continued on their way through normal services. Godley and his wife at Bulawayo wrote frequently to each other during the siege, and found afterwards that only one letter had gone astray. Godley's wife also sent in supplies of saccharine 'which were most welcome'. In this way also, after the first few weeks of silence, news of home, and of the progress of the war, reached Mafeking. At the end of November Cecil received news by a special runner, hastened on his way by the Boers, of the death of his mother, the wife of the Prime Minister.

The main hazard was still the weather. On 5 December nature succeeded in doing in a few hours what war had been unable to achieve in more than seven weeks: the defences of the town were breached.

The day broke with a glowering haze of heat, which, to the local people, indicated trouble later. Fleeting wisps of black cloud were observed on the far horizon from Cannon Kopje and other high points; high winds followed, blowing hard across the plain; doors slammed, and shutters creaked, and chin-straps were adjusted. A deluge could be seen passing over the plain and over the Boer camps, the wind before it hurtling across the grass bits of scrub and twigs and broken branches. The black clouds moved over Mafeking and

---

[1] In his own sketch-map of the investment, widely reproduced, Baden-Powell drew a 'Boer cordon' around the town.

battered the place with a furious rain. Then, from the gentle slopes around the town, came a vast torrent of water: it came with extraordinary speed.

The earthworks which had been constructed all round the town were swept away as the torrent poured across the soggy veld. Nearly every trench and dug-out and basement was sought out by the torrent in its rush for resting places. The stores of Cannon Kopje floated hopelessly all the way into the town with the personal belongings of the men stationed there. Carts attempting to salvage articles from the flood were unable to move when presented with the full force of the waters. Struggling animals were pushed along helplessly, and some were killed against the new rocky barricades of Cannon Kopje. Shoes and boots were removed and men paddled the streets up to their knees. Many houses were inundated. The Molopo stream, gurgling with its surfeit, became a wide, fast-flowing river.

Through the hiss of the rain and the roar of the river, the occasional pop-popping of a machine-gun and the boom and thud of an artillery piece could be heard; but no one cared, all efforts were concentrated on the salvaging of belongings. As many of those present agreed, it was the best opportunity the Boers had had for taking Mafeking. A mist remained after the storm had departed; it rose up from the river and soaked the ground and swirled about in great eddies. But the Boers never came. They, too, were bedraggled, dispirited and awash; many departed for Johannesburg as soon as they could.

＊

While Captain Wilson, like the other staff officers at Baden-Powell's headquarters, had been living a life of no great hardship for officers on active service in time of war, his wife, Lady Sarah Wilson, had been all this time on the farm of Mrs Keeley, to which she had fled at the outbreak of war. The only book in the place was George du Maurier's *Trilby*, a work which she was reduced to reading many times. One line in particular seemed to echo her own predicament: 'The days are so long, and there are so many of them.'

Her first communication with the town was when the *Daily Mail* reporter, on his way south, had called at the farm with letters from

Mafeking. Soon however she established regular communication with her husband through the good services of 'a trusty old nigger called Boaz'. Mrs Keeley also corresponded with her husband in the town, and the two women paid Boaz £3 a journey, which at that time was a very generous sum indeed. One day Keeley himself arrived at the farm, having tired of 'the siege' and having impudently ridden out of the town.

At length Lady Sarah decided to go to Vryburg to discover the strength of the Boers there. Her excuse to local farmers, most of whom were pro-Boer, was that she had toothache which needed attention. She wrote: 'I thought nothing of undertaking a sixty miles' drive in broiling heat and along a villainous road . . . Then suddenly the carriage drove into the main street, which boasted of some quite respectable shops. The first thing which attracted our notice was the Court House, almost hidden in trees, through which glimmered the folds of the gaudy Dutch [i.e. Transvaal] standard.' There were not many signs of occupation : a few armed Boers, and a notice fixed on a tree. The occupying Boer force had left the town long before, except for a token garrison. Lady Sarah visited some wounded British at the hospital; these were the men who had fallen into Boer hands when one of the armoured trains had been ambushed right at the start of the war. She learned there that 'Boer doctoring was of the roughest description, the surgeon's only assistant being a chemist-boy, and trained nurses were replaced by a few well-meaning but clumsy Dutch girls, while chloroform or sedatives were quite unknown.'

Lady Sarah drove to the Central Hotel, where she got 'capital rooms and was most civilly received by the manager, an Englishman. The latter, however, could hardly conceal his surprise at my visit at this moment . . . For fear of exciting curiosity, I did not walk about much, but observed from the windows of my sitting-room the mounted burghers patrolling the town, sometimes at a foot's pace, more often at a smart canter . . . I never could have imagined so many men absolutely alike : all had long, straggling beards, old felt hats, shabby clothes."

On the return journey Lady Sarah's carriage was stopped by a party of Boers, who asked to see her pass. She had made efforts to disguise her appearance, but produced her British passport and was waved on by the uncomprehending patrol. At this time the Boer invaders and local rebels were making efforts to administer their newly won territory.

With rumours mounting as to her true identity, Lady Sarah and her maid moved to a farm in another district : one rumour had it that she was a grand-daughter of Queen Victoria who had been sent to the area by the Queen to report on the doings of some of her rebellious subjects. At the new farm she met the Reuters correspondent returning to Cape Town from Mafeking. This enterprising gentleman had with him a basket of carrier-pigeons with which he hoped to communicate with the town on a return visit. He offered one to Lady Sarah as an unusually swift means of communicating with the garrison. She accepted. A letter was sent to Baden-Powell, attached to one of the birds, informing him of her new position and suggesting that she could forward any information that he might wish to send. She did not, of course, know that by this time the town was in fairly open communication with Cape Town via Bulawayo. 'I had never had any experience of such birds and was delighted to think how much quicker they would travel than old Boaz. When the pigeon was released, however, I must confess it was rather disturbing to note that it did not seem at all sure of the direction it should take, circling round at least twenty times in the air.' However, the Reuters man assured her that this was the usual habit of such birds and this particular one had won several prizes.

Not long after the departure of Reuters' correspondent for Cape Town, a party of Boers rode up to the farm. They had been drinking a good deal of looted liquor on the way and, on their arrival, amused themselves for a time by setting up bottles and shooting at them from a distance of about fifty yards. Lady Sarah and her hosts watched from behind the curtains. At length the Boers approached the house, where they received further refreshment. 'A proclamation was read out in the living-room : "This country now being part of the Transvaal, the residents must within seven days leave their homes or enrol themselves as burghers".' Afterwards three of them remained : not as caretakers of the farm but as guards for Lady Sarah. The pigeon, she now learnt, had not only flown straight to the Boer camp, but had alighted on the roof of the farmhouse which was Snyman's headquarters; there it had been shot and Lady Sarah's message, with its offer of help to Baden-Powell, read with interest. Lady Sarah, a heavy smoker who always seems to have been well supplied with cigarettes, offered some to the guards and waited. Nothing happened. The days went on as before. Despite all her efforts to take a more active part in the proceedings of the siege of Mafeking, it seemed that this lady, very much a Churchill, was fated to remain on the sidelines. But this fate was not agreeable to her : she decided to get into Mafeking itself. She was strengthened in her determination by the knowledge that the *Daily Mail* reporter had made his trips to the area once too often and had been sent by the Boers to the prisoner-of-war camp in Pretoria. Lady Sarah had offered her services to the *Daily Mail*, and they had been gladly accepted.

Lady Sarah Wilson persuaded, or ordered, her guards to take her to Snyman, forty-five miles away. At the end of her journey she was accompanied only by some African boys, and : 'About four in the afternoon we came to a rise, and, looking over it, saw the white roofs of Mafeking lying about five miles away in the glaring sunlight . . . Seeing not a solitary soul on the flat grass plains, I felt very much tempted to drive in to the native village.' Unwisely deciding against this, she continued to the main Boer camp and, surrounded by two or three hundred fascinated Boers, found herself outside Snyman's commandeered farmhouse. Snyman's secretary, who spoke perfect English, emerged from the door and enquired as to the purpose of her visit. 'After an interminable wait among the gaping crowd, the aforementioned gentleman returned and informed me I could see the general at once. He literally had to make a way for me from the cart to the house, but I must admit the burghers were very civil, nearly all of them taking off their hats as I passed through them.' She was in a low, dark room. Seated on a bench were two old-looking men with enormous, untidy beards : Snyman and Botha. Snyman said he would consider her request to enter the town. She was taken to a cottage half a mile away, which had been set up as a field hospital. Lady Sarah was taken into the operating-room and told she could sleep there. There was no bed : only a broken-down sofa, the operating table, a washstand in the corner, and a table with bottles of drugs and ointments. Two Boer girls entered the room and told her to undress, which she did; they then searched her clothing and her suitcase and small dressing-case. A little later a messenger came from

Snyman saying that he would be willing to exchange her for a certain Petrus Viljoen, who had been in jail for theft in Mafeking since before the war. Lady Sarah thought it unlikely that Baden-Powell would agree to such a suggestion, and instead of addressing him personally, as was her custom, she wrote a comparatively rare letter to her husband:

MY DEAR GORDON——I am at the laager. General Snyman will not give me a pass unless Colonel Baden-Powell will exchange me for a Mr Petrus Viljoen. I am sure this is impossible, so I do not ask him formally. I am in a great fix, as they have very little meal left at Setlagoli or the surrounding places. I am very kindly looked after here.

She then went to sleep on the sofa. At noon on the following day her guards handed her a reply:

MY DEAR SARAH——I am delighted to hear that you are being well-treated, but very sorry to have to tell you that Colonel Baden-Powell finds it impossible to hand over Petrus Viljoen in exchange for you, as he was convicted of horse-stealing before the war . . . GORDON WILSON.

During the afternoon Lady Sarah witnessed the arrival of a coach from Pretoria 'with much horn-blowing and whip-cracking'. She was delighted to be able to read a newspaper only two days old.

Then a letter from Baden-Powell arrived, rather more informal than that from her husband, in which he said that he had hoped to save her 'the unpleasantness of the siege', and that they were 'all very well, and really rather enjoying it all'.

A suggestion that Lady Sarah should be exchanged for a Boer woman in Mafeking was put to Snyman. The Boer commandant ignored it, and the matter was dropped when the woman explained that she had no intention anyway of leaving 'the shelter of the town'. Dispirited and indignant, Lady Sarah said she wanted to return to the farm where she had been staying.[1]

---

[1] Three letters from *South African Memories*, Lady Sarah Wilson. The inconsistency regarding the nature of the siege is not untypical of Baden-Powell.

At this point Snyman suggested to Lady Sarah that she should go to Pretoria, where she would find 'pleasant ladies' society'. 'Seeing my look of angry surprise, he hastily added that he only wished he had a house of his own to place at my disposal ... I remarked that I had no intention of visiting their capital ... I would not for an instant admit they had a right to detain me or to send me to any place against my will ... I went to bed once more on the wretched sofa.' Several days went by, during which Lady Sarah pestered Snyman—normally a quite imperturbable man—with vigour. Soon he was corresponding with her in 'enormous' and sealed official envelopes.

Two people at the camp particularly displeased her. One was a woman doctor of the field hospital, '... the first of her species I had ever come across, and with whom I was not favourably impressed'. She considered this unfortunate woman untidy, ill-kempt and badly dressed, although she felt that 'this lady had been a handsome woman' before becoming a doctor. Lady Sarah voiced her distaste of the woman doctor as frequently as she could, 'partly from the irritation I felt on hearing her addressed as Doctor'.

On the afternoon of her fifth day at the hospital she saw 'a fine-looking burgher' ride up. Speaking in perfect English, he said he had known her brother, Lord Randolph Churchill. His name was Spencer Drake—descended from the family of Sir Francis Drake; he had lived for many years in the Transvaal and was now fighting on its behalf. Although she regarded him with displeasure, Lady Sarah enlisted Drake in her cause, and soon he was speaking for her to Snyman and acting as go-between. She also met a German soldier of fortune who claimed to have served in the British Army and to have charged with the Light Brigade, but she was unable to put him to any use.

On the morning of 7 December, at 6.0 a.m., Lady Sarah Wilson was awakened by Spencer Drake knocking on her door. He told her to get dressed and be ready in half an hour.

There had been considerable argument about Lady Sarah at Baden-Powell's headquarters. Many of the British officers in the town either knew her personally or were familiar with her reputation; not all of them were anxious for her to join them. Lord Edward Cecil, on the other hand, had thought it looked very bad for an Englishwoman to be left so long in the hands of the Boers while they did nothing to help her. The town authorities, meanwhile, had refused to take the responsibility of releasing a criminal who had been jailed under the jurisdiction of the civil authorities. Baden-Powell had been vacillating between the arguments. At last Cecil, according to Lady Sarah herself, using his position as the Prime Minister's son, had told Baden-Powell that he would take all responsibility and would take any consequent blame on his own shoulders. Baden-Powell had agreed to this plan, and had informed Snyman that the exchange could take place after all.[1]

A truce had been arranged only until 8.0 a.m., and Lady Sarah was extremely agitated about missing it. When, therefore, she was taken to Snyman for farewells, she was somewhat impatient. He had been suffering from inflamed eyes, and she expressed the hope that they were better, shook his hand and left him there. Snyman, it seems, was not inclined to detain her.

She went with a group of her captors, if they could be described as such. Just over a mile from the town they were met by a party which had emerged from the defences bearing a white flag and escorting Viljoen. Horse-thief and lady were formally handed over, 'and at a gallop we rattled into the main street', Baden-Powell and Cecil having met her at the defences. Captain Wilson was fully occupied elsewhere.

She was taken to the house of Mr Weil, where she was to stay; by Mafeking standards it was a place of some luxury.

Baden-Powell dispatched a letter to Snyman:

Sir——I beg to thank you for having handed over Lady Sarah Wilson in exchange for the convict P. Viljoen. At the same time, I beg to point out that I have only consented to the exchange under protest . . .

He went on to criticize Snyman, in petulant tones, for having objected to his use of natives in the defence. He said it was primarily because the Boers had been raiding the Africans' cattle.

. . . While on the subject of Natives, please do not suppose that I am ignorant of what you have been doing with regard to seeking

---

[1] Lady Wilson, p. 153.

the assistance of armed natives, nor of the use of the Natives by you in the destruction of the railway line south of Mafeking. However, having done my duty in briefly warning you on these points, I do not propose to further discuss them by letter.

I have the honour to be, Sir,

Your obedient servant,

R. S. S. BADEN-POWELL.

On her first day Lady Sarah ordered a bomb-proof shelter. It was completed, under her directions, within a few days, and it was the most remarkable shelter in Mafeking: 'a triumph in its line', as she herself proudly said. Neatly lined in white-painted panelling, it had thick beams overhead and heavy pillar supports. Bed, linen and dressing-table were the best the town had to offer. One wall was entirely covered by a vast Union Jack, which Lady Sarah very much appreciated. It was not only known as the coolest place and the safest dug-out in town, it was the equal of any room above ground in Mafeking. A splendid dinner was served by Lady Sarah to the senior officers as a 'house-warming'.

A direct-line telephone was installed from Lady Sarah Wilson's shelter, the talk of the town, to Baden-Powell's headquarters.

*

Four days after Lady Sarah's arrival, Baden-Powell sent a remarkable document over to the Boer lines. It was a manifesto, signed by himself, asking the Boer rank-and-file to disperse to their homes, or at any rate to evacuate their positions. He pointed out the hopelessness of attempting to take a place as easily defended as Mafeking; that thousands of British troops were pouring into South Africa (this was true), and that the Boers ought to depart before trouble fell on them. This declaration was sent out by eight messengers from all parts of the defences. Baden-Powell, in later years, normally insisted that the major incentive for his arranging to be invested in Mafeking was to detain large numbers of Boer forces there. By pointing out the uselessness of the investment, Baden-Powell could not have been helping the cause:

... In a few weeks the South African Republic will be in the hands of the English; no sacrifice of life on your part can stop it ... Is it worth while losing your lives in a vain attempt to stop their invasion or to take a town beyond your borders which, if taken, would be of no use to you? ... The Staat Artillery have done us very little damage, and we are now well protected with forts and mines. Your presence here, or elsewhere, under arms, cannot stop the British advancing into your country ... The duty assigned to my troops is to sit still here until the proper time arrives and then to fight and to kill until you give in ... my advice to you is to return without delay to your homes ... To those who, after this warning, defer their submission till too late, I can offer no promise, and they will only have themselves to blame for any injury or loss of property that they or their families may afterwards suffer.[1]

The following day Snyman replied with not unnatural asperity. Another, more pointed, reply was signed by Botha and Spencer Drake: 'We wish to inform you that we are perfectly prepared to meet your troops, and that you must therefore let them loose as soon as possible.'

Two reasons have been given in the past for Baden-Powell's manifesto: it has been seen as a joke, or as an attempt to increase disaffection among the enemy. It has only been reproduced once, in 1900, and read differently to either of these suggestions; Baden-Powell, however, insisted both at the time and later that it was to create 'dissension and desertion' among the Boers and necessitate reinforcements being sent to Snyman. If this is so, it did not succeed.

For some days before this, shelling of the town had practically ceased, the Boers being by now well aware of the difficulties inherent in taking the scattered town by bombardment. As if in answer to Baden-Powell's manifesto, shelling was immediately stepped up. By this time, however, most of the people in the town had become careless about precautions, so infrequent and ineffective had the shelling become. On one occasion a Boer battery had opened up, with shells streaming over the town itself and landing among Boer positions on the other side, which replied with frantic messages enjoining caution.

---

[1] Baillie, 11 December 1899.

After the manifesto there was a sudden flurry of casualties and several deaths. By the middle of December twenty-three white combatants in Mafeking had been killed, of whom eighteen had lost their lives in the skirmish at Five-Mile Bank, in Fitzclarence's raid, and in the Boer assault on Cannon Kopje. The few deaths by bombardment had been in the native village, where no protective measures had been taken. Suddenly casualties increased; they were to fade away again after Christmas.

One shell went through the bar of Dixon's Hotel in the early hours of the morning: at almost any other time it would have been a disaster, for the bar—there being no lack of liquor as yet—was always crowded during the day. Many shells never exploded on arrival in Mafeking; one casualty was caused when a town councillor was tampering with one of 'Creaky's' many unexploded shells. The shell went off as he was extracting the fuse, killing him and one passer-by, and severely injuring another. Baillie wrote in his diary: 'Everybody was much depressed by this; it seemed so sad that more damage should be caused among the whites by an accident than had hitherto been the result of six weeks' shelling by the enemy's heavy gun.' Another unexploded shell was found to be uncharged. It contained a message for Baden-Powell:

MR BADEN-POWELL——Please excuse me for sending this iron message i have no other to send at present. He is rather exentric but forgive him if he does not behave well. I wish to ask you not to let your men drink all the whisky as i wish to have a drink when we all come to see you. Cindly tell Mrs Dunkley that her mother and vamily are all quite well. I remain, Yours trewly, A REPUBLICAN.

The plight of the Africans was humanely described by Hamilton: 'We have had many more natives killed than whites, and the element of tragedy in this becomes the greater and more acute since, as a rule, the native, employed in building bomb-proof shelters for the whites, lacks the energy to turn to his own profit his knowledge of the manner in which shell cover should be constructed. They lie about under tarpaulins, behind zinc palings, wooden boxes, and flimsy sheds of that description, and perhaps for days their shelter may escape the line of fire; but there comes a moment made hideous by the scream of shell as it bursts in some little gathering of dozing, half-listless natives. At such a moment their bravery is extraordinary—is indeed the most fearful thing in the world. The native with his arm blown off, with his thigh shot away, or with his body disembowelled, is endowed with extreme fortitude and most stoical resolution. Unless he is seen, he lies where he is struck, not caring to take the trouble to make his wounds known to someone who could sympathize and assist him. When the gaze of the curious is turned upon his mangled and wounded form, he attempts to laugh, makes every effort to assist himself, and even if he knows that his injuries be fatal, he makes no sign. There is thus much to admire in these natives, but for the most part people are quite indifferent to their sufferings.' Vere Stent, Reuters' correspondent, accused one of the doctors, Dr Hayes, of operating on Africans without using anæsthetics, and implying that native patients were otherwise ill-treated. The matter was referred to Baden-Powell, who dismissed the whole affair as 'childish'[1]; he had a poor opinion of the correspondents in the town, who were always making their presence felt, whether it was with success on the polo ground or in presumptuous questions.

One of the worst incidents in the renewal of shelling occurred when a shell entered a chemist's shop and killed an African who had been inside. 'Mingled with the fragments of glass and the contents of the shop were shreds of cloth and infinitesimal strips of flesh, while the entire environment of the scene was splashed with blood. The poor native had lost an arm, a foot lay a few yards from him, and his other leg was hanging by a few shreds of skin.' Hamilton went on to describe the white spectators who 'were standing about without the inclination to help, or even a smattering of first aid to the injured . . . The bleeding body was put on a stretcher and the mangled extremities gathered together. . . . Despite his fearful injuries, which were beyond the scope of human power to aid, he was not dead, feebly exclaiming as they put him on the stretcher, "Boss, boss, me hurt." ' A second shell immediately after this killed a corporal who had witnessed the scene in the chemist's and who was going to have a 'pick-me-up' at the bar of the adjoining Reisle's Hotel.

The hospital was busier than ever before, almost entirely with

---

[1] *Staff Diary*, 30 November 1899.

African casualties. Fortunately for them, Dr Anderson, the Army doctor who was attached to the Protectorate Regiment, had purchased before the war a large quantity of medical stores at his own expense; without his foresight the medical supplies would undoubtedly have become exhausted. As well as the civilian doctors of the town, and the nuns, volunteer nurses and sisters of the hospital, he was assisted by a Dr Dowling, a Cape Town physician who had arrived in Mafeking just before the war and who had offered his services. There had been few bullet wounds, but some of those that had occurred had been caused by the new explosive Martini bullet—which caused internal injuries—rather than the Mauser bullet, which usually went straight through the body in a comparatively clean perforation. The Martini bullet was very much feared. Two men, one an African and the other a railway employee, were shot through the head with Mausers and lived. Many of the Boer marksmen had their rifles fixed on strategic points, or were able to fire by lifting sights over parapets without showing themselves. This was standard practice among the Boers in other theatres of the war. The rifle with which they were armed enabled them to keep aim on an object until the magazine was expended, the rifleman having nothing to do but pull the trigger; with the British rifle, a bolt action had to be worked after each shot, deranging aim and losing sight of the target on each occasion, and making a movement which could draw the attention of the enemy.[1]

The British artillery, inadequate as it was, was well used by the extremely able Major F. W. Panzera, of the British South Africa Police, who had been put in charge of the guns. Carefully husbanding his ammunition, he seldom engaged in fruitless duels with the Boer guns which could easily outrange him; from time to time this brought him into friction with Baden-Powell, who was always keen on 'show'. An antiquated naval gun, made in 1770, was brought into use; its cannon balls, fired by powder cartridges sewn by women, including the willing nuns of the convent, travelled for well over a mile. The main work of the artillery was keeping the Boers from

---

[1] A letter from Lieut.-Colonel Hector Macdonald to Kitchener, in January 1900, complained bitterly about this (*Kitchener Papers*, P.R.O.), but nothing could be done.

manning positions close to the town; this work, aided by snipers, they did effectively.

＊

The increase in shelling was not enough to shake the ineffable good spirits of the commander in Mafeking, or the confidence of the people. Hamilton's 'picnic' continued much as before. Attending a dinner-party at Dixon's, Lady Sarah was delighted to find little or no change since before the war, 'the stock of Schweppes' soda-water appearing inexhaustible—besides this luxury, we had beautiful fresh tomatoes and young cabbages.' Meat was almost entirely beef, but no one complained of that; eggs were plentiful; the main complaint was that tinned butter, a result of Cecil's and Weil's store-gathering before the war, had now replaced fresh butter. While rations were collected daily, everyone added to them freely at the various stores, many things still being unrequisitioned and a flourishing 'black market' taking care of most needs. Few, at this stage, questioned whether the rationing system was rigid enough to tend to a long siege; it seemed that the town was superbly stocked.

At parties and fêtes Baden-Powell himself—thoroughly in his element, as Lady Sarah said—dispensed the tea for all and sundry from a large urn. Often he seemed more like the host at some huge, jolly party than a military commander. At his Sunday concerts he continued to take part in all kinds of buffoonery; he now played the mouth-organ as well as the other musical instruments with which he had accosted the ears of the besieged, and his most popular act had become an impersonation of the pianist Paderewski, with a mop of false hair and many high-pitched shrieks. He also enjoyed dressing up as a Cockney and singing 'Cockney songs'. As always, he took every opportunity of dressing up, and sometimes posed for the photographer; sometimes he was seen in his beloved scouting outfit, with flannel shirt with rolled-up sleeves and revolver in holster, which reminded everyone of his love for adventure and initiative. At the pony races he appeared in another favourite costume, that of a ringmaster, in white tie and tails, with an enormous whip thirty feet long.

Mafeking had never known such an orgy of sports and entertainments. All the concerts and shows had cards and programmes printed as neatly as if they had come from Leicester Square :

1 March, *Athalie*, Mendelssohn, by Members of the Amateur Orchestral Society.
2 *A Little Bit of All Right,* Mr. Pat Taylor.
3 *The Romany King . . .*
Another Afternoon Concert, Under the Patronage of Col. R. S. S. Baden-Powell. Commencing at 5 p.m. Admission : two shillings. A limited number of reserved seats—see plan . . .

At the cycle races, Lady Sarah Wilson presented the prizes, which included such desirable articles as a silver glove-buttoner, a painted fan, a clock, a candlestick mirror, silver-mounted pipes and amber cigarette-holders. Much to everyone's dismay, the playing of open-air games, and particularly of polo on Sundays, was threatened. Snyman had sent a strongly worded note to Baden-Powell : he objected, for religious reasons, to such frolicking on the Sabbath. If they continued he would be obliged to shell them.

Baden-Powell stopped polo on Sundays.

However, townspeople and garrison were not alarmed, and other Sunday games and sports continued as before.

*

As Christmas Day fell on a Monday, Baden-Powell carefully decided to observe Christmas on the preceding day. A notice was posted to this effect :

It is notified for general information that Christmas will be celebrated on Sunday next the 24th instant, instead of on Monday; the exigencies of the service and the state of siege preventing the observance of Monday as a holiday.

In the same notice it was announced that one Telegelo, a Kalahari native, was sentenced to death for theft.

There were morning and afternoon church services on 24 December, all with packed congregations. At the Church of England the

May Xmas find you glad and well.
In spite of Kruger's Shot and Shell.

Ye Mafeking Hotel.

BRITISH BECHUANALAND·

G. RIESLE   PROPRIETOR.

MENU.

Xmas Daye 1899.

Anchovy Croûtons.
Olives.

Consommé Windsor.

Oyster Patties.

Smoked Calves Tongue.
Giblet Pie.
Tournédos Parisienne.
York Ham and Madeira Sauce.
Fricasée of Veal.

Roast Fowl and Bread Sauce.
Boiled Fowl and Bacon.

Joints.

Baron of Beef and Yorkshire Pudding.
Veal and Ham.
Roast Side of Lamb and Green Peas.
Sucking Pig and Apple Sauce.
Roast Saddle of Mutton.
Boiled Mutton and Capers.
Boiled Bacon.
Corned Beef.
Tongue and Ham.

Vegetables.

Marrow, Green Peas,
Baked and Boiled Potatoes.

Xmas Pudding.
Mince Pies.
Sandringham Jellies.
Victoria Sandwich.

Dessert   Café Noir.

RULE BRITANIA.

Rev. Weekes played the harmonium and also conducted the service. In the afternoon Weil entertained 250 children to tea around the Christmas tree, the need for which he had even foreseen in October. Cartloads of cheering children went to and from the women's camp. Feeling it safe to ignore Snyman's susceptibilities on this special occasion, sports were also held in the afternoon. Parties of men drifted from shelter to shelter in search of good cheer and alcohol. Rationing was suspended for the day. Baden-Powell and his staff had their Christmas dinner at Lady Sarah's dug-out: turkey, plum-pudding, wine and brandy: afterwards—a group photograph. At Reisle's Hotel, 'We had quite a royal Christmas dinner. It included everything conceivable; we revelled in plenty.' They did indeed. The dinner menu at the hotel (reproduced opposite), had nearly all come from Weil's amazing stores, which as yet had not been depleted by a third. At the hospital, the staff enjoyed tinned duck and Christmas pudding. Bell, the local magistrate, wrote in his diary: 'Whiteley [the Mayor] provided some toothsome viands and soul-inspiring drinks. We did ourselves well and rose from the table full of Christmas sentiments. Attended church . . . The sermon was delightfully short, for which I commended Weekes. Singing good. Ladies in fashionable attire, men as usual: altogether a creditable turn-out. The Wesleyan Church is closed, the Parson having given up the Bible for the Sword . . . A good deal of champagne was put away by different fellows in the town.'[1] (In his official Report on the defence of Mafeking, Baden-Powell wrote of 'the entire absence of all luxuries.')

During the day a gunner showing off his Maxim to a girl inadvertently fired off eight rounds towards the Boers. An apology was duly delivered.

Next day the festivities continued only slightly abated, for the Boers had decided to observe Christmas on the obvious day—25 December. They had ordered a truce. Baden-Powell wrote: 'By tacit consent no shots were fired, and both sides kept Christmas Day as a holiday.'[2]

In the evening there were a number of concert parties. At the

---

[1] Bell, 24 December 1899.
[2] *Staff Diary*, 25 December 1899.

native village, Jim Mbalo was shot by a firing squad for 'being out-side the lines without a pass'.[1]

On Christmas night Bell wrote: 'I am considerably worried during all hours of the day by hungry Natives, who lean against the garden wall and stare at me, exclaiming at intervals—*Baaije hongore Baas*; at the same time the fact is demonstrated by the supplicant smiting with his hand the black empty leather bag which represents his stomach. These people will soon be a source of anxiety to us . . .'

But for the Europeans the two days were a pleasant break in the defence. For Baden-Powell's efforts to avoid monotony among the garrison enjoyed, perhaps, more effect on the children and the women than among most of the non-commissioned troops, who did not care for polo and other sports and did not frequent the concert parties as much as before. There was a widespread feeling of bore-dom. Hamilton wrote: 'How wearily the time passes.' Young men 'vied with each other in begging for permission to join scouting parties at night'. Lady Sarah, in Churchillian vein, noted that, 'the soldiers in Mafeking were disposed to grumble at the small part they seemed to be playing in the great tussle in which England was en-gaged'.[2] Baillie, as usual, took it all less seriously: 'In this war of "sit down" I, for one, have worn out much patience and several pairs of trousers.'

Years after the siege, Baden-Powell wrote in *Sketches in Mafeking and East Africa*: 'We acted as much as possible on the principle that aggression is the soul of defence.'

At the time Hamilton wrote: 'The siege, as it progresses, seems to give fewer opportunities for coming into positive contact with the enemy; such occasions as there have been are few and far between, and although Colonel Baden-Powell holds out the promise of such a venture, it has been so constantly deferred that we are for the most part becoming incredulous.'

But conflict was coming sooner, and bloodier, than Hamilton imagined; a number of events were now about to urge Baden-Powell to action.

---

[1] *Weil Papers*. But Bell wrote that he was really executed because he had said that the big gun had been taken away by the Boers: it hadn't.

[2] Lady Wilson, p. 96.

8. The British Defeated

Elsewhere in South Africa, Christmas had been a less traditional affair. For the British the war to date had consisted of a series of most unpleasant shocks . . .

The carefree confidence with which the country had gone to war had been shaken even before the arrival of Sir Redvers Buller. The main Boer thrust, into Natal towards the coast and the ports so coveted by the Transvaal, had been met by the main British force, which had come under the command of General Sir George White, a sixty-four-year-old Ulsterman who had once been Commander-in-Chief in India. After some initial success White tried to outdo the elusive Boers and suffered defeat at Nicholson's Nek, losing over 800 prisoners to the Boers. The dismayed and nonplussed Sir George concentrated his force of over 12,000 men at the town of Ladysmith, where the Boers were busily surrounding them on the day of Buller's arrival at Cape Town with his staff. Left to defend Natal were little more than one battalion of the Dublin Fusiliers, some assorted cavalry and oddments of infantry and artillery, and an armoured train. White came in for a good deal of odium both during and after the war for accepting siege.

Faced with this situation, the unfortunate Buller had to recast his previous ideas on how to win the war. First of all, Ladysmith, with its large and essential British force, obviously had to be relieved. In Ladysmith were 13,496 troops, with 51 guns, 5,400 civilians and 2,400 Africans and Indians—a total of some 21,300 souls, not least of whom was 'Dr Jim' Jameson himself.[1] From then on Buller was like a man for whom events always seemed to be about one day's grasp ahead of him. He sent the only force yet available to Durban. From there it was to proceed up the railway to Ladysmith, to an

---

[1] *Official History*, Vol. II, Sir F. Maurice (Hurst & Blackett, 1907).

area for which it had not been prepared, and for which it only had small-scale maps.

With scant knowledge as to the whereabouts and strength of the Boers ahead, the armoured train, from which much was hoped, was sent forward to discover what it could, like a blind man's stick. On board, but apprehensive as to the manœuvre, was the correspondent of the *Morning Post*. Churchill wrote: 'Nothing looks more formidable and impressive than an armoured train; but nothing is in fact more vulnerable and helpless. It was only necessary to blow up a bridge or culvert to leave the monster stranded, far from home and help, at the mercy of the enemy. This situation did not seem to have occurred to our commander.'

It did, however, occur to the Boers; after a desperate and hard-fought action in which Churchill took a prominent part he and about fifty others were taken prisoner.[1] But in less than a month Churchill had escaped from the officers' prison camp in Pretoria. After a number of daring and audacious adventures, narrowly escaping death or detection on several occasions, he presented himself at the office of the British Consul at Lourenço Marques in neutral Portuguese territory. On reaching Durban, Churchill found himself the hero of the day. His escape had received a great deal of publicity, for not only was it extremely courageous, he was also, after all, the son of a late famous politician and had recently stood at an important by-election. The harbour was decorated with flags, the quays were thronged with crowds, and bands welcomed him with rousing tunes. At last the public had someone in the war whom it could unreservedly admire; and if ever there was a genuinely dare-devil action which justified public approbation it was Churchill's sensational escape from Pretoria.

Meanwhile, in the Cape, Cronje's forces had taken villages and posts inside the border for a length of some hundred miles, and sometimes at a considerable depth. The taking of Vryburg had been the prelude for serious efforts to take the great diamond-mining city of Kimberley. Among the 50,000 people in the town was the greatest name in South Africa: Cecil Rhodes. Although far from well, Rhodes embarked on a long series of castigations of the military commander,

---

[1] The Boer who took him prisoner was Louis Botha, at that time not in high command: the future Prime Ministers later became firm friends.

Lieutenant-Colonel
Herbert Plumer

Plumer's force leaving Bulawayo, October 1899

The lookout

Baden-Powell on the lookout

Baden-Powell at the
sports

At the Sunday sports

A Mafeking bank-note.
These were exchange-
able for cash within up
to six months of the re-
lief, but most were kept
as souvenirs

10s. *Mafeking* Siege Note. 10s.

March,
1900.

THIS NOTE IS GOOD FOR

Ten Shillings

(STERLING)

6385 DURING THE SIEGE; 6385

AND WILL BE EXCHANGED
FOR COIN ON RESUMPTION
OF CIVIL LAW AT THE

Standard Bank,
MAFEKING.

March,
1900.

Issued by authority of Col. R. S. S. Baden-Powell, Commanding Frontier Forces

R. Urry

H Greener Capt
Chief Paymaster.

A British Amazon in the trenches at Mafeking—a popular view

Benjamin Weil, who fed
Mafeking for more
than half a year,
clothed and supplied
the defence force, and
organized communica-
tions with the outside

Winston Churchill as a
war correspondent in
1899 *Radio Times Hulton Picture Library*

Lords Roberts and Kitchener arriving at Cape Town, 4 January 1900

Lady Sarah
Wilson approach-
ing Mafeking after
her exchange for
the Boer prisoner
Viljoen

Lady Sarah at
the entrance to
her shelter

The interior of
Lady Sarah's
shelter

Christmas Dinner, 1899. Standing, from left: Colonel
Baden-Powell, Captain Fitzclarence, Captain Moncreiffe,
Ben Weil, Lord Edward Cecil. Seated: Captain Wilson,
Major Goold-Adams, Major Godley, Lady Sarah Wilson,
Colonel Walford, Major Hanbury-Tracy

Boers inspecting the British dead at Game Tree Hill

Lieutenant-Colonel R. G. Kekewich, about the defensive arrangements and the prospects of a relief. With Kekewich was half a battalion of regular infantry as well as the newly raised irregulars and town
guard. For artillery he was no better off than Baden-Powell, having
only fourteen muzzle-loading seven-pounders. Unlike that of
Mafeking, however, Kimberley's position did place it in direct
strategic relevance to an invasion of the Cape. Rhodes, stamping about
like a caged giant, cabled to Milner : 'If Kimberley falls everything
goes.' And Milner cabled home : 'If Kimberley falls we cannot hold
the whole of the Colony; perhaps we shall only be able to hold a small
bit of it.'[1] A relief force, under the command of Lieutenant-General
Lord Methuen, was prepared. But such arrangements, as Rhodes was
frequently informed, take time.

All this time British reinforcements were pouring into South Africa.
At Cape Town, Buller was entertained by Lady Violet Cecil and
Lady Charles Cavendish-Bentinck at Rhodes's house—Rhodes having
requested them to look after it for him during his enforced absence.
Buller, despite all his preoccupations, found time to comfort these
ladies as to the fate of their husbands in Mafeking. Lady Violet had
written home on 2 November : 'We think they have been fighting
there every day since the war broke out.' She had received a letter from
M. Georges Clemenceau, the French politician and journalist (later
Premier), who wrote to apologize at the gloating of the French press
over the British defeats. Lady Cavendish-Bentinck, who had come to
South Africa in order to be near her husband, was one of the most
admired beauties of her day. The two women spent much time at
the Town Hall, in Cape Town, distributing rations and clothing for
British refugees from the Boer republics. Lady Violet was seeing a
great deal of the High Commissioner, Sir Alfred Milner, who was
naturally entertained frequently at Rhodes's house. Three or four
times a week hastily written, informal notes arrived for her from
Sir Alfred, who was, as it happened, a most eligible bachelor.

Early in December, in order to speed the relief of Ladysmith so
that he could get on with the campaign, Buller went to Natal himself.
His men were both glad and alarmed to see him, for, despite his habit
of knowing the correct decision but taking the wrong one, he was

[1] 18 October 1899 *Milner Papers*, Vol. II, p. 24.

always liked by his troops and even by most of those who worked closely with him. He had many admirable qualities : generalship was not one of them.

The Boers were entrenched at the foot of hills on the far bank of the Tugela River, where the railway crossed it at the township of Colenso. Confusing his force as to both its command and its orders, Buller ordered a frontal attack—he had previously declared, rightly, that such action could not succeed. It did not—much to the despair of the besieged in Ladysmith, who could hear the guns of the battle. It was a horrible and bloody action. By now Louis Botha, Churchill's captor, was in command of the Boers; he was no mean opponent.

In the same week, Methuen, in his bid to relieve Kimberley, had been defeated at Magersfontein. That the greatest army ever to leave Britain should have sustained this double blow was received at home as the most devastating shock of the Victorian Age. But 'Black Week' released new reserves of patriotic fervour. If only Mafeking could hold on . . .

Inside Ladysmith, the defenders were worse off than those in Kimberley, who, in turn, were not so well placed as those in Mafeking. In Ladysmith many commodities were unobtainable and tobacco was selling at fantastic prices; eight new potatoes sold at thirty shillings. Water was a grave problem. Many people had gone down with enteric, which had got out of the control of the medical authorities. Depressed, confused and tired, Buller cabled the War Office that he did not think he could relieve Ladysmith; he got orders through to White to fire off all his ammunition and get the best surrender terms he could. White declined to do so, and Buller himself thought better of it two days later.

Christmas Day in Ladysmith was a mixed affair; some contrived to make the traditional festival of it; others manned the trenches with no difference in their ordinary routine. There were over a thousand sick at the hospital camp. During the morning there was heavy firing.[1]

In London, the Cabinet had become disillusioned with the hapless Sir Redvers. On 16 December Salisbury and the Cabinet decided to send out Lord Roberts, with General Lord Kitchener as his chief-of-staff. The Robertsites were overjoyed : at last the Boers would be taught a lesson. Wolseley was thunderstruck. He had not, he wrote

---

[1] MS. *Diary*, Brig.-General Hon. C. G. Fortescue (Family).

to his wife, heard 'an inkling' of it till after the Cabinet meeting. Lansdowne said that his name had been considered first, but that he could not be spared from the War Office ('all nonsense').[1]

Roberts had that day lost his only son, in Buller's force; Lieutenant Roberts was later posthumously awarded the v.c. A week later 'Bobs' sailed from Southampton, a leathery little man of 67, looking older than his years, in deep mourning—his dejected appearance not lessened by his enormous drooping moustache. Would even his great reputation crumble before the untamed Boers?

After Black Week, nothing excited the British more than the fate of Mafeking. As the *Spectator* said afterwards : 'The Siege of Mafeking was played on a public stage. It was carried on with the breathless attention of the whole nation focused upon it.' There was something attractive about its very remoteness : Kimberley and Ladysmith could be envisaged as more ordinary places, like small provincial towns at home, but Mafeking seemed to typify the pioneering aspect of Empire so treasured by the British public. Dispatches from Mafeking, censored by Hanbury-Tracy and Baden-Powell, took about two weeks to reach London, and when they did so they often took precedence over all other war news and were placed in the most prominent position on the page. Most of the correspondents realized they had 'a good story' and wrote their reports accordingly. Only Hamilton continued to pour cold water on the emotion at home, but elsewhere in *The Times* a different impression was given. Hamilton's reports appeared almost once a week and spoke of 'the timidity of the enemy', 'our feeble-hearted foe', 'nothing has happened', and pointed out that 'distress is wholly absent and danger is largely a question of accident'.[2] Baden-Powell's reports to G.H.Q. were also published at frequent intervals; they received very great publicity. They were written in racy, often humorous vein, but it appears that Baden-Powell was astonished when he learnt they had been published; he always insisted that they had been written for official readers only, or for the Boers who might intercept them. They usually began 'All well here', and they made Baden-Powell famous. On 4 December he reported: 'Boers have fairly large daily loss of life from rifle fire',[3] a message

---

[1] *The Letters of Lord and Lady Wolseley* (Heinemann, 1922), pp. 377–8.
[2] *The Times*, 7 December 1899.
[3] Baden-Powell, 4 December 1899: *The Times*.

which would not have impressed the Boers had they intercepted it. With disasters occurring in the war almost every day, there was something reassuring about Baden-Powell and the Siege of Mafeking.

Buller, meanwhile, was planning another crossing of the Tugela. This time it was to be done by a flanking movement, near a hill which hitherto neither side had thought worth taking : Spion Kop.

Churchill, at Buller's headquarters, had persuaded the Commander-in-Chief to give him a commission as an officer in one of the irregular regiments; this was highly improper, as the War Office had laid down that correspondents could not be officers on active service (a ruling which had, indeed, been largely made owing to Churchill's own previous mixing of journalism and military service). Buller, however, made the proviso that Churchill would receive no military pay. This did not concern Churchill in the least, as he had delighted the *Morning Post* with his reports, which were now resumed after the break enforced by his captivity. Now that he was the first hero of the war, his dispatches became even more widely discussed and influential. He made full use of his new fame. Soon after his sensational arrival in Durban, he said in a report : 'We must face the facts. The individual Boer, mounted in suitable country, is worth from three to five regular soldiers. The power of modern rifles is so tremendous that frontal attacks must often be repulsed. The extraordinary mobility of the enemy protects his flanks. The only way of treating the problem is either to get men equal in character and intelligence as riflemen or, failing the individual, huge masses of troops.'

Churchill realized that the important theatre of war was, for the present, in Natal; but he was not unaware of what was happening on the West Front or at Mafeking, the commander of which he had seen three years previously in very unlikely circumstances, and from where his aunt was writing newspaper dispatches. He knew there was a good dispatch to be had about Mafeking, but he was prepared to wait his time.

In the north, far away from any newspaper correspondent, almost ignored by the Commander-in-Chief, and certainly forgotten by the public, the little force of Colonel Herbert Plumer was riding south-west; out of the near-jungle and towards the great plains; towards Mafeking.

9. Blunder and Boredom

Late on Christmas night there was much coming and going among the military in Mafeking. As dinner parties broke up and concerts ended, men paraded in readiness for the long-awaited attack on the Boer positions. The newspaper correspondents, not all of them entirely sober, were assembled in Lord Edward Cecil's room and told that an assault was to be made that morning.

It was not unexpected news. It was known that for weeks officers had been persuading Baden-Powell to take a more active part in the war. As the official biography puts it: 'The officers were eager to strike. They were getting impatient from their enforced idleness.' More than a week previously Hamilton, of *The Times*, had lain out all night in expectation of an attack on Game Tree Fort, a Boer defensive position about two miles from the town's northern defences. Now Game Tree Fort was to be attacked at last. Scouts and patrols reported it 'poorly constructed, poorly defended'.[1]

A number of reasons have been given for the choice of this fort by Baden-Powell for his attack. Some of those present at the time, and many of the accounts of later years, including the *Official History,* have given the primary reason as a wish to divert attention from Plumer, then known to be moving into the area of the railway. If so, this would be feasible, as Game Tree Fort was in the direction from which Plumer, Holdsworth, or both, could be expected to approach; but at that time they were a long way from Mafeking. One of the official biographers for instance, says that the 'sortie' was 'to relieve the pressure on Plumer'. Baden-Powell, in his report to Lord Roberts on the siege, makes no mention of this reason. He is

[1] Hillcourt, p. 185.

quite clear about the reason for attacking Game Tree Fort. 'Some shells thrown into it a few days previously had caused enemy temporarily to vacate it, showing it to be a weak open work; this had been confirmed by reconnaissance by our scouts, but as the enemy had been seen strengthening it during the past few days, I determined to attack before they should make it impregnable.' If taken, it would have been a very difficult position to hold, even more so than Cannon Kopje, being well isolated from the perimeter.

The Boers had indeed been strengthening the position, forewarned not only by the episode of over a week before, but also by messages smuggled out from their own people in the town. Of the former, Hamilton wrote: 'That attack, however, did not take place and, although the town and garrison were disappointed, there was a very strong feeling that it would not be long before they were compensated for their disappointment.'

By 26 December Botha had been expecting an attack at Game Tree Fort for two weeks.[1] Since the shock of Fitzclarence's night raid with the bayonet, all Boer defensive positions had been strengthened, and it was remarkable that Baden-Powell's intelligence had not informed him of this earlier. But by 25 December he was aware of the situation. He wrote on that day: 'The busyness of the enemy in repairing all their works, and putting extra wire entanglements round them, as they have done today . . . point to their having had information of our intending a night attack shortly.'[2] He did not, however, cancel the planned attack.

As it happened, Game Tree Fort was not only unusually well defended, it was extremely well placed on top of a rise, with an easy command of all its approaches.

Two hundred and sixty men were detailed for the attack, which, bearing in mind Baden-Powell's limited numbers, was ambitious enough to satisfy his impatient military critics. This force consisted mostly of men of the Protectorate Regiment, with artillery and the Bechuanaland Rifles in support. Oddly, considering his reputation for unconventionality, Baden-Powell still placed great trust in the armoured train; in the early hours of the morning, packed with

[1] *The Siege of Mafeking*, J. A. Hamilton, pp. 182–3.
[2] *Staff Diary*, 25 December 1899.

riflemen and with two machine-guns, it moved quietly out of Mafeking.

Meanwhile the men of the Protectorate Regiment had left the perimeter and lay waiting for dawn, hidden in the grass some distance from the enemy fort. Panzera's guns were also taken forward to get within range. In Mafeking they waited. Bell wrote: 'awoke at dawn, hearing no firing I congratulated the Garrison that we were not going to sacrifice the lives of good men and waste ammunition in attacking a useless place.'

As daylight showed in the sky Panzera's artillery opened a heavy fire on the Boer position. Among the projectiles fired were the round-shot of the ancient cannon. The African morning was rent with the boom and thunder of explosives. Hamilton wrote: 'It was yet dark, although there came a faint glimmer of light from the east, but not sufficient to prevent the flashes from the muzzles of the guns and the glow of the bursting shells from being plainly visible. Until that moment there had been no sign of any living thing.'

The armoured train, which had been progressing slowly up to that time in order that its clicking over the rails might not be heard by the Boers, came to a halt. The Boers, not surprisingly perhaps, had pulled up the line, closer to the perimeter than hitherto. The train, therefore, was unable to give the effective flanking fire on the fort which had been devised as an essential part of the plan.

The barrage from Panzera's little battery continued for only a few minutes. It had been arranged that a whistle from the train would announce to the artillery that the attacking troops were moving forward; the artillery was then to stop. The train was no longer in a position to give this information accurately, and it did so, prompted by the commander of the leading squadron of the assaulting troops, Captain R. J. Vernon, too early. The whistle blew. The artillery fire ceased. The Boers crowded the loopholes at their parapet and opened a rapid fire on the approaching troops, whom Vernon now ordered to advance up the slope.

The short barrage had not essentially damaged the position at all. What the British believed to be a simple earthen-work barricade was in reality an immensely strong blockhouse, with a roof of steel rails on which sandbags were piled, hidden from the front by the deceptive height of the outer wall. There was a double row of loopholes, and the only entrance was blocked up by sandbags. It was, as Baden-Powell recorded in his official diary, 'quite impervious' to the British artillery. As Hamilton put it:

> The damage inflicted upon the fort did not materially aid the charge which our men were so gallantly to make, and which, when completed, revealed the fact that Colonel Baden-Powell had also organized a frontal attack upon an entrenched and impregnable position, with most lamentable results . . . The character of our attack needed a movement which was quietly delivered, and which was in the nature of a surprise . . . our gunfire simply warned the garrison in the fort to stand to their arms. There is no doubt the employment of the guns was a blunder in keeping with the conception of the attack. Colonel Baden-Powell, one has to say regretfully, upon this occasion was instrumental in bringing about quite needless loss of life.[1]

The time of attack coincided with the time when the day guard had just arrived at the fort to relieve the night one : another fact which Baden-Powell's intelligence staff might have been expected to know. The garrison in the fort was therefore double its normal strength. As Vernon's squadron, rushing forward, got to within 200 yards of the Boer fire, they began to fall. With great courage and discipline for irregular and newly raised troops, they continued while their comrades fell all around them. Many of those who reached the Boer position were already wounded and bleeding profusely. Attempting to scale the parapet, they were horrified to discover the whole position roofed over. Moving around desperately, officers emptied their revolvers into the apertures and men thrust their bayonets inside. Vernon, already wounded twice, was finally killed with a shot through the head. The wounds inflicted by firing at point-blank range were terrible. The two other officers present were also killed while firing through the apertures. Command fell on a sergeant.

It was now obvious that the position could not be taken that way, but in the absence of orders to withdraw there was nothing for it but to throw in the second squadron of the Protectorate Regiment, under

---

[1] Hamilton, p. 178.

Fitzclarence. Stumbling over the bodies of their dead and dying comrades, Fitzclarence's squadron made their own efforts to penetrate
the sealed fort which was bristling with bullet-cracking rifles.

Baden-Powell had moved from his H.Q. to the perimeter of the
Mafeking defences for the attack. He could not see what was happening, and did not know. He was content to wait for news. When news
came it was in the form of a breathless messenger, who informed him
that 'the position is practically impregnable to infantry'. Only then
did a withdrawal begin. The *Official History* says: 'The attempt had
long proved hopeless when the remnants of both units were ordered to
draw off.'

Of the sixty men in Vernon's squadron, more than two in three
were casualties. The British casualties totalled fifty, including
twenty-four killed or who died of wounds: a very serious loss to
Baden-Powell's best-trained troops. The Boers lost three men killed.[1]

The Red Cross flag was immediately taken out to the battlefield, and
Anderson, the Army doctor, with Doctor Hayes, did what he could
for the dying and for the less seriously injured. The Boers came out
of the fort and helped carry the British dead and wounded down the
slope towards the armoured train. The correspondents were allowed
to go to the scene of the fighting, and Hamilton wrote:

> The heavy vapour from the shells still impregnated the air, and
> hanging loosely over the veldt were masses of grey-black and
> brown-yellow smoke clouds. Boers on horseback and on foot were
> moving quickly in all directions . . . The fort itself showed no
> traces of the shelling . . . The scene was intensely pathetic, and
> everywhere were dead or dying men . . . The attitude of the Boers
> around us was one of stolid composure, not altogether unmixed
> with sympathy. With their rifles up on their backs and two bando-
> liers crossing each other on their chests, they appeared a stalwart
> body of men; for the most part they were big and burly, broad in
> their shoulders, ponderous in their gait, and uncouth in their
> appearance, combining a somewhat soiled and tattered appearance
> with an air of triumph.'

---

[1] *Staff Diary.*

Their composure, however, was not above a little looting of dead and injured here and there, as witnesses, including Hamilton, recorded. One Boer unwisely attempted to relieve the redoubtable Fitzclarence, badly wounded, of his sword while he was being borne away on a stretcher, an ambition which was 'successfully resisted' by Fitzclarence himself.

Among the Boer forces on the battlefield was Drake, and when he was heard speaking English there was temporarily some difficulty in maintaining the cease fire. But on the whole, as Hamilton recorded, 'People who had been pitted against each other in mortal combat the moment before were now fraternizing with every outward sign of decency and amity.'

At about 10.0 a.m. the armoured train arrived back in Mafeking with a cargo of dead and wounded. It was greeted by a large, silent, depressed and somewhat bitter crowd. Bell wrote : 'A fearful mistake was made . . . all due to our not having carefully found out what we were going to attack . . . lives had been thrown away for no purpose.' It was a day which came to be known for years in Mafeking as Black Boxing Day. Everyone had been convinced of the superiority of British arms. What had gone wrong? The *Official History says* : 'The strengthening of the fort, too elaborate to have been accomplished in haste, bore out the enemy's assertion that he had long expected attack in this quarter; yet means had not been lacking of obtaining more accurate information about a work so small and so close to the lines.' What had happened to the Army's great exponent of scouting?

Throughout the action the inexperienced troops had shown remarkable bravery in carrying out their orders. After the relief this was recognized in the award of two Victoria Crosses to men of the Protectorate Regiment for courage shown while carrying away wounded comrades (in one case the man's brother) while under fire.[1]

The *Mafeking Mail,* in an official report the next day, gave three objects of the attack : to break the Boer 'cordon' with 'a view to opening communications with the north'; to extend the grazing area; and lastly to compel the enemy to call reinforcements. The last is an im-

---

[1] Mafeking was thus granted all its three applications for the award. The two recipients on this occasion were Sgt H. R. Martineau and Trooper H. E. Ramsden. There was one Victoria Cross awarded for action at Ladysmith, and none at Kimberley.

portant early statement of one of Baden-Powell's favourite reasons for the defence of Mafeking; a surprising lapse on the part of the censor, whom the correspondents normally considered outrageously strict. The attack on Game Tree Fort, however, succeeded in none of these objects. Baden-Powell liked to describe his very rare sorties as 'kicks', but on this, his most ambitious sortie, he had succeeded only in kicking his own troops.

In his General Orders, Baden-Powell described the attack as 'a brilliant example', although he did not specify of what. In his report on the siege, he made an acceptance of responsibility, somewhat unnecessarily, and very unusual for a commanding officer, but complete none the less : 'If blame for this reverse falls on anyone, it should fall on myself, as everybody concerned did their part of the work thoroughly well, and exactly in accordance with the orders I had issued.'

That night Baden-Powell sent off a dispatch concerning the engagement. With bland aplomb remarkable even for him, he said the action had been satisfactory in that the enemy would have noted 'the fatal results of storming a position'.[1]

*

Mafeking was in the height of the rainy season. For days on end the sky was dark with cloud. The dismal, drizzling days were lit only by the occasional glimmerings of lightning or the orange flashes from the guns. When it was not raining it was stifling and hot, with temperatures of nearly a hundred degrees.

After the disaster at Game Tree Fort, distrust in the ability of their leader, a new respect for the Boer, and lack of confidence quietened the malcontents who had been calling for action. Once more such martial activity as there was continued in largely ineffective artillery duelling. At the end of December 'Creaky' attempted to eliminate one of Baden-Powell's most forward guns, but was unable even to do that.

New Year's Eve, conveniently enough, was on a Sunday. There were special events and races, and in the evening the old century was left to history with many toasts in all the bars, hotels and shelters of the

---

[1] *Staff Diary*, 26 December 1899.

town. At midnight 'Auld Lang Syne' drifted away across the damp veld to the Boers huddled in their wagons and tents as the rain pattered down everywhere.

At 10.0 a.m. on the first day of the twentieth century the Boers began a six-hour barrage, one of the heaviest of the siege. Snyman, hardly surprised at the food supplies continuing to be available in the town (Baden-Powell, in his Manifesto, had told the Boers he had supplies for 'several months') was not yet dismayed, but like Baden-Powell he too felt obliged to satisfy the hot-heads among his officers. By the end of the day, the 635th round from 'Creaky' had fallen on Mafeking since the start of the war; less than one in a hundred had caused any physical harm. The damage was still as incommensurate as ever with the number of shells used. On that day one white man and three Africans were killed—one of the most severe days of the defence. Anyone who took cover during bombardment was always perfectly safe. The greatest danger now seemed to be from a new type of phosphorus shell being employed by the Boers; the fire risks from this appeared to be considerable, but they never developed owing to the scattered buildings and wet and muddy terrain.

On 2 January Hamilton held a dinner party for the correspondents, and for Baden-Powell's staff, at Reisle's Hotel. Baillie commented: 'How so good a dinner could be served after about four months' siege is indeed extraordinary.' Lady Sarah was not invited; the other correspondents considered her an 'amateur', no doubt much to her relief.

The following day, on Baden-Powell's orders, a 'counter-demonstration' was held by the British artillery in return for the Boer bombardment on New Year's Day. Four guns were trained on the emplacement of 'Creaky'. About one hundred shells, as well as cannon balls from the ancient naval gun, were fired in the vicinity of the big Boer gun. Understandably, Baden-Powell was very keen on such demonstrations for morale purposes. For the occasion, he dressed in one of his favourite outfits, a linen 'ditto suit', girdled by a many-coloured belt—'beautifully arrayed', as Neilly said. Standing nearby, he had gathered all his staff, and the correspondents, to see the effect of the barrage. The most impressive sights were the cannon balls, fired according to principles discovered in an edition of one of Captain Marryat's novels; they bounced several times to some height before coming to rest.

According to a native who came into the town that night, the damage suffered by the Boers was five men hurt, one wagon damaged and a group of horses thrown into confusion. For this Baden-Powell had used up nearly a quarter of Panzera's remaining rounds for the artillery. However this excellent officer was not completely dismayed; he was at work organizing the manufacture of shells, and reconditioning shells thought useless, in the railway workshops and at the local soda-syphon factory; at Weil's remarkable warehouse he found two tons of gunpowder and any number of fuses. He also ordered work on a five-inch howitzer made from a steel tube. After a preliminary failure, this weapon eventually became an addition to the defence, and was named 'The Wolf' after the natives' name for Baden-Powell.[1]

More effective than the artillery were the sharp-shooters of the Bechuanaland Rifles, who from time to time lay out all day in the veld to discourage the Boer gunners. Whether as a result of them or of Baden-Powell's 'counter-demonstration', or a combination of both, 'Creaky' was moved from its position to a new one two-and-a-half miles east of Mafeking. The *Official History* records that 'when it reopened fire its accuracy was markedly less than before'. Baillie, on the other hand, wrote in his diary, on 18 January: 'There is no doubt that since the change of position of the gun a far greater proportion of damage has been done.'

On 20 January the siege entered its hundredth day. Till that time fifty-four white combatants had been killed, almost half of them at Game Tree Fort, and most of the remainder in the actions at the beginning of the war. About nineteen natives had been killed, mostly from bombardment.

At this time the Boers had less than eight guns around Mafeking,

---

[1] It was the subject of an acrimonious correspondence after the war, Panzera claiming its ownership and seeking its presence in Mafeking as a memento. The authorities decided that the gun had been 'manufactured at Baden-Powell's own expense' and that it belonged to him. Panzera, who had become Resident Commissioner in Mafeking, objected vigorously, claiming that the gun had been built in the workshops from his own plans, materials coming from public funds. Baden-Powell was approached by Sir Edward Ward, Under-Secretary of State at the War Office, and was asked to return the gun. He declined to do so, and presented it to the Royal United Service Institution, where it remains. (*War Office Papers.*)

five of them almost totally ineffective. On 26 January the most
spectacular damage yet was done when Bradley's Hotel was partly
wrecked by a shell from 'Creaky'. In the afternoon of the same day
the roof of the convent was hit once more; Lady Sarah and her husband, Gordon Wilson, were both in the room below, where they were
convalescent, she from tonsillitis and he from fever. Lady Sarah
wrote: 'A terrifying din immediately above our heads stopped all
power of conversation, or even of thought, and the next instant I was
aware that masses of falling brick and masonry were pushing me out
of my chair, and that heavy substances were falling on my head.'
Neither was seriously hurt, however, and 'Needless to say, we left
our ruined quarters that evening, and I reposed more peacefully in
my bomb-proof than I had done for many nights past. The air at the
convent had accomplished its healing work. We were both practically
recovered.' They were not the only invalids to make sudden miraculous recoveries at the convent, which, being one of the few landmarks
clearly visible to the Boers, was frequently hit by shells. No one during
the defence was more heroic than the calm and efficient nurses of the
hospital; Nurse Craufurd's diary speaks continually of others, with
distress at the horrors of war, but no one could have been more continually exposed to danger than the hospital staff themselves. This,
and the arming of Africans, continued to occupy Baden-Powell and
Snyman in their continual, extensive and indignant correspondence.
(Nearly 500 natives were now armed and enrolled in Mafeking.) The
shells which fell on the women's camp outraged Baden-Powell even
more, and he was forever complaining to Snyman about it. The
fact was, however, that if the Boer gunners were hitting the women's
camp it was quite certain that they could not be aiming at it.

Despite the random and incompetent gunnery of the Boers, the
town was now beginning to have a definitely knocked-about appearance. Many windows were boarded up, roofs and rooms of some
houses were shattered; but even the ninety-four-pounder shells
were not powerful enough to destroy totally a flimsy Mafeking
building.

One difficulty was that the regularity of shelling was no longer as
reliable as it once had been. Neilly wrote: 'At first we got our supplies
of shells much as a patient gets his pills—at regular hours and in fixed
numbers. The people became so used to the times at which the gun

was fired that I heard of some who timed their watches by the fire, and occasionally when somebody heard the gun he would say: "There's the afternoon gun. My! I must hurry. I'm ten minutes late already for an appointment." When the commandant discovered that his gunfire was more or less a convenience to us in this way, he began to serve us out with shells at irregular periods and surprise times.' But 'Creaky's' barrel could still be seen raising itself before delivery, and ample warning was in every case given.

The supply situation in January was better than had been anticipated. The stock of foodstuffs in private hands was greater than had been originally reported. At a stock-taking on 19 January, Weil still had such items as 144 lb. of tinned salmon, 2,450 lb. of sardines, 10,488 lb. of boiled mutton, as well as many other tinned meats, and a huge stock of corned beef, all of it brought up from Cape Town on Cecil's credit before the war. At the end of the month it was calculated that there was still enough meat for seventy-seven days and enough meal for seventy-five days, besides vegetables, groceries, preserved fruits and fish.[1] The *Official History* states: 'Reduction by starvation, therefore, seemed even more remote than reduction by attack, and almost as remote as relief.'

Baden-Powell had heard from Roberts, via messenger from Plumer, soon after the new Commander-in-Chief's arrival at Cape Town. He held out no prospect for immediate relief. Roberts congratulated Plumer and Baden-Powell, but Mafeking was 'too far to attempt relief at present'. Baden-Powell replied that he could hold out for about another hundred days, until about 18 May. Very wisely, therefore, further rationing was made during February. Tinned milk was always valued; and whisky, five shillings a bottle before the war, was now being sold at eighteen shillings. Matches, of which Weil had a stock of 35,400 boxes at the beginning of the war, were strangely unobtainable, but in their stead small paraffin lamps were supplied to almost every person, and these burnt night and day—the supply of liquid fuel being very large. Vegetables—still rationed at one pound a day—were becoming less plentiful, but rice could be used in their place; the bread ration was decreased to five ounces a day, plus biscuits. Natives from the village, however, successfully brought in

---

[1] *Official History*, pp. 164–5, and *Weil Papers*.

Boer cattle. For the Africans, horsemeat was made into a stew. A kind of porridge made from the husks of oats, a food which was suggested by a Scotswoman, began to be eaten.

Lady Sarah noted that, 'People looked graver; a tired expression was to be noted on many hitherto jovial countenances; the children were paler and more pinched.'

A case of typhoid had occurred in the women's camp, and now a special field hospital was set up for the women and children at a cottage, to be run by Nurse Craufurd. She wrote: 'It is a brick cottage with mud floors, very dirty at present, and full of black ants, but is to be done up.' She was soon tending to typhoid cases, and also pneumonia, dysentery and diphtheria. A dug-out was provided for her, but 'I have never been in it. I could hardly go myself and leave them in their beds.' Soon roof and walls were hit. Miss Craufurd, like the rest of the medical staff, seldom had an hour off duty, even on Sundays, during the daytime. There were many sick in the women's camp. Deaths from malaria and other diseases had never been infrequent at Mafeking: now there were more.[1]

The Africans were suffering the most. Goold-Adams, and later Vyvyan, who took over their welfare, supervised a strict system of rationing and a soup kitchen. The Africans were the first to be provided with horsemeat, to which they very much objected, declaring that it made their heads swell. They continued to go in and out of the town much as they pleased, passing information to both sides. By February three Africans had been executed in Mafeking for spying. On 30 January a Boer emissary with a white flag arrived at the native village and suggested to the headman that he take his people over to the Boer side. This invitation was declined; whatever the rigours of the defence, the British were notably less harsh to the Africans than were the Boers.[2]

Runners continued to get in and out, although sometimes they were caught. On 3 February, for instance, runners were sent both north and south. On the 5th, two parties of runners arrived from the north, they brought, among other letters, a bill for Hanbury-Tracy

---

[1] Out of more than 650 people in the women's camp, including servants, 24 died during the defence, but none from enemy action.

[2] q.v. *My Experiences of the Boer War*, Count Sternberg.

readdressed from his regimental depot at home. On the 9th a runner arrived from the south. And so it continued. Even the post to Kimberley, only a little more energetically besieged than Mafeking, was maintained. Baden-Powell had received a letter from Cecil Rhodes. He had already sent him a report of the situation in Mafeking. Lady Sarah also, one day, received a letter from the great man :

DEAR LADY SARAH—Just a line to say I often think of you. We play bridge every evening. I wonder do you; it takes your mind off hospital, burials and shells . . .

On 29 January a civilian was killed by a 'Creaky' shell while working in the square. On 1 February a soldier was killed by a shell at Cannon Kopje, still the most exposed place in the defence. During February affairs continued much as they had in January, and the greatest hardship was still the unutterable tedium of the days. The *Official History* says : 'Throughout the month of February there was little to record. Daily, and often nightly, shelling, sleepless vigilance, and the constant round of duty in the trenches formed the life of the garrison, to whom the siege dragged on only less wearily than to the non-combatants, condemned at once to inactivity, discomfort and danger.' Some days the big gun was completely silent. Once the battery at Jackal Tree Hill was silent nearly a week, and it was believed that the guns had been withdrawn. A truck, armed with a stove-pipe as a dummy gun, was rolled out of the town, and at the sight of this the Boer guns opened up again, thus proving their presence to Baden-Powell.

Lady Sarah wrote :

Often of a hot afternoon, when I was sitting in my bomb-proof, from inclination as well as from prudence—for it was a far cooler resort than the stuffy iron-roofed houses—while women and children were walking about quite unconcernedly outside, I used to hear the warning bell ring, followed by so much scuffling, screaming and giggling, in which were mingled jokes and loud laughter from the men, that it made me smile as I listened; then, after the explosion, they would emerge from any improvised shelter and go gaily on their way, and the clang of the blacksmith's anvil, close at hand, would be resumed almost before the noise had ceased and the dust had subsided.

The practical-joke side of Baden-Powell had become increasingly absent. He spent longer than ever staring away across the veld through his binoculars, and lay stretched out on the veranda of his head-quarters, apparently dozing. Apart from his almost incessant, obsessional whistling, he became prone to long periods of silence. Just as his perky, flamboyant dispatches were creating a frenzy of interest in the siege at home, so his untypical taciturnity created re-newed confidence in him in Mafeking. Neilly wrote: 'He warbled operatic airs and music-hall ditties from morning till night . . . you saw him snatching half an hour's leisure with a book, lying on the veranda of his headquarters, or relieving his brain by working a sketch or painting.' Hamilton wrote:

Colonel Baden-Powell [has] a keen appreciation of the possibilities of his career, swayed by ambition, indifferent to sentimental emotion. In stature he is short, while his features are sharp and smooth . . . He does not go about freely, since he is tied to the multitudinous cares of his command . . . He seems to close every argument with a snap, as if the steel manacles of his ambition had checkmated the emotions of the man in the instincts of the officer. He weighs each remark before he utters it, and suggests by his manner, as by his words, that he had considered the different effects it might conceivably have on any mind as the expression of his own mind. As an officer he has given to Mafeking a complete and assured security, to the construction of which he has brought a very practical knowledge of the conditions of Boer warfare, of the Boers themselves, and of the strategic worth of the adjacent areas . . . Outwardly he maintains an impenetrable screen of self-control, observing with a cynical smile the foibles and caprices of those around him.

Sometimes, at night, Baden-Powell, who had, of course, a reputa-tion as a scout, would walk through the lines to study the Boer dis-positions; since the ill-reconnoitred Game Tree Fort fiasco, no attack on these was contemplated, and all Boer movements could be observed from the lookout at headquarters or from Cannon Kopje.

The most serious shortage in the town was of small change. Bank notes were produced from a drawing by Baden-Powell, with determined-looking defenders surrounding the gun which had been made at the workshops. Stamps were also running short. The larger denominations, for letters to Rhodesia, the Cape and Britain, were in good supply, but cheap stamps for the busy internal service—mainly from the outposts of defence to the town—were running out. It was decided that a stamp should be issued and that it should depict Baden-Powell's head : according to Godley, who said he was one of three who decided on this, it was done 'in joke more than anything else . . . entirely as a stunt'; according to the official biography the decision was taken (by four men) because it was thought that to use the Queen's head would be *lèse majesté* and probably illegal. In any event, the original decision was not Baden-Powell's, although, according to the official biography, the stamps were presented to him first for approval. It appears that he authorized their issue.[1] Baden-Powell himself, in *Lessons From The 'Varsity of Life,* said that the stamps were issued entirely without his knowledge. But writing to his mother from Mafeking, Baden-Powell described the town as 'quite a little republic'. He explained how he made his own 'laws and orders', how he had issued his own banknote; and 'today we are making' the new stamps, which with some pride he said would have his head on them instead of the head of the Queen—or of Kruger.

The design for another stamp depicted one of the boys of the Cadet Corps, who were doing such useful work. It was known as the 'Cadet Penny', the other being the 'Colonel Threepenny'. Baden-Powell had followed Cecil's careful training of the Cadet Corps boys, who were now invaluable for messages and errands; but he considered that Cecil was 'not much use'. Cecil was often ill, and Panzera deputized.

---

[1] Baden-Powell later came in for some criticism over this, and was touchy about the subject. Details of the stamp affair are given in Hillcourt, pp. 191–2, 432. But Baden-Powell's entry in the D.N.B. says the stamps were printed 'without his knowledge . . . he had these withdrawn at once' and replaced them with Cadet stamps. On 7 April 1900 in a message to Plumer he said : 'Try and send us some ferricynide of potassium, 1 lb weight to be sent 4 oz at a time for making our own stamps.' (*Roberts Papers.*)

In mid-February, 'by express order of the Colonel Commanding', all bars were closed for seven days inclusive. Baden-Powell had noticed several cases of over-indulgence in the town; he himself never drank. After protestations, he reinforced his order by declaring in General Orders that if there were further cases of drunkenness when the bars reopened he would have them closed permanently and would consider confiscating all liquor. An attempt was later made to carry out this threat, but it does not appear to have been very successful. Baden-Powell had no objection to tots being issued to troops on wet nights, but nearly three months before he had warned the garrison that he considered a seven-day sentence of imprisonment with hard labour 'a light sentence' for drunkenness, and that such generosity had only been allowed because of the accused's previous gallantry in action.[1] Under Martial Law an order had been passed declaring that : 'Any person who shall in any way hinder the troops or defence forces in performing their duties shall be liable to summary punishment on the spot.' During the defence 115 sentences of corporal punishment and 91 imprisonments with hard labour were passed, as well as 5 death sentences.[2] One of those in jail was the notorious blade of the day, Ronald Moncreiffe : cricketer, social gadfly and heavy drinker. Moncreiffe had been so anxious to get to Mafeking before the war that when the guard of a train tried to remove him owing to his travelling without a ticket, he had seized the guard's whistle and set off the train. He was 'most unhappily incarcerated . . . for conduct which had exhausted the patience of Baden-Powell'.[3]

The rains began to cease. It became again sunny and hot. And the investment dragged on.

Now everyone lived for the cease-fire of Sundays. The relief at the ending of another dreary week was enormous. All religious susceptibilities of the besieged or of Snyman were swept aside. There were games, exhibitions of art in which the best exhibits were very clearly those of the Colonel himself, an agricultural exhibition, a horticultural show, a 'golf match', a baby show . . . Neilly wrote : 'We had a good time strolling about, and having afternoon tea and chats . . . On

---

[1] *General Orders*, 24 November 1900.
[2] Not including executions of natives for spying.
[3] Montmorency.

the whole we enjoyed ourselves hugely, and in the evening returned to await awakening at the sound of the big gun when she sang her song at dawn.' Hamilton wrote : 'We drink, we accept one another's invitations to meals of unsurpassing heaviness, we even invite ourselves to one another's houses . . . we flirt, we live in every second of the hours which constitute Sunday, and upon the passing of the day it is as though we had entered into another world . . . For six more days we stand-to-arms and wonder when the devil the enemy are coming on.'

But the enemy were not coming : not yet.

During the week irritation became intense. It was recorded that not one woman in the town had a friend left of any of the others. Rumours abounded. On being informed (incorrectly) that Kimberley had been relieved, Neilly retorted : 'Oh, hang Kimberley and relieving columns, and everything else. All I know is that I am in a besieged town with enemies around who want to kill me, and I hope with good luck to get out of this and back to civilization within five years. Good morning.'

'The main occupation of the garrison just now,' wrote Hamilton, 'is to speculate on the progress of the work of trench-building, which is being rapidly pushed forward in the brickfields upon the south-eastern face of the town.' Trenches were being dug to within two hundred yards of a Boer position. Such proximity to the enemy had not been encountered—except during attacks—before. What was Baden-Powell up to now?

Another message was received from Lord Roberts. As the demands of the war elsewhere were keeping him fully occupied, he welcomed Baden-Powell's offer of holding out till 18 May.[1] But Baden-Powell told the town that, 'Even should any unforeseen delays occur, our supplies will last a good deal over the date specified.'[2] This was just as well, because on 20 April another message was received from Roberts in which he tried to withdraw his promise of relief by that

---

[1] 30 March 1900. 'Many thanks for your letter of 20 Feb. I trust to be able to ensure your relief by 18 May, date named in your telegram of later date. Delighted to hear your good news.' (*Roberts Papers*.)

[2] Notice, 12 April 1900: *Weil Papers*.

date. 'Matters,' he wrote, 'have turned out somewhat unexpectedly.'[1]

Baillie wrote in his diary : 'The news had no depressing effect on the town or garrison, and everybody is resolved to undergo anything sooner than surrender.' But it was the particular quality of the investment of Mafeking that the necessity for surrender seemed quite as remote as the likelihood of relief.

If Roberts could do nothing from the south, there was always Plumer in the north. And now, like an unleashed mongrel prowling round some sleeping animal restricted to a cage, Plumer had arrived in the vicinity of Mafeking.

---

[1] G.H.Q., 9 April 1900: P.R.O. Roberts of course also saw the many dispatches Baden-Powell sent to G.H.Q. Baden-Powell had worked out a code system for place names which he had circulated in October. Roberts wrote on the bottom of one of the dispatches: 'Colonel Baden-Powell might be asked to discontinue this form of cypher. The Boers have been reading it the last six months.'

10. South from Rhodesia

The long and arduous journey from the Limpopo to the railway, undertaken by Plumer, was worse than anyone had expected. But as they moved westward the country became easier, the dense bush of the Limpopo area giving way to more open ground. And then at last the grassy plains, with their frequent winds, were reached. For men who had come straight from the torrid, steaming swamps of the remoter regions of the Limpopo valley, the vast veld offered a brilliant and refreshing scene. The journey of about 175 miles to the base at Palapye was accomplished in ten days.

Plumer had left a small force behind him at Rhodes Drift, and had with him 480 men. He added these to those already operating in the railway area, under Colonel Holdsworth, mostly British South Africa Police and Rhodesian Volunteers, and the force under his immediate command was now about 1,000 strong. His move had been an imaginative one; it would, moreover, have been far easier to have stayed where he was, for which none would have blamed him. As the *Times History* says, 'a less bold leader than Plumer might have been afraid to take the responsibility of leaving Tuli, where he had been instructed to stay, while there was still a chance that the Boers might return for the invasion of Rhodesia.' With the police under Plumer was Richard Godley, younger brother of Alex Godley in Mafeking. The younger Godley put the situation well: 'Since Colonel Baden-Powell, commander of the frontier force, was being besieged with the garrison in Mafeking, the whole responsibility of keeping communications open to the north and countering any attempt at invasion of Rhodesia, and for the safety of Bulawayo, devolved on Plumer and his force.' Baden-Powell, however, was well informed of all Plumer's moves, and from now on made an increasing contribution to the latter's plans and movements. Nicholson,

Holdsworth and Llewellyn had all felt obliged to send official reports in to Mafeking, from time to time, for their 'besieged' commanding officer. Baden-Powell, for his part, was able to air his outraged feelings about the shells dropping into the women's camp. There were times when he was so deep in argument and correspondence with Snyman that he appeared to be conducting the war by post. In a message to Plumer he said: 'Snyman practically admits he ordered the shelling.' But Plumer had his own problems.

The Boers in Plumer's area were split up for some hundreds of miles into groups of one or two hundred men. Their total numbers fluctuated a great deal and were much affected by the whims of Snyman at Mafeking; some had originally come from Cronje's force and had become detached from it when it had left the area; others were under the command of Grobelaar, still ambitious to make his mark in the war and tiring of keeping his watch on Rhodesia. Grobelaar had a plan to take Bulawayo by approaching it through Bechuanaland, but the local chieftain, Khama, had refused to give him access to his land for this purpose; as a result there was further friction between African and Boer in the area, and the possibility of serious conflict.

Before the arrival of Plumer the British force had confined itself to keeping as much of the railway open as possible. Before Christmas their base had been forced farther and farther back up the line until they were almost 200 miles from Mafeking. But by the arrival of Plumer, in mid-January, Holdsworth was some 160 miles north of Mafeking and was patrolling to within ninety miles up the line from the town. Plumer moved down to Gaberones, about sixty miles from Mafeking, with 750 men, four field guns, two machine-guns, and one armoured train and one partly armoured train. The main Boer force opposing his further advance was just south of Crocodile Pools Station, where the Boers had destroyed a bridge.

Plumer's intentions were to take the offensive in the area in order to draw enemy attention away from Rhodesia, still busily arming itself, to create a nuisance value to the Boers and to probe the possibilities of relieving Mafeking.

Roberts, alarmed at the apparent vulnerability of Rhodesia, had wired Nicholson at H.Q. in Bulawayo and said that 5,000 men should be raised for the defence of the territory. This, for such a tiny population in a still undeveloped area, was ridiculous, and

Plumer, on being informed, wired back on the same day that only 800 more could be raised in addition to those who had already joined.[1] (In the end 1,500 Rhodesians were raised.) Meantime, faced by the lack of action by the Government (which was anxious to concentrate its available forces under Roberts rather than disperse them), the British South Africa Company was allowed to raise and equip the Rhodesian Field Force. After some diplomatic wrangling with the Portuguese, it was agreed that this force of some 5,000 men (which in the end the Government provided itself) of English, Dublin and Belfast Yeomanry, with Australians and New Zealanders, under Lieutenant-General Sir F. Carrington, should go to Rhodesia via Beira. Plumer himself had been considered too junior for this command. In Rhodesia, it was expected that Carrington would relieve Mafeking, but there was no sign of him or of his force.[2]

Plumer's immediate objective was the repairing of the railway bridge at Crocodile Pools, about six miles south of Gaberones.

From the start Plumer saw his main problem as one of supply. Considering the distance involved, and the exposed position of his force, this must have seemed at first an insurmountable obstacle which would fatally hinder his ambitions and perhaps lead to the destruction of his force. But Plumer was not intimidated by it. In conjunction with Baden-Powell, he decided on a sensible move, and carried it out brilliantly; he would have several bases, well-placed and guarded, to any of which he could retire speedily and at will.

Believing Plumer to be more vulnerable than he was, the Boers never fully comprehended this scheme, and although they came near to destroying Plumer, they never looked like really doing so. Thus Plumer was able to exert an influence in a large area out of all proportion to his puny force.

A night attack was made on the Boer position at Crocodile Pools; it went into barbed-wire entanglements, came under heavy fire and had to withdraw after severe losses.[3] The Boer position was an

---

[1] White male population of Rhodesia about 10,000 in 1898 (Colvin, p. 181).

[2] War Office approval of the Rhodesian Field Force was given on 11 January 1900: Carrington arrived at Cape Town on 9 April 1900.

[3] Variously reported as follows: *Official History*, 28 (8 killed); *Times History*, 29 (5 killed); Montmorency (who was there), 32 (9 killed); the final War Office figure for Plumer's total casualties from the beginning of the year to 25 February is 31 (7 killed).

extremely strong fort on rising ground, and had been insufficiently reconnoitred by the British. For this Plumer was responsible. There were no Boer casualties.[1] However, the bridge was repaired, a party of brave men working on it under cover of rifle fire.

Plumer now busied himself preparing another base, about forty miles away, and well west of the railway; this was at the native capital village of Kanya, some sixty miles north-west of Mafeking. (The natives there had received news of Martial Law in Bechuanaland by means of a carrier pigeon dispatched by Baden-Powell.) Plumer was determined not to confine himself to the railway line, where all his movements could be discerned by the enemy. Fearing for their now exposed position, and alarmed by this unexpected initiative on the part of Plumer, the Boers retired. Soon Plumer, leaving Holdsworth to guard the line at Crocodile Pools, had reached Lobatsi, only about forty-five miles from Mafeking. His camp there was under frequent shell-fire from Boer field guns. From there two expeditions, totalling 500 men, struck out by different routes towards Mafeking. Snyman, infuriated by all this, took a large part of his force from Mafeking to destroy the intruders (according to the *Times History* it was 'most of his forces around Mafeking'). One of Plumer's detachments got as far as Ramathlabama, within twenty miles of Mafeking—an extraordinarily cheeky venture, deep into Boer-held territory. Pursued by a large Boer force of over a thousand men on horseback, the British of both Plumer's detachments hastily withdrew. Plumer decided he could not hold his forward base at Lobatsi against the pursuing enemy. It was now that the full effect of his plan of dispersed bases was rewarded. Instead of having to retire up the railway again to the next base, at Crocodile Pools, he struck camp, under heavy shelling, and made ready to move to Kanya, where the reserve base was ready and prepared. Unmounted men, guns and stores were quickly entrained for Crocodile Pools and for Gaberones, while the mounted men kept off the Boers at the outposts; then Plumer's mounted force drifted away westwards into the veld. The Boers were so bemused that they were bombarding Lobatsi with the field guns they had brought up long after it was deserted.

[1] Montmorency.

Next morning 550 men, with two guns, arrived at Kanya after a night's ride; and 350 men, with two guns, steamed into Crocodile Pools. According to *The Times*: 'The Boers appeared to have been thoroughly nonplussed by these manœuvres, as they did not even damage the line above Lobatsi, but retired back again to Mafeking.'

Young Godley was with the troops withdrawn by rail to Crocodile Pools. He had communicated by letter with his brother in Mafeking, and he wrote home: 'He is quite well, but feeling very bored with being shut up. However I don't think it will be for very much longer, as from information we get there seems little doubt but that the enemy are beginning to dribble away from there'.[1]

Plumer, retaining a base at Kanya, now moved his mounted force to Sefetili, some thirty miles south of Kanya and thirty from Mafeking. Sefetili was in real Kalahari Desert country; arid, hot, dusty, merciless. Plumer and nearly all his men had been living rough since the previous October, and had not spent a night under a roof in that time or slept in a bed for five months. Here Plumer's supply-line stretched for 1,100 miles to Beira, finishing with creaking ox-wagons being lashed across the desert. Communications with Gaberones and Kanya were maintained by a series of cyclists' posts. As always, the supply line was kept filled and working by the implacable Nicholson at his desk in Bulawayo.

From Sefetili, Plumer ventured deep into the Transvaal. On this reconnaissance 'in strength' he covered seventy miles in twenty-six hours without losing a single horse, an outstanding achievement in the prevailing conditions. Once again Snyman was forced to diminish his troops at Mafeking in order to chase him. Then Plumer himself led a strong party to Ramathlabama. He got to within sight of Mafeking. The Boers moved in quickly to surround him. Owing to faulty information he had received from Baden-Powell, Plumer believed that a relief force was already approaching the town from the south. Too late he discovered that his was the only British force in the field. A small demonstration made by Baden-Powell at the same time did not disturb the Boers, and only resulted in one wounded horse.[2] The bodies of three of Plumer's men were brought

---

[1] *Khaki and Blue*, R. S. Godley, p. 71.
[2] Neilly, p. 242; Plumer's dispatch 15 April 1900, *Roberts Papers*.

in by the defenders and were examined by many local men to see if they had known them. 'Next morning we buried them,' Neilly wrote, 'and thus the first messengers that came to tell us that help was actually outside were these three troopers, whose bodies came to friends who knew them not.'

Plumer was sent scurrying back, with severe casualties, and himself wounded in the arm.[1] It would have been much worse except for 'the masterly handling of the squadrons in successive rearguard actions'.[2] Despite this serious loss, Plumer considered he was in a position to contemplate joining up with Baden-Powell, for none of his moves so far had been made with his full strength. Baden-Powell, with his larger force, would of course have to play a major part in the operation. The *Times History* said:

> With a force always at a numerical disadvantage, containing no Regular troops and very few Regular officers, working all the time on the borders of the enemy's territory, with miserably inefficient artillery and constant anxiety for supplies, he succeeded by daring, which never exceeded the limits of due precaution, in stopping most effectively any attempt against Rhodesia and in dissipating the energies of the force arrayed against Mafeking. His timely trek from Tuli, and his unexpected diversion to Kanya and Sefetili are remarkable instances of military judgment, and the chorus of approval which greeted the defenders of Mafeking might justly have been diverted in part to the patient worker for its relief.

On 27 April the younger Godley wrote home: 'Here I am with Plumer's advance camp, only about 28 miles from Mafeking. We can occasionally hear a bombardment going on, but only on very still days. We, I believe, are going to sit here, where we are strongly entrenched, until the southern relief column arrive, and shall then co-operate with them.'

Plumer sent all Baden-Powell's messages back to G.H.Q. via

---

[1] Among those killed was a well-known Yorkshire cricketer of the day, Frank Milligan. Plumer reported (8 April 1900) 49 casualties, 8 being killed.
[2] *Official History*, p. 201.

Nicholson and the Consul at Beira, and himself sent back meticulous returns—even recording when Trooper Thompson lost his way
in the bush—often carefully written out in his own handwriting.
Nevertheless, little had been heard of his operations at home. While
everyone had heard of Baden-Powell, few had heard of Plumer;
but the frail little man with the bad eyes was now the hero of all
Rhodesia.

*

When the public at home was not pondering, in awe, on the defence
of Mafeking, it was being increasingly depressed by wretched news
from Natal; it was not surprising that it much preferred the former
to the latter. At Tugela things had gone, at first, from bad to dis-
astrous. The attack at the hill known as Spion Kop had duly taken
place; the British force, conducting itself with unflinching courage,
had been mismanaged to a most unusual degree; having, at great
cost, taken the twin peaks of the hill, the survivors were ordered
down again, a useless operation which resulted in 1,733 casualties.
The will of Redvers Buller was no match for that of Louis Botha.
Having thus failed miserably in frontal attack at Colenso and in
flanking movement at Spion Kop—failures due mostly to deficien-
cies in command—Buller tried again. And again he failed. The
defenders of Ladysmith, now on starvation diet and racked by
disease, waited in some dudgeon. In the first week in March there
were 708 enteric cases in hospital in Ladysmith and 341 cases of
dysentery.[1] Buller's men were prepared to follow him to death, and
a large proportion of them did. When at last he bludgeoned his way
from the river and approached Ladysmith, he left behind him, lying
dead on the battlefields for many miles, some of the best troops of
the British Army. The combination of the amiable Buller and the
utter determination of the Boers to gain the great and tantalizing
prize of Ladysmith had been almost too much, but not quite. Buller
was nothing if not persistent; at last he had pushed Botha aside; his
casualties since he had first set out to relieve Ladysmith were more
than the entire Boer force opposing him. A young cavalry officer,

---

[1] *Official History*, Vol. II; also for Spion Kop casualties.

Captain Hubert Gough,[1] rode into Ladysmith on 28 February, more than a month after Spion Kop; he was greeted in the main street with friendly but controlled imperturbability by Sir George White, with the words: 'Hello, Hubert, how are you?'

Two weeks before, a patrol of Australian horse had ridden into Kimberley, the relief column under Methuen having successfully engaged Cronje's force; more than 1,500 had died during the siege, nearly all from disease. Cecil Rhodes, who had been smouldering within the town, was free at last. But for some months the memory of the strain that had been put on his patience was enough to fire him with anger. Within days, however, he purported to have forgotten the existence of Kekewich, who had commanded the defence of Kimberley. ('You don't remember the man who cleans your boots.')

Then Cronje had himself been besieged, at Paardeberg. He had surrendered there on 27 February with 4,000 men. And so, when everything had seemed so hopeless to the British, suddenly, in two days in February, everything seemed victorious.

Ladysmith had been relieved, however blunderingly. The relief of Kimberley had led to the first great British victory of the war.

Could Mafeking also hold out? The Boers, it was felt, had twisted the lion's tail enough. Suddenly, to many people, that Mafeking should not fall to the Boers became the most hoped-for thing in their lives.

---

[1] Later General Sir Hubert Gough. *Brasshat*, B. Collier (Secker & Warburg, 1961).

11. In the Trenches

It was the night of the Beleaguered Bachelors' Ball. At eight in the evening the streets near the Masonic Hall, where the Ball was to be held, presented 'an animated, even a gay, picture'. Officers in uniform, and ladies, both young and not so young, 'in charming toilettes, were making their way to the scene of the festivity, each with a careless happiness which made it impossible to believe that within a thousand yards of the town were the enemy's lines'.[1] The dance began with a rendering of 'Rule Britannia!' by the band of the Bechuanaland Rifles, which was accompanied by 'immense cheering'. It was a pleasure to dress up and dance the night hours away, under the brilliant lights inside the hall, as if the war had never been begun. There were several such balls during the defence of Mafeking. On that particular occasion everything was well under way when above the strictly tempoed music of the band came a familiar whistling sound and then a shudder. It was—most unexpectedly, as it was Sunday night—'Creaky'.

The doors of the hall were opened and a group of people stood around outside under the starlit sky. Orderlies were galloping through the streets sounding a general alarm. The reserve squadron of the Protectorate Regiment was running to form up at headquarters. Officers, in mess footwear and dress uniforms, left their partners and ran off for their positions in the defences. 'It was a fine night and the moon was full. Here and there, silhouetted against the skyline, those who were watching could see the reinforcements marching to the advanced trenches. There had been little time to think of anything, to collect anything . . . ' The correspondents gathered before the steps of H.Q. and learnt that a Boer attack was

---

[1] Hamilton, p. 233.

149

expected at the brickworks. Like so many other alarms, it proved ill-founded. There was wild and heavy firing all night from the Boer positions, but no attack developed. The trenches were manned till breakfast time, when the morning mist of the Molopo mingled with the scent and steam of hundreds of mugs of coffee and drifted across the positions.

Such activities in the brickworks, which usually included the harmless use of a great deal of ammunition, had become the major source of excitement in Mafeking. The brickworks, which included a number of sturdy kilns, were in the south-eastern sector of the perimeter. As the defensive arrangements had not included them in their entirety, they offered an obvious and irresistible place of infiltration to the enemy; being so close to the town, they were an excellent position, particularly for snipers who, during February, had once more become a menace to the defenders. No mines had been laid there and the Boers had been able to creep forward and build a number of trenches and strongpoints. According to Baden-Powell's report: 'The enemy's trenches were of a very good design and made in well-selected positions.' Moved to activity by this un-expected initiative on the part of the Boers, Baden-Powell and his staff had also directed the construction of a system of trenches. They were named with such familiar names as Oxford Circus and Regent Street. Much rifle firing took place, but apparently to little effect (although Baden-Powell suggested that ten Boers were killed each week during this period). The obvious danger was that the Boers might launch a rush from these new positions, and to discourage them grenades were devised by the inexhaustible Panzera; these were old meat- and jam-tins filled with dynamite and powder, and fitted with a fuse. The unreliability of these bombs was a source of as much apprehension to the throwers as to the recipients, which no doubt explains why a Sergeant Page, champion bait-thrower of Port Elizabeth, bombardier, delivered his missiles by 'casting' them with his fishing rod (an act which was taken up with glee by the British press as a typical example of unconquerable English sports-manship, and which was sketched in appropriate style by Baden-Powell. Page figured in many accounts as having cast his line in the Thames at the East End of London, a confusion no doubt with the South African port of East London). The Boers, on the other hand, had the use of German grenades, but their aim seems to have been as inaccurate as that of their artillerymen. During this time of operations in the brickworks, Baden-Powell reintroduced his megaphone ploy, and orders—particularly 'Fix bayonets!'—boomed across to the Boer trenches at night.

Among the troops manning this sector were men of the Cape Police, perhaps the most reliable men in the garrison, and the Cape Boys (i.e. the half-breeds of European and African descent). The latter always engaged the enemy with especial interest and vigour; they kept up an incessant chanting of taunts at the Boers, whose trenches at some points were less than a hundred yards away, and offered 'insults of an exceedingly personal character'. This did not at all amuse the Boers, who lost a number of lives by needlessly raising themselves above their parapet to retaliate. On St. Patrick's Day the Cape Boys had a sing-song with an accordion and shouted invitations to the Boers to join in; when the latter raised themselves to do so, two of them were promptly shot through the head. Baillie said of the Cape Boys: 'They had a distinct sense of humour, though possibly a somewhat grim one.' On 25 February the Boers were so goaded that they opened fire on a Sunday in daylight, previously an almost unthinkable event.

Slowly the defenders pushed out their trenches and the Boers withdrew: it was slow work and took place over several weeks. Two kilns were blown up by British raiding parties, one of them led by Panzera, at night. Baden-Powell took the closest interest in the progress of sapping, planned much of it himself with carefully drawn maps, and visited the scene of action. Sapping and counter-sapping took place all the time on the British side under the protection of steel shields devised by Baden-Powell, with hardly ever a raid by either side. The most serious occasion on the British side was when a contingent of Cape Boys withdrew from their position owing to a misunderstanding; it was only regained after a hard fight. After this the already legendary 'Fitz', only half-recovered from his wounds at Game Tree Fort, was put in charge. More of Baden-Powell's steel plates, with loopholes only two inches square, and improved defensive positions, lessened the dangers to the garrison. Sapping activities decreased. The intermittent Boer shelling continued; now it was being directed by a deserter, a certain Trooper

E. J. Hay. 'I shouldn't care to be Hay after the war,' Baillie commented, 'as there is £50 on his head, and the Boers are hard up.' There had been three previous deserters from the military forces in the past month.

On 23 March, ceaselessly harassed by British sharpshooting, the Boers gave up all idea of holding the brickworks and departed. It may be considered as the greatest and about the only operational success of the defence; however, in the setting of the siege as a whole, the operations were on a very small scale, for, as Neilly said, 'From the fight at Game Tree till the last day in March there was no occurrence that bore the semblance of even a skirmish.'

Baden-Powell himself probably saved the lives of the men who took over the main Boer redoubt by warning them of the dangers of mines: 250 pounds of nitro-glycerine were found in it. He considered the position too isolated for his own defences and had it demolished. From then on, however, the whole sector was covered by Panzera's artillery: a seven-pounder, Panzera's own home-made howitzer and the ancient cannon being brought up.

At the same time Baden-Powell had been pushing the perimeter out here and there as the Boers had evacuated more positions. On 23 March the Boers also evacuated the strongpoint which had been raided by Fitzclarence's bayonet party five months previously. The perimeter, which six months before had been not more than seven miles, was now nearer ten; there were some sixty forts and earthworks on the perimeter, and some dummy forts with life-size dummy figures. 'From these evacuations, and other signs, it was plain that the numbers of the investing force had decreased.'[1] Had the time come for Baden-Powell to break out of the increasingly hungry, bored and frustrated town, combine with Plumer and open up the campaign?

*

---

[1] *Official History*, p. 172. Hamilton (p. 289) said less than 2,000. The *Times History* (p. 210) gives the total of Snyman and the Boer forces to the north facing Plumer and Holdsworth as about 2,000. Count Sternberg (*op. cit.*, p. 59), who was with the Boer army, gave 1,000 to 1,500, with a large percentage absent from December. See also figures on next page.

It was at this time that Plumer began asking Baden-Powell whether he should make a serious effort to break through, as there appeared to be no question of Baden-Powell forcing his way out; if Plumer went through with two or even three thrusts, and Baden-Powell attacked at a number of points with all his resources, it seemed that the remaining Boers must be dispersed and probably even defeated. Plumer made the request on a number of occasions. He was very keen to take the offensive. As early as 23 March he had offered to advance and engage the besiegers. Baden-Powell had replied that his circumstances were not critical enough to justify such a move.[1] On 4 April Plumer told Roberts, 'I have told Baden-Powell I can advance at once.'[2] Roberts had supported Plumer: 'I hope to hear that you and Plumer have joined hands.' Baden-Powell had earlier left the Commander-in-Chief in little doubt about what he thought of such suggestions: 'As a precaution I on my account say this, in case of unsuccessful relieving we shall require for the southern flying column 2,000 to drive off the enemy and admit Plumer. Will you send convoy, and if Plumer severely defeated, a column 5,000 with fresh convoy? . . . Our supplies last till May 18 and therefore if you have no news by April 12 of our joining hands here and other conditions remain as at present, it would be well to send relief from the south.'[3] Baden-Powell, since the arrival nearby of Plumer, and the presence of Holdsworth on the railway, now had a larger force at his disposal than had Snyman; in a report to Roberts he himself put the Boers facing him and Plumer at 1,200.[4] Moreover, he was well placed to attack the Boers from the rear while the latter were attending to Plumer. It might have been thought, indeed, that the Boers' position had become untenable. But Baden-Powell insisted that such an operation could not be countenanced, and after Plumer's risky reconnaissance in force had nearly met with disaster outside Mafeking, he forbade any further ventures of that kind. Meanwhile the

---

[1] *Official History*, p. 200.
[2] *Roberts Papers*.
[3] Roberts's message, *War Office Papers*, 9 April 1900; Baden-Powell's, *Roberts Papers*, 17 March 1900. Baden-Powell seems to have been the first to have used the expression 'flying column' for the relief force.
[4] 23 March 1900, *Roberts Papers*. In his official report and in his other accounts Baden-Powell insisted that never less than 2,000 Boers invested Mafeking.

Boers languished in their camps, with their reduced numbers even less able to mount a proper investment than before.

Plumer, for the first time in the war, found himself playing a static and defensive role. He contented himself with building up supplies at Kanya for the large exodus of Africans which was now expected there from Mafeking. For there was famine at the African village.

*

Early in April, Lieutenant F. Smitheman, of Plumer's force, had entered Mafeking, at night, to see conditions there, and to make arrangements for the Africans to be got out of the town. One of the first people he met was Baillie, of the *Morning Post,* to whom he said: 'How do you do? I am bloody glad to be in.' Baillie could always be relied upon to make an adequate reply, and he said: "How do you do? I am glad to see you but I should be bloody glad to be out.'

Smitheman, who had been an explorer before the war, had much influence with the natives and was able to persuade many to leave; quite a few, however, needed but little persuasion. The system of rationing for the Africans had not been a success; most of them were required to pay (threepence for a pint bowl of soup), and few of them had sufficient money.[1] The more humble natives, who were treated almost as slaves by the Baralong tribesmen, were in a pitiful position. Hamilton, as could be expected, was filled with both anger and compassion (although not all his views on the subject ever appeared in *The Times*). 'Whatever motives of philanthropy direct the policy of the executive in this question of distributing food allowances to natives, it cannot be said that the Government or its administrators err upon the side of liberality.' He claimed that the charge of threepence, which he did not think the natives could raise, was only imposed to get them to leave for Kanya. 'There can be no doubt that the drastic principles of economy which Colonel Baden-Powell has been practising in these later days are opposed to and altogether at variance with the dignity and liberalism which we profess, and which enter so much into the pacific settlement of native questions in South

---

[1] Receipts from the soup kitchens during the defence were £3,242.

Africa.' Even Neilly, normally a carefree fellow, was horrified at the condition of the Africans:

I saw them fall down on the veldt and lie where they had fallen, too weak to go on their way. The sufferers were mostly little boys —mere infants ranging in age from four or five upwards . . . Hunger had them in its grip, and many of them were black spectres and living skeletons . . . their ribs literally breaking their shrivelled skin—men, women and children . . . Probably hundreds died from starvation or the diseases that always accompany famine. Certain it is that many were found dead on the veldt . . . Words could not portray the scene of misery; five or six hundred human frameworks of both sexes and all ages, from the tender infant upwards, dressed in the remains of tattered rags, standing in lines, each holding an old blackened can or beef tin, awaiting turn to crawl painfully up to the soup kitchen where the food was distributed. Having obtained the horse soup, fancy them tottering off a few yards and sitting down to wolf up the life-fastening mass. and lick the tins when they had finished. It was one of the most heartrending sights I ever witnessed.

Neilly wrote that critics in the town had suggested to Baden-Powell that the Africans should have a share of the rations, still comparatively plentiful, allocated to the whites. Baden-Powell issued an order saying that he would be grateful if anyone hearing these 'grousers' would 'apply the toe of the boot'. Neilly continued:

The blacks were informed they could go over the lines in comparative safety . . . They picked up meat-tins and licked them; they fed like outcast curs. They went farther than the mongrel. When a dog gets a bone he polishes it white and leaves it there. Day after day I heard outside my door continuous thumping sounds. They were caused by the living skeletons who, having eaten all that was outside the bones, smashed them up with stones and devoured what marrow they could find. They looked for bones on the dustheaps, on the roads, everywhere.[1]

---

[1] Neilly, pp. 227–30.

Europeans had a difficult task preserving their pet dogs and cats from Africans; and Neilly saw one African stone a dog and then grab the bone which it had dropped. The dog cemetery, on the outskirts of the town, was raided for its remains and bones . . .

On 19 March an African was executed for stealing a horse.

Even the Africans with employment and money were in despair. Baillie wrote in his diary : 'My kaffir wishes to go and join Plumer. He doesn't approve of the food supply in Mafeking. I thought I should never get rid of him. Thank goodness the brute has gone now. He has been a sort of "old man of the sea" to me. I only kept him because he appeared generally in small health, but when he flung his rations into the middle of the square yesterday I thought it was high time for him to be off.' Rations for native servants and grooms were regulated at one quart 'siege porridge', four ounces of meat and half an ounce of salt per day—more than double the ration of less favourably placed Africans.

Before even the start of the year, Weil had received a begging letter from one of his servants, probably a 'coloured' boy. '*I wish to ask you to allow me rations*. . . . Surely good very dear and I and family cannot come out now, with salary without rations. Please allow me rations as before . . . I ever will trust to be safe in your hands. Sorry I couldn't express fluently in talking so I write to you open my feelings, I remain, I am sir your dear boy.'[1]

After three days Smitheman left, with two natives, by the way he had come. During the succeeding weeks he returned to the town on a number of occasions.[2]

On the nights following his first visit, women and children were sent out in large parties, and told to head for Kanya. According to the correspondents, many of these were shot by the Boers *en route*, no attempt at concealment being made, and Snyman regarding large parties differently to individual runners. Snyman was apparently under the erroneous impression that Baden-Powell's supplies were giving out at last. He reported to Pretoria : 'All the Kaffirs are being driven out of Mafeking by force by Baden-Powell. I have seen some of them, they are in a miserable state on account of hunger.'[3]

[1] *Weil Papers*, 12 December 1899.
[2] R. S. Godley, p. 72.
[3] 26 February 1900, *Boer Dispatches*.

In a sworn declaration made in the Transvaal some Africans declared: 'If we ask the English for food, we receive an answer: Go over the border of the Transvaal and steal from the Boers.'[1] On 8 April 600 women were nearly all caught by the Boers. They were all stripped and saw their clothes burnt. They were then flogged and driven back, naked, into the town. Only between sixty and seventy succeeded in getting to Plumer.[2]

In his official report Baden-Powell said that Plumer's presence enabled him to 'get rid of' 2,000 native women and children in order further to conserve his supplies. There are conflicting records of how many reached the food waiting for them sixty miles away, but on 24 April Plumer reported that 600 had reached him, and on 27 April Baden-Powell reported that 803 had succeeded in reaching Plumer's camp.[3]

Baden-Powell, who had ample supplies for the Europeans, was not prepared to endanger the comfortable military position of his garrison by sharing them with the Africans.

*

The higher caste and enrolled Africans were in a better state, and it was these who took an active part in the defence; indeed, as the investment progressed they became more active than the whites. Almost every night armed bands left the native village to maraud the veldt in search of food.[4] The first native raid on the Boer lines, directed by the British, was as early as October the previous year: 'a brisk little engagement'.[5] In April a party of Africans captured by the Boers said that they had been ordered to raid the Boer camps 'for the purpose of assisting the English to drive away the Boers from around Mafeking'.[6] Frequently they brought back cattle from the

---

[1] *Weil Papers.*

[2] Baillie, 8 April 1900; Plumer's dispatch 8 April 1900, *Roberts Papers.*

[3] The *Official History* (p. 202), and the *Times History* (p. 208), give a total figure of 1,200 reaching Plumer. Plumer's report in *Roberts Papers.* Baden-Powell's figure from *The Times*, 9 May 1900.

[4] Baden-Powell assured Snyman that they were 'certainly not acting under my orders' nor 'so far as I am aware' the orders of his officers (7 April 1900, *Weil Papers*).

[5] Bell, 18 October 1900.

[6] *Weil Papers*, 13 April 1900.

Boer herds, and these added a much appreciated supply to the tables of the whites. On several occasions they were in running fights with the Boers, who sometimes caught them in their work, and often they gave as good as they got. Snyman continued to protest bitterly about this to Baden-Powell, but to no effect. Once a party of thirty armed Africans held out for twenty-five hours against the Boers, and were only subdued after two machine-guns and a field gun had been brought up to destroy them in the dried-up water-hole which they were using as a defensive position. There was one survivor. On another night they attacked one of the main Boer forts from the rear and engaged the hundred-odd Boers who garrisoned it, only withdrawing after finishing their ammunition, with the loss of one killed and two wounded.[1] During much of March and April most of the activity on the British side was by Africans, most of them famished, some starving. Hamilton wrote:

> They have fought for us; they have preyed upon the enemy's cattle so that the white garrison might have something better than horseflesh for their diet; they have manned the western defences of the village and they have suffered severe privations with extraordinary fortitude . . . In the history of these people there is not much in the consideration which we have shown them to justify their allegiance . . . let us at least remember the debt of honour which we owe them.

The most daring operation conducted by the Africans was the stampeding of a herd of cattle into the town. Baillie described the episode in his diary on 15 April:

> Colonel Plumer selected some hundred head of cattle in good condition, and it was these that the party endeavoured to bring in. When they were some distance out, it was reported to Mathakong [the chief in command] that the Boers knew that they were coming and were going to try to intercept them. However, as he had been given to understand that it was desirable to get the cattle in, he determined to make the attempt, as at any rate they might get some in, and if he stayed where he was the Boers would probably

---

[1] Baillie, 8 April 1900.

surround him. The Boers got on both flanks of the cattle, assisted by rebel natives, and heavy firing began. The Baralongs pushed forward with cattle falling all round them, and behind the bodies of the cattle kept up a running fight until all their ammunition was gone. They stuck to them till only fifteen head were left, and then, when they left, the Boers came up cheering loudly . . . Mathakong was much upset by the loss of the cattle, but the fight did not worry him at all and he said that had the cattle not been in such good condition he would have rushed them along faster and got most of them in. This, however, is only one of the many cases in which the Baralongs have done, or have endeavoured to do, good service. They lost four killed and seven wounded, and account for their small loss by the protection afforded them by the herd.

After this the Boers stood up in their trenches and held up legs of beef for the disappointed garrison to gaze upon.

Next to the Africans those suffering most in Mafeking were the Boers in the town. Many died of disease and malnutrition; most of the women, who from start to finish were always suspected of spying, were confined to a stinking and unhygienic section of the women's camp, and the men, with one Irish nationalist, were locked up in the jail every night. Baillie, standing in the market square one day noticed 'a very weak-looking child, apparently as near death as any living creature could be. It transpired, on inquiry, that this infant was a Dutch one, Graaf by name. His father, a refugee, died of fever; his brother was in hospital and he had been offered admission, which he refused because he said that he must look after his mother. Even then, though scarcely able to cross the road, the kid was going to draw his rations. He was taken to hospital, but I think that this is about the pluckiest individual that has come under my notice.'

If one was neither an African nor a Boer, life was not so bad. On 13 April Stent, Reuters' correspondent, sent out a message saying: 'We are able to look forward with cheerful patience to another fortnight, or perhaps three weeks, of siege.' The main trouble, as always, was the unutterable boredom of the days. It was now six months since Baden-Powell had set up the investment, and half a year in such conditions is a not inconsiderable slice of life; to those in

Mafeking it was beginning to feel like a lifetime itself. Owing to the lack of nourishment and the lack of activity in the latter part of March and during April, many people had settled into a kind of trance. Several of the diaries mention, almost with resignation, that the relief, which had once been expected almost immediately after the relief of Kimberley, might never come and they would be left to end their days in Mafeking.

In the Boer lines figures were seldom seen; it was uncanny. It seemed as if there were hardly any Boers in whole sectors around the town. After a brief flurry of shelling during the first few days of the month, and a particularly heavy bombardment on 11 April, even the guns stopped, and were not heard from for several days on end. That night 'Creaky', at long last, was taken away to Pretoria, from whence it had come; it had fired 1,497 shells into Mafeking and killed less than twenty people; possibly never in the history of war had one such apparently formidable weapon discharged so much ammunition to so little effect; but the staff at the battered hospital felt a very particular relief.

'The Boers became tired of war for a spell and lazed and gave us a quiet time. Those were happy days for us. It was like being born again into a more enjoyable world than ours, this getting out on the veldt for a ride or a delicious walk without being potted at every yard of the way . . . it was heavenly to wander along the valley of the little River Molopo and sit on the bank, where the big stones offered an obstruction to the stream . . . '[1] Lady Sarah summed up this time as : 'Inferior food, and very little of it; divine weather; bridge in the afternoons; and one day exactly like another.'

An Anglo-Boer wedding took place; the bride could not speak a word of English, the bridegroom, a Private in the Bechuanaland Regiment, could not speak a word of Afrikaans. The *Mafeking Mail* commented : 'This celebration is another proof of the pluck and courage which, in the garrison, is available for any event. A diploma of honour was given to a baby for being born during the siege, and certainly nothing short of the v.c. should be the award of bravery that enables a man to undertake matrimonial responsibilities with rations so scarce.'

---

[1] Neilly, p. 226.

Another man died through fiddling with one of the many unexploded shells . . . the Court House was set up as a reading room where the London and Bulawayo newspapers could be perused . . . the posts to and from home were delivered and received (Baillie was infuriated when informed, on 24 April, by 'the Rhodesian postal authorities', that there would be a delay on press telegrams to London owing to pressure on the lines: 'The postal arrangements throughout the campaign have been most infamous.') . . . on Easter Day there were no hot-cross buns, but crosses were stamped on the bread rations . . . new uses were found for every part of slaughtered animals . . . dog licences were instituted for those owners anxious both to gain rations for their pets and to preserve them from bone-protruding Africans who wandered the streets with sacks . . . a growing shortage of wood was felt, and substitute fuel was made by mixing coal dust with cow dung . . . a swarm of locusts provided many tables with the Indian dish of curried locusts . . . horse sausages, minced horsemeat and oat-husk porridge were becoming familiar.[1]

The *Official History* states:

On April 23, when a board of officers took stock, there were still in hand breadstuffs (oats and meal) sufficient for fifty-two days, and meat for ninety days; horses, donkeys and mules being counted as available for the latter, in addition to cattle, calves and sheep . . . The troops, indeed, thus assiduously cared for, received rations such as have been rarely enjoyed by men so long besieged . . . Of actual sickness there was not much; but there was visible in the ranks that inevitable lassitude of men long confined on low diet.

---

[1] For Europeans, horsemeat was not widely eaten till April. As late as 31 March 1900 Hamilton wrote: 'Horses have not become our daily ration yet, although they form the basis of a curious soup which is made and served out to the natives.' On 1 May 1900 he reported to *The Times:* 'Excellent brawn is now being made and is eaten by both whites and blacks. It is made from ox and horse hides.' On 30 April 1900 it was announced that horsemeat sausages and mince would be issued three days a week, 1 lb of beef on four days: on 5 May 1900, horse and beef on alternate days. (In his report, Baden-Powell said that horsemeat was issued three days a week 'during the last two months'.)

The daily fresh-vegetable ration was reduced to half a pound on 1 May, but on the 4th the sugar ration was increased to one and a half ounces a day. The meat ration was still one pound a day. The Boers could not credit that Mafeking's resources could last much longer. They were not alone in their surprise at the situation. In London, Mr Balfour had been asked in the House of Commons how it was that the siege had lasted so long. He had replied that it was partly due to the foresight of Cecil. In Mafeking, Vere Stent wrote: 'I mentioned to Weil that I should like to interview him on the question of provisioning of Mafeking. Who was responsible for the fact that we had been able to hold out for six-and-a-half months and yet had sufficient provisions for another sixty days?' Weil told him that, with Cecil's authority, he had been able to bring up not only enormous food stocks, but enough provisions to ration, clothe and reclothe the troops; at the start of the war the Army Service Corps had possessed only enough to supply the garrison for three weeks. Weil had also brought up from the Cape large quantities of military stores, including ammunition. In February he still had such vast quantities of tinned meat in stock that he had asked Baden-Powell personally for permission to sell it, but had been refused. There was still liquor, although on 10 May Hanbury-Tracy was moved to write to Weil: 'I hear that you propose sending more wines and spirits to Colonel Plumer. I trust that this is not the case.' Weil had already contrived to supply Plumer's force with some much-needed refreshment; this had not endeared him to some in Mafeking.[1]

One event which did much to raise everyone's spirit was the receipt of a telegram from no less a person than the Queen herself:

I continue watching with confidence and admiration the patient and resolute defence which is so gallantly maintained under your ever resourceful command.

Mayor Whiteley had also received a telegram from the Queen, seven weeks before. But only now did everyone begin to realize the impact the siege was having at home. They were heroes, but they had not known it. Baden-Powell's jolly messages had the nation in

[1] *Weil Papers.*

an orgy of admiration. On 22 April he sent out by runner : 'During the past week there has been no bombardment with the exception of an occasional shell. One bottle of whisky raffled and fetched £107 10s. od.' Owing to letters from home, Baden-Powell must surely now have been aware of the publication of his 'official' communiqués, although he denied it. On 10 April he had received many letters from home, including one from his sister informing him, with pride, that he was 'the hero of the day' : his photograph, he was told, was in all the London shops, and sold better even than those of Roberts. His effigy was at Madame Tussaud's.

This was some consolation for the bad news he had received at the time of Plumer's sortie to Mafeking. 'The Boy' McLaren, who had been with Plumer and who had no doubt hoped to enjoy a reunion with his old friend, had been wounded and was a prisoner of the Boers. On hearing this, Baden-Powell's immediate reaction had been to rush over to the Boer lines to see McLaren; the only thing that prevented him from doing so was Cecil and the staff refusing to let him go across. It was explained to him that if he went under a white flag the Boers might easily abuse the truce and hold him prisoner. This had been a severe blow to Baden-Powell. He sent messages to 'The Boy' enquiring as to his welfare, his needs in clean pyjamas, books, etc. In a correspondence with Snyman he tried to get McLaren exchanged for one of the Boer civilians in the town. When Snyman refused, Baden-Powell wrote : 'I would be greatly obliged if you would allow my doctor to visit him.' Every day a messenger with a white flag went out from the town with Baden-Powell's daily letter to his friend. His protracted correspondence with Snyman proving of no avail, Baden-Powell sent a letter and a telegram to President Kruger, pleading that 'The Boy' should be sent in to Mafeking, and undertaking that McLaren would not take up arms again during the campaign.[1]

In the town, boredom and frustration had brought dissension. The correspondents, who had not expected to be away from Cape Town and Kimberley so long, were almost penniless. Reuters, however, could be relied upon to look after their man, and they did so by wiring him £150 via Weil's Cape Town office, which passed the

---

[1] Hillcourt and *Weil Papers*.

authority to Weil in Mafeking (telegrams from Bulawayo at this time took about seven days). Stent was 'extraordinarily busy at present, dispatch runners leave nearly every day, and I have to make bricks without straw in the shape of dispatches without news.'

Weil's stores, which were full of luxuries as well as necessities, were open to all who could get the written permission of Captain Ryan to purchase—but Weil naturally expected to be paid. Bitter letters and threats of legal action passed to and fro. The Colonel commanding was not immune. People complained he was hoarding food unnecessarily, withholding news and bringing upon the town unnecessary damage. Baden-Powell was by no means insensitive to criticism. He issued a long, sharp and personal statement, answering the charges, and threatening the 'grumblers—most of whom are known to me (as they will find when their claims for compensation come up for adjudication)—and it is these gentlemen that I desire to warn to keep quiet as otherwise I shall have to take more stringent steps against them . . . I would ask, after perusal, that this notice be destroyed as I should be ashamed if the fame of Mafeking and its heroic defence should be marred by any whisper among envious outsiders that there was any want of harmony and unity of purpose among us.'[1] The warning had no effect, for a few days later he received a strongly worded letter from the Mafeking Town Council, signed by Weil, Whiteley and others, about the compensation they would insist on.

In mid-April Hamilton wrote :

Our nerves are altogether raw, our tempers soured, our digestions failing . . . In the situation itself there is nothing to write about, it so constantly repeats itself until the absolute monotony of the days settles down upon the nerves, depressing one's spirit like a wet blanket. The Boers still fire at us and we still sit tight, nursing our hopes by a sublime confidence in the relief column. But in reality there are but few people who believe in the practical existence of any relief column.

Baillie was less puzzled about the relief, which he had given up

---

[1] *Weil Papers.*

as hopeless, than what the Boers thought they were doing. 'Why they should wish to take Mafeking is hard to say. Their chance of invading Rhodesia is gone, the crossings of the Vaal river are in our hands.' Perhaps it was that the few Boers remaining were content to continue 'investment' just as long as Baden-Powell wished to stay.

Meanwhile the Africans and the captive Boers swelled and swelled, and died.

April turned into May : hot, dusty and dry. At the hospital, Nurse Craufurd entered in her diary :

So many of the natives have died lately after swelling all over. They have an idea it is the horse soup that is the cause, and that there is something in it which is poisonous. This, however, is not the case, I think, but that the swelling is caused from lack of sufficient nourishment in it, and that the swelling is a sort of scurvy. I had a small Dutch boy called Graaf in a few days ago who was swollen in the same way, and died after a few hours. Poor little chap! He was one of a huge family, and I think he and a brother (who was found in the Market Square the day after so weak that he could hardly stand) must have given most of their share of rations to their younger brothers and sisters. Major Baillie and Colonel Vyvyan found the elder boy. He told them he was ill but could not go to hospital as there was no one else to help mother. The doctor thought he could not live, but I hope he may. Poor little lad! He is wonderfully brave and patient, although he has dysentery very badly and is so thin that it is a marvel his bones do not come through.

Away towards the Kalahari, Colonel Plumer, receiving groups of emaciated Africans, counted his stores and waited. Commandant Snyman, at the farmhouse over the hills, sat in the semi-darkness and pondered on his continually diminishing force and waited. And high on his platform, whistling through his teeth, for ever scanning the horizon with binoculars, stood Colonel R. S. S. Baden-Powell, the hero of the day—waiting.

*

Then, right at the end, someone arrived on the stage who was pre-pared to take action—before it was too late.

Whereas in Britain the siege of Mafeking had become the most glorious episode of the war, to the Boers it had become a disgrace. Snyman and his men were the cause of ribald laughter among all other forces. As the *Official History* says, they 'had become the scorn of the rest of the Boer army'.

On 24 April Commandant Sarel Eloff, with a detachment, joined Snyman's depleted force. As leader of a commando, he was now ranked Commandant. He was young, he was indignant, he was the grandson of the President himself. Outraged at the Boer indifference at Mafeking, he determined to take the place at once, if only now as a matter of pride. On the day after his arrival Eloff had launched a demonstration in which he had been in the van, riding and shoot-ing around the British lines. Wan, dispirited and listless, the British waited throughout the day, but no attack developed. A few days later another skirmish was attempted, but it was called off. Eloff, it seemed, was just like all the other Boers. The British yawned and forgot about him. But they were wrong. Eloff was quite differ-ent. He had been attempting to draw British fire (fairly unsuccess-fully, owing to the shortage of ammunition in Mafeking) to ascer-tain the strengths of their various defences. On 6 May the Sabbath truce on shelling was violated for the first time. Using his influence as Kruger's grandson, Eloff virtually took over Snyman's command.

Bloemfontein, the capital of the Orange Free State, had fallen to Roberts on 13 March. It was obvious to most by then that the Boers' chance of forcing a favourable settlement on the British had gone already, their policy of investing British forces, and wasting precious time while much larger forces streamed into South Africa, being devoid of common sense as well as of sound strategy. Their capitulation was a matter of time (a much longer time than most people thought, as it turned out); but before that happened Eloff was utterly determined to wipe out the shame of Mafeking.

Then a note was received from the young man :

Dan Kolonel Baden-Powell——I see in the *Bulawayo Chronicle* that your men in Mafeking play cricket on Sundays and give con-certs and balls on Sunday evenings. In case you would allow my men to join in the same it would be very agreeable to me as here outside Mafeking there are seldom any of the fair sex and there can be no merriment without their being present. Wishing you a pleasant day, I remain your obliging friend, S. ELOFF, *Commandant.*

Up till then Baden-Powell had enjoyed a monopoly of humour in the correspondence between the two sides. Of late, however, there had been little of the accustomed spark in him. He now replied, in suitable terms, saying that he would be glad to oblige with a cricket match, but not until the present game—in which his side had scored 200 days not out—was completed.

Baillie watched all this with some asperity. 'With such mild jokes we pass the time away . . . A bad joke in these times is worth more than a good pint of porridge, as the former will go round whereas the latter will certainly not. It is very edifying work trying to get fat on laughter.'

Would the relief ever come?

12. The March of the Relief Column

For six weeks the bars of Kimberley had been buzzing with rumours of the assembly of a column to relieve Mafeking. But nothing had happened.

The truth was that the Commander-in-Chief, Lord Roberts, had been too preoccupied to give much time to the thought of a relief; he had always hoped that Plumer and Baden-Powell between them would be able to solve the situation. But as time went on, pressure on him began to mount. The public at home was dissatisfied and restless; the Government was worried as to public reaction if Mafeking, unrelieved, should fall. Even the investment of 1,500 British troops at Wepener, in the Orange Free State, during April, had not succeeded in distracting world attention from Mafeking.

Roberts later explained to Lansdowne his reasons for not mounting the relief long before. He said he had been detemined to carry out his plan of campaign and 'not to be led into diverting from it, for operations of subsidiary importance, the troops which I required to attain my main objective—namely, to advance in adequate strength through the northern portion of the Orange Free State and Johannesburg and Pretoria'.[1] Roberts was convinced that the defenders had 'ample supplies to support them till the middle of June'.[2]

At first Roberts had hoped to assign the task to Methuen after the relief of Kimberley. Rhodes himself took an interest in the matter, but many of the men in Kimberley had already had enough of the war and had been loth to leave the city when it was benefiting from the presence of a British Army in the locality and when there had been much to be done after a long investment. There had been a number of men more than anxious to take part in what—it was

[1] Lord Roberts to Secretary of State for War, 21 May 1900.
[2] *The Life of Lord Roberts*, Sir G. W. Forrest, p. 275.

by then realized—would be a dramatic and perhaps even historic occasion, but not sufficient to raise a mounted column, and Roberts had not been able to spare the men from his own troops. His next scheme had been that a relief should, after all, be operated by his main forces in the area as part of a general movement, but owing to other operations this had been delayed. And all the while there was the possibility that, if Baden-Powell could hold out long enough, Carrington might be able to join with Plumer and relieve the town from the north. Indeed, when Carrington had at last arrived at Cape Town, on his way to take up command of the Rhodesian Frontier Force, he had been told that his most urgent duty was the relief of Mafeking, and to assist Plumer in any way he could. But it was now clear that public demand would not wait till Carrington's force was established in Rhodesia. Plumer's main need was guns. A battery of the Royal Canadian Artillery had recently arrived from Canada, in February, as part of four shiploads of Canadian troops, with half a dozen accredited newspapermen.[1] It was in camp thirty-three miles from Cape Town. The story of its progress is one of the most remarkable of the South African War. The battery of six guns had left Canada, under the command of Major Hudon, on 21 February. It had disembarked at Cape Town on 26 March, and went to camp. On 14 April, Good Friday, it had marched thirty-three miles back to Cape Town and had begun re-embarkation at 3.30 a.m. and completed it by 12.15 p.m. the next day. The ship sailed at 3.0 p.m. and arrived at Beira on 21 April. Two hours after the last man disembarked the battery was on the train for Rhodesia. From the railhead it travelled 285 miles by mule wagons and coaches, changing mules every few miles (there being then no rail link with Bulawayo). The contractor for coach services in Rhodesia had agreed to suspend all services and had collected all his mules in the country to expedite the battery's progress. At Beira the Canadians had been joined by an advance party of Carrington's force, 100 men of the Queensland Mounted Infantry, who had recently arrived there from Australia. It was decided that two guns would have to follow more slowly, but the remainder of the little force arrived at Bulawayo by

[1] C Battery, R.C.A.: enrolled at posts of the North-West Mounted Police in Ontario, and at Winnipeg, Manitoba; officered almost entirely by volunteers of the North-West Mounted Police and regular Canadian Artillery Officers.

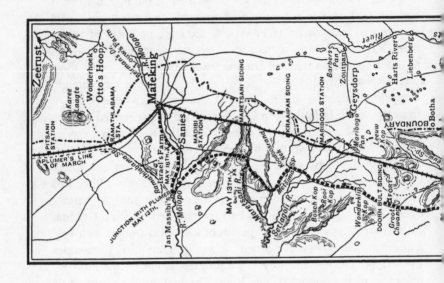

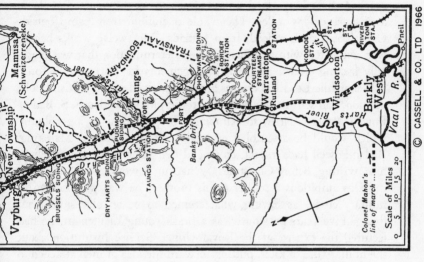

THE MARCH TO THE RELIEF OF MAFEKING

© CASSELL & CO. LTD 1966

7 May. At Bulawayo they entrained again, going south 460 miles to within forty miles of Plumer's camp at Sefetili, which they reached on 14 May—twelve days after leaving the railhead at Beira, a distance of 785 miles. The whole operation, from camp outside Cape Town and, indeed, from Canada only twelve weeks before, was conducted with an efficiency and determination that was markedly lacking elsewhere in the arrangements for Carrington's force.

Meanwhile Lord Roberts, as a well-conceived sop to British public opinion, had sent Baden-Powell's brother, Major Baden F. S. Baden-Powell, Scots Guards, to Kimberley to prepare a 'flying column' which would be assembled especially for the relief of Mafeking. Baden-Powell had, in fact, envisaged that his brother might relieve him, writing, before Christmas, 'What fun it would be.'[1] Baden was quite as ambitious a soldier as his brother; he was well known in military circles as having what seemed to be an obsession about flying. Five years previously, as a brash young Lieutenant, he had lectured the experts at the Royal United Service Institution about the military use of kites, putting forward the idea of men attached to kites going above and beyond the enemy lines.[2] Some people thought him a crank, but he had an original mind and a good appreciation of the trends of modern warfare. He was more genuinely interested in military matters, and more concerned with military theory, than his elder brother.

Baden found that a column could now be assembled from existing units, and, accordingly, the local commander, Lieutenant-General Sir Archibald Hunter, who had been prominent in the defence of Ladysmith, was instructed to form a 'flying column', to be commanded by Colonel Bryan Mahon. Mahon had left Egypt in January, having finally defeated the Khalifa in Kordofan; on arrival in South Africa, he had been sent by Roberts to take command of Methuen's mounted troops. He had a reputation as a most dashing commander. He was widely known as the Mahout (i.e. 'the elephant-driver').

---

[1] 12 December 1899: Reynolds, p. 106.

[2] In 1910, at the same place, he said: 'Let us not forget that machines are now actually in existence that can come over, without warning, from the Continent, and it is more than possible that they may be the cause of considerable damage to us, even risking their own loss thereby.' (*R.U.S.I. Journal*, 1895, 1910)

Rumours now multiplied. As long ago as the second week in March the correspondents with the main army at Bloemfontein had been informed that a relief for Mafeking would be leaving Kimberly on 20 March. Hastening to Kimberley, they had found that no such arrangements had been made. Then the five correspondents, who had waited many weeks, were at last summoned to the Press Censor's office : Charles Hands, of the *Daily Mail,* A. W. A. Pollock of *The Times,* Filson Young of the *Manchester Guardian,* Charles Falconer of the *Daily Telegraph,* and John Stuart of the *Morning Post.* There a sealed envelope, marked SECRET, had been opened and the information that a relief column would leave at dawn next morning read out to them. They were pledged to secrecy.

Tuesday evening [Young wrote] was full of romance for anyone who knew what was about to happen. The dining-room of the club was gay with yellow and brass and scarlet and the subtler colours of wine and flowers; but conversation grouped itself into the low choruses that indicate far more truly than one united sound indicates the presence of some common and thrilling interest.

When the news eventually spread out to the Empire from Kimberley, in innuendos and hints, that a relief was on its way, there were several days of tension and pride almost unsurpassed in the Victorian era. There was not only the defence of Mafeking, which had for so long seemed to typify everything that the British admired about themselves, there was also the romantic reputation of the Anglo-Irish colonel in command of the relief, and the very term 'flying column' seemed to convey a specially dramatic military operation. Was the event which the public had longed for to come about at last? Only the Boer could prevent it, but with the Boer one never knew . . .

*

The column, which was to rendezvous with Plumer, assembled at Barkly West, more than twenty miles north-west of Kimberley. It consisted of the Imperial Light Horse, one of the most famous units in

South Africa, the Kimberley Mounted Corps, part of a battery of the Royal Horse Artillery, two machine-guns and one hundred infantry that had been specially selected for the occasion from Fusilier battalions—twenty-five men each from English, Scottish, Irish and Welsh regiments. Thus it had carefully been arranged that after the junction with Plumer men from all the home countries, from Australia, Canada, New Zealand, Natal and Cape Province, would take part in the relief. The total strength was nearly 900 mounted troops, 100 infantry, four guns and two pom-poms : accompanying it were fifty-two mule-wagons (ten mules each) so that the column would be able to supply itself *en route*. Altogether there were 1,149 men. The Imperial Light Horse, which had come from Natal, had been in the van at the relief of Ladysmith, and its men had been among the first to enter that town. Once Roberts had finally made up his mind that there was no hope of Plumer and Baden-Powell disentangling themselves, it seems it was easy enough for him to spare a relief column.[1] Somewhere, sometime, during the previous six weeks Roberts, who had previously shown little interest, had decided, or been persuaded, to let the public have what it wanted— not just a relief, but a relief managed as if on the stage at Covent Garden itself, with Baden-Powell as stage-manager.

The main defect in the composition of the column was that, although it was to cross extremely difficult and parched country, it did not include any Royal Engineers.

Among those with Mahon, in various staff capacities, were Prince Alexander of Teck,[2] Sir John Willoughby, Colonel Frank Rhodes (brother of Cecil), Major Sam Weil (brother of Benjamin), Major Baden F. S. Baden-Powell and Captain G. T. M. Bridges.[3] Also present was Major W. D. Davies, a hero of all British people in South Africa as he had been on the Jameson Raid and had refused to come to terms with the Boers afterwards; as a result he, with one

---

[1] By that time Roberts had an army of nearly 250,000 men at his disposal, including 107,726 regular British troops.

[2] Later the Earl of Athlone, Governor-General of South Africa, 1923–31.

[3] Nephew of the poet Robert Bridges. Later Lieutenant-General Sir Tom Bridges; at St. Quentin, in 1914, he rallied two battalions with a toy whistle and drum.

other of the raiders, had been imprisoned in the Transvaal for over
a year. Frank Rhodes and Willoughby had also been on the humiliating Jameson Raid. Willoughby had been with Jameson at the
siege of Ladysmith and was not in the Army at all; he was a retired
regular soldier. Hunter took the responsibility of making him a
major and appointing him to Mahon's staff.

Mafeking had been the base for the Jameson Raid. The careful
composition of the relief force, therefore, was calculated to add even
more emotion to the event.

In the early morning of 4 May the long, straggling column pulled
out of Barkly West. On the first day it covered twelve miles; on the
following days it went much faster.

As speed was judged to be the essential aspect, it was important
to avoid a clash with the Boers. The most obvious route, beside the
railway line, was therefore, not taken; instead Mahon at first took
his column along a track some miles to the west of the railway. But
it was too much to keep such a column a secret. The land was dry
and dusty. As the column wound its way north, snaking over the
arid veld, a great cloud of dust rose into the sky above it, marking
its relentless progress. From distant hills lone Boer scouts watched
its advance.

At the same time Hunter and Methuen had begun their main
advance, as part of Roberts's general offensive into the western
Transvaal; and Sir Charles Warren had arrived at the Orange River
to begin operations against the rebel commandos of the area. On
5 May Hunter had a successful engagement against the Boers at
Rooidam, about twenty miles from Barkly West, and this did
succeed in distracting the Boers from Mahon's initial move.

The Boers from the Rooidam area now tried to catch up Mahon,
but this was not easy as Mahon's infantry were travelling in the
wagons and sometimes his whole column moved at a trot rather than
at a marching pace. Owing to the intense heat, the column travelled
at night and in the early morning. After a while the route joined
with the railway, and on 9 May the flying column entered Vryburg
without having fired a round, having covered the 129 miles from
Barkly West in just over five days without incident.

The Boers had evacuated Vryburg not long before, and the
citizens of the place had only just had time to replace the flag of the

Republic with the Union Jack. As the column rode into the main street, it was given a tremendous welcome from such a small population, with flags, streamers, a band, and much cheering, drinking and rejoicing.

Having used up all the town's stock of wood for its cooking-fires the column moved out of Vryburg again the following evening 'in a cloud of purple dust', wrote Young; 'as long as the light lasted we could see the rather pathetic-looking little crowd of residents waving handkerchiefs and flags.' Pathetic, perhaps, but the people of Vryburg, as they watched the great men pass them by for Mafeking, their own somewhat inglorious part in the war now at an end, sensed something in the air which was soon to sweep across the Empire.

There were still 100 miles to go.

At this point the first mishap occurred. Immediately on nightfall the column got lost. Water, which it had been expected would be found after three hours, was not found after eight. Those who had believed the whole affair was going to be a party were disconcerted, that night, to find themselves camped beside some dried-up water-holes, surrounded by complaining and suffering horses and mules, with no fires or lights—not even a cigarette—permitted, and having to rise again and move off after only three hours' rest. That night they had gone eighteen miles, and they did four in the morning; thirteen the following night, and eight in the morning. The Mahout's reputation, it seemed, was all very well—except when one served under him.

On 11 May Lieutenant Morsum joined the column. He had been sent by Plumer to Baden-Powell on liaison duties, and he had then left Mafeking and reported to Plumer who had sent him off to the relief column. He now acted as a much-needed guide to bring Mahon to the rendezvous with Plumer at 'JanMassibi's' deserted farm, on the Molopo River. Morsum's journeying seemed to indicate that the Boers' watch on the town, now that they were thoroughly aware of Mahon's approaching force, was even less than usual.

Mahon sent Plumer and Baden-Powell an account of the strength and details of his force, for which Baden-Powell, waiting in Mafeking, had asked. There was no agreed code. Mahon was puzzled about how to satisfy Baden-Powell's curiosity without risking passing information to the Boers. At the suggestion of Frank Rhodes, he sent the following message:

Our numbers are Naval and Millitary [*sic*] Club multiplied by ten; our guns, the number of sons in the Ward family; our supplies, the O.C. 9th Lancers.

This was interpreted by Plumer and Baden-Powell as: numbers, 940 (94 Piccadilly x 10); guns, 6 (the Earl of Dudley and his five brothers); supplies, few (Lieut.-Colonel Little).

It was expected that Lord Dudley's brothers would be known, as his brother-in-law, Ronnie Moncreiffe, was still in Mafeking. What Mahon and Rhodes did not know was that Moncreiffe had spent nearly the entire siege in jail.

Routine in a fast-moving column had to be meticulously observed. Filson Young described it:

When the time for the five minutes' rest in the hour has arrived, *"Halt!"* is passed down the column, and one hears the word running down squadron after squadron until it is lost among the lines of the ammunition column. The connecting files pass it for-forward to the advance guard, who send it out to their scouts and patrols, until the great serpent that winds over the country is completely at rest. Then follows a sound of horses cropping grass and men talking. Then *"Stand to your horses!"* runs down the column, followed by a shuffling of feet as men scramble from the ground where they have been lying; *"Prepare to mount!"* and there is a general gathering up of reins; *"Mount!"* and a long rustle and jingle as the men swing into their saddles . . . and the serpent is off again, feeling his way before him. Three miles in front of us the furthest scouts of the advance guard are working cautiously in the bush, and from the officer in command of the guard a note occasionally comes back to the Brigadier, carried from squadron to squadron until it reaches the head of the main squadron.

The 500 Boers from Rooidam had now caught up Mahon and were marching parallel to him; on 12 May they were joined by 400 more who had come down from Mafeking.[1] On the following day the Boers entrenched themselves in a strong position both sides of a defile on the line of Mahon's advance and awaited his arrival. Mahon, however, heard of their position and realized its strength; with hardly a minute's delay he changed direction, left the main road and veered off from it at an angle to the left of almost forty-five degrees. The column struck out across the bush.

Just when it was thought the Boers had been completely shaken off, they opened fire from rising ground on the right of the flying column at one of the rare moments when it had been allowed to straggle and get split up. Mahon concentrated his convoy, immediately reinforced his right flank and got his guns unlimbered and into action. He was a man of quick and decisive command. The Boers had almost as many men as he had, and also a field gun. It might have been a disaster, but by taking the detour, and now by his command of the situation, Mahon averted it. There was a fierce little action lasting three-quarters of an hour and, according to Baden Baden-Powell, the Boers 'were easily driven off'. Mahon's losses were five killed and twenty-six wounded or missing; the Boers lost at least twenty-two killed.[2] Among the most serious British casualties was Hands, the *Daily Mail* correspondent.

As the column regrouped itself, a night's march was lost; but on 15 May, just after daybreak, the vanguard sighted Plumer's tents and flag in the brown valley of the Molopo below. Plumer had arrived a few hours before.

The first message from the combined force into Mafeking was sent by Sam Weil to his brother Ben, telling him, in code, to inform Baden-Powell that they hoped to be co-operating with him from 9.0 p.m. on the next day.

Plumer had not received certain news of Mahon's column until 12 May, in a telegram from Roberts; on the 13th he had received the message from Mahon himself. On the evening of the 14th he had left Sefetili, where his force had languished for six weeks, for Jan Massibi's twenty-eight miles away. He had received considerable reinforcements of late, including 200 men of the British South

---

[1] Mahon's report to Lord Roberts, 23 May 1900. *War Office Papers*.
[2] *With Six Generals in the Boer War*, A. W. A. Pollock, p. 247.

Africa Police; but disease and sickness had been rampant and he could still only muster 800 men. The Canadians had arrived only two or three hours before Plumer struck camp. There was no transport for them, or for Plumer's other dismounted men and infantry, (which included some of the Queenslanders and men of the Rhodesia Regiment), and these had to march the distance, which they did through the night in eleven hours.

Plumer's force consisted of British South Africa Police, the Rhodesia Regiment, Queensland Mounted Infantry with fifty New Zealanders, a small party of Rhodesian Volunteers and eight guns, including the four of the Canadians. Captain Montmorency was in charge of the largest gun, and referred to those of the Canadians as 'most indifferent weapons'.

The fact that these two forces, starting from bases more than 650 miles apart, had been able to reach a rendezous at nearly the same time, having crossed almost throughout 'hostile territory' and having only had one small engagement on the way, illustrates the lack of control and determination shown by the Boers in that sector.

Mahon, being senior to Plumer, took command of the combined force.

They were eighteen miles to the west of Mafeking.

News of the attempt at relief had now reached most Boer Commandos in the area, and about 2,000 Boers had arrived and gathered under Commandant de la Rey, now the bright new hope of the Boer forces, and shortly to become Assistant-Commandant General. Mafeking had become, even for the Boers, a matter of prestige; to continue the siege or to take Baden-Powell's force was of no conceivable use to them. It was, it seems, a matter of honour. Snyman, morose and taciturn, who had made so many look so foolish, was in disgrace.

Baden Baden-Powell noted all this and, referring extremely briefly to 'the siege' in a military textbook he wrote on the campaign after the war, noted, briskly: 'The uselessness of investing places is to be noted.'[1]

One lone horseman now rode up from the south to join the force. He was Lieutenant Watson of the Kimberley Mounted Corps, who

---

[1] *War in Practice*, B. F. S. Baden-Powell (Isbister, 1903).

had been on sick leave at Cape Town when he had heard that his regiment had left for Mafeking. He had rushed back to Kimberley and, determined not to miss the relief, had somehow managed to catch up with the column, covering 220 miles in five days.

All was ready for the relief. But if Baden-Powell's orders were to detain Boers while the campaign in the south developed, and given his attitude to the Africans, why—when Mafeking still had supplies for over a month—was the relief taking place at all?[1] For if there was one time when Roberts would have needed the Boers kept occupied in the north, it was during May and June 1900, when he was attempting to clear the Transvaal. But Roberts never attached much importance to the Boers around Mafeking, as is revealed by his willingness to let Plumer mount the relief earlier in the year. Could Roberts really afford the disruption of his plans even by a force so small as Mahon's? As Hands, the wounded *Daily Mail* correspondent, wrote : 'Had Mafeking fallen it would to a certain extent have simplified the military situation, for the necessity of relieving the little town so remote from the main line of advance could not but complicate Lord Roberts's task.'[2] But this was written by Hands before Baden-Powell said what his orders had been.

Eighteen miles away, Baden-Powell was on his platform that morning as usual : whistling, surveying the distant landscape, waiting. Three days before it had looked for a moment as if he had waited too long . . .

---

[1] This may have been on Roberts's mind when he wrote his dispatch of 21 May 1900. He wrote first: 'The supplies in the town would only last until 18 May.' This was changed in Roberts's own writing to : 'He stated that supplies in the town would only last until about 18 May.' This in turn was scratched out and replaced by: 'I had previously inquired from him how he stood as regards supplies, and he informed me in reply that they would, in all probability, only last until 18 May.'

[2] *Souvenir of the Siege of Mafeking* (Mafeking, 1900).

13. A Finishing Touch

At moonrise on 11 May nearly 300 Boers crept up the bed of the Molopo River, unnoticed by the outposts of the defence. It was the route into Mafeking that young Eloff, after a careful study of the entire perimeter, had realized was tactically the best; the huts of the native village came right down to the river, and these offered further cover for penetration of the town.

Eloff did not consider Mafeking impregnable. His plan, which had been carefully worked out, was to infiltrate the area of the native village and to establish positions in it; reinforcements could then be pushed through the gap into the town itself, Baden-Powell's headquarters stormed, the defence thrown into confusion and units isolated, and surrender forced on the garrison. It was a good plan. All depended, of course, on the prompt arrival of reinforcements to take advantage of the break in the defences which Eloff hoped to establish; in view of this, Eloff had insisted that Snyman, of whom he had a poor opinion, should put his agreement to the plan in writing; Snyman had done so.

Out of the 700 Boers who should have assembled with Eloff that night for the attack, less than half appeared. Of these, forty were German and French soldiers-of-fortune under Baron von Weiss, including a formidable Frenchman, the Comte de Frémont, and guided by Trooper Hay, the deserter. Some of the French had arrived in the area only a week before, and had seen the Canadian battery for Mafeking's relief at Beira. The knowledge that a serious effort was to be made to relieve the town acted as a spur to Eloff, if not to all his compatriots; and at first, apart from the not unexpected decrease in his force, all went well for him.

It had been arranged that a feint should be staged by Snyman on the opposite side of Mafeking, and at 3.50 a.m. a half-hour of heavy rifle fire was opened on that quarter. When the firing died out, most people considered it the usual abortive demonstration and returned to sleep. It was, perhaps, only natural that the defenders were not as wary as they once had been—the investment having continued for so long without any attack by the enemy. According to Lady Sarah, the general alarm was a long time coming, not until the firing had been going on for some time;[1] according to the *Official History*, Baden-Powell sounded it immediately, suspecting that the shooting was a feint for an assault elsewhere.

Meanwhile Eloff and his men, crawling on their bellies, had reached the native huts. They began darting through them, most of the unsuspecting Africans being asleep. First one was fired, then others. Crackling flames leaped up, lighting the scene. It was the signal for Snyman that the defence had been breached; but it was a serious mistake, for it roused the garrison to the situation as well.[2] Eloff's other mistake was that he omitted to capture the two outposts which he had eluded when creeping up the Molopo; these—now aroused—covered his line of retreat, and would no doubt have something to say to the reinforcements when they came. Snyman now put down a mild shelling on the town, but was understandably reluctant to increase it in case he was firing on his own men; however the effect of such bombardment was always small, and since the departure of 'Creaky' many of the people in Mafeking had given up their shelters and had returned to their homes or normal living quarters.

Eloff's men, filtering through the native village, split into three parties. The largest section, under Eloff himself, advanced towards the nearby headquarters of the Protectorate Regiment, which had been the old police barracks, a quarter of a mile from the town. It was in that time after the setting of the moon and before the rising of the sun; it was extremely dark.

On the British side, although most people by now were aware that something was happening, few apart from the Africans, fleeing before Eloff, knew exactly what. Baden-Powell's careful arrangements for communication had proved momentarily inadequate. In

---

[1] Lady Wilson, p. 206.
[2] *Times History*, p. 594.

One hundred days of siege—the Town Guard at prayers

Baden-Powell sketching on his veranda

Africans waiting for their daily rations of horse stew and 'siege porridge' at 3*d* a pint; few could afford it every day

Starving Africans besieging Weil's store

(*Above*) A Native on trial for his
life. At the table are Lord Edward
Cecil (with black armband) and
C. G. H. Bell, the magistrate

(*Below*) The same native's death-
warrant. His crime, stealing a goat

Africans shooting dogs for food

The taking of Pretoria. Roberts saluting the flag made by
Lady Roberts, in the main square of the Boer capital on
5 June 1900

Colonel Bryan Mahon

Sisters Craufurd and
Buchan, the two brave
volunteer nurses at the
hospital and auxiliary
hospitals, where they
often came under shell-
fire

MISS CRAUFURD.

MRS. BUCHAN.

The march-past of the relief column

After Eloff's attack—
ruffianly Boers being
marched to jail by
upright Englishmen,
sketched by an artist
after the relief. On the
right are boys of the
Cadet Corps

Field-Marshal Lord
Roberts

Leaving for a world
tour *Radio Times
Hulton Picture Library*

B.-P. posing for his
photograph
*Radio Times Hulton
Picture Library*

the barracks were Colonel Hore, commanding officer of the Protectorate Regiment, with three other officers and eighteen men. Seeing men rushing towards them in the dim light, they believed they were troops of the garrison. Not until they were all but surrounded did they realize the situation and begin to fire. Hore, astounded at the sight of the enemy after seven months, somewhat promptly decided to surrender. He and his men spent the remainder of the day partaking of the accumulated stores of the regiment, opening a number of cases of whisky and wine. With them was Hamilton, who had been captured when investigating the area, not realizing the barracks was in enemy hands. Eloff had now acquired a splendid strongpoint within the defences; putting his prisoners in the storeroom, he quickly placed his men at the loopholes of the barracks and in the various outbuildings attached to it. He settled down to await Snyman's force, which would no doubt be coming upon the scene before long.

Baden-Powell, meanwhile, was attempting to find out what was taking place; it was more than half an hour since Eloff himself had set fire to the first of the native huts. Repeated telephone calls to the Protectorate Regiment headquarters produced no answer. Then the clerk of the Protectorate Regiment orderly room telephoned H.Q. and said, to the dismayed staff waiting there: 'Boers are all in among us.' Baden-Powell thought it unlikely, but on putting the telephone to his ear he heard gruff Boer voices, which convinced him soon enough.[1]

Baden-Powell realized that his key man now was Godley, who was not only in command of that whole sector of the defences but was also the most competent officer in the garrison. But he could not contact Godley right away, as the telephone line to Godley's headquarters ran through Hore's area, which was now in the hands of the Boers. A new line direct to Godley had to be run out, and this took time, particularly in the confusion still existing in the western part of the town.[2]

---

[1] Churchill interview in the *Morning Post*, 28 June 1900.
[2] In Baden-Powell's Report, and in the *Official History*, this is not mentioned, and the effect of immediate orders being transmitted by Baden-Powell to Godley is created. The *Official History* writes of 'the incredible speed' of the defensive measures.

Godley had, in fact, already taken action. Before the line had been broken he had sent a message back for the reserve squadron of the Protectorate Regiment, always kept ready to fill a breach in the defences. Under the irrepressible 'Fitz', it had arrived. The garrisons at Cannon Kopje and the brickfields were called in. Meanwhile Baden-Powell sent further reinforcements for Godley's command. When Baden-Powell finally got in touch with him, Godley was told that 'I must do my best to round up the Boers' on this anxious day'. Godley does not seem to have had many specific instructions; perhaps it was as well, for he was a quick-thinking, bold and highly trained officer, for whom Baden-Powell had considerable respect. On the telephone—the link having now been re-established—he gave Godley command of all units in the area, including reinforcements and artillery.

As the garrison rushed to and fro there was a great deal of gaiety and laughter. People seemed half-delighted and half in disbelief that something really serious was happening at last, after all those weeks of boredom and with the relief believed to be almost on hand. Weil, whose stores seemed to be comprehensive and inexhaustible, busily opened up crates and boxes and distributed firearms of all kinds to civilians. At the jail, the prisoners, including Lieutenant Murchison —charged with murder—were released and given rifles. The jailer was the only civilian killed during the day.[1]

Lady Sarah, who had been awakened by the original fusillade on the other side of the town, wrote:

To this awe-inspiring tune I dressed, by the light of a carefully shaded candle to avoid giving any mark to our foes . . . I had a sort of idea that any moment a Dutchman would look in at the door, for one could not tell from what side the real attack might be. In various stages of deshabille people were running around the house [Weil's] seeking for rifles, fowling pieces, and even sticks, as weapons of defence . . . The Cockney waiter,[2] who was such a

---

[1] Most later accounts say he was killed by shell-fire, but in the Churchill interview in the *Morning Post,* 29 June 1900, vetted by Baden-Powell, it is stated that he was shot.
[2] Several civilians in the town had military orderlies, including the doctors, nurses and the Weil household.

fund of amusement to me, had dashed off with his rifle to his redoubt, taking the keys of the house in his pocket, so no one could get into the dining-room to have coffee except through the kitchen window.

She went off to the hospital to offer her help and (as she admitted) to find security, coming under heavy fire on the way. Baillie, emerging from his *ennui* at last, wrote in his diary:

I got on the roof of a house and saw a very magnificent sight. Apparently the whole native village was on fire, and with the sunrise behind us and the village in flames in front, the combination of effects was truly magnificent, if not exactly reassuring. However nobody seemed to mind much. Our guns, followed by the Bechuanaland Rifles, hurried across the square, men laughing and joking . . .

By now Snyman's commandos had arrived beside Godley's western defences, but they made no serious attempt to get through to Eloff, contenting themselves with taking up positions and answering Godley's fire. As they did not assault, Fitzclarence and his squadron were sent back again into reserve.

Three hours after the attack began, at 8.30 a.m., Baden-Powell was aware of the situation of the three Boer groups inside the perimeter, and he moved his troops so as to cut them off from each other and the outside.

In the barracks, Eloff was still waiting for Snyman's promised support. Fierce rifle firing was kept up all morning (although the British contrived to partake of breakfast as usual). Inside the buildings the situation was desperate. The Boers had no food and no water. They had many wounded. One of the prisoners, the veterinary surgeon of the Protectorate Regiment, tended to them. Liquid nourishment was found in the Officers' Mess, and one of the Frenchmen was unwise enough to take a bottle of burgundy on to the roof and engage the British riflemen in badinage: he was shot in the stomach. The officers' quarters were thoroughly looted. Trooper Hay was swaggering about with his former colonel's sword and belt strapped on him. Bullets, coming in through the windows, flew about in all the rooms. Throughout the heaviest firing, the Comte de Frémont, well fortified with wine, played chansonettes on the piano.

Hamilton described Eloff, 'chatting brightly to the prisoners and sympathizing upon the fortune of war. He sat within the door upon a case of burgundy, his legs dangling, his accoutrements jingling, and his spurs echoing the tick-tack of the Mauser rifles . . . within our presence the drama was slowly passing; orderlies came and went, but the commandant, still tapping with his spurs, continued to issue his instructions and his orders. He seemed to possess the complete mastery of the situation; his buoyant face was impressed with the confidence of youth . . . At times he lost control of himself and complained querulously, in Dutch, about the non-appearance of his reinforcements; at other moments he regaled the prisoners with scraps of information.' Hamilton, always the professional, chatted with Eloff and then asked him whether, should things go well for the Boers, he could have permission to communicate with *The Times*.

Snyman had decided not to press an attack. When one of his Field-Cornets begged him to storm the town, he muttered: 'Tomorrow is another day.' If Eloff and his men were taken prisoner, it would not only help Snyman's patient plan to starve out the garrison, but it would also place the brash young man out of the Commandant's way and perhaps teach him a lesson, too. It was the crucial decision of the day, although it may have been too late anyway for Eloff's initiative to be successfully followed up.[1]

Godley now had the situation entirely under control. Having ordered a thorough reconnaissance, he surrounded one of the Boer groups, twenty-seven strong, which had been sheltering in a ruined cattle yard about a third of a mile from the barracks. Three squadrons of the Protectorate Regiment encircled it and the Boers were called upon to surrender. They refused. But when the place was charged by many Africans who had come upon the scene, as well as by the troops, the Boers quickly raised the white flag. Some difficulty was encountered in preventing the Africans from slaughtering all the prisoners, and Captain F. C. Marsh, of the Protectorate Regi-

[1] When President Kruger was told of Snyman's decision, he asked to be informed whether the Commandant had been drunk.

ment, was mentioned in dispatches for 'great personal gallantry' in interposing himself between Africans and Boers. It had been the Africans who had directed Marsh's squadron to the position. It was not their only aid during the day. A party of them captured a dugout which had been taken by the Boers, and successfully defended it, losing four killed; another party cornered a group of Boers endeavouring to slip away from the town, and forced them to surrender; other parties occupied positions on the river bank, which they held all day under heavy fire, thus preventing Boers getting in or out of the town by that route or from getting water. The Africans, in fact, played a part only just second to that of the four squadrons of the Protectorate Regiment during the fight.[1]

Godley now concentrated his attention on another Boer position —a stony hillock, where the Boers had also refused to surrender. Six rounds of shrapnel were fired at it, and the Boers fled towards the Molopo, intending to get out of the perimeter by the same route as they had used to come in. But Godley had been prepared for this, and Lord Charles Bentinck, with a troop of the Protectorate Regiment, was waiting for them. But Bentinck received an order from Baden-Powell to let the Boers go; he was no doubt conscious of the effect of prisoners on his food supplies, and now thankfully confident that no help was coming to Eloff.

Only the police barracks remained in Boer hands. Many of the Boer defenders, to Eloff's disgust, had left and scattered in attempts to get out of the town. Only seventy-three exhausted and thirsty men remained to him by the late afternoon. Now much use was made of the white flag to enable Nurse Craufurd, at her women's and children's hospital, which was near the fort, to receive the Boer wounded. Miss Craufurd had no experience of dressing wounds, having tended only fever cases or been on night duty when at the main hospital, but she did what she could, helped for some of the time by her sister, Mrs. Buchan. The little cottage became a battle dressing-station, with dying men, and an amputation taking place on a table. She even visited the British prisoners in the barracks, twice taking them tea, and did her best to encourage them. This remarkably courageous woman found herself under fire several times, and at length a truce

[1] *General Orders,* May, 1900: several Africans were mentioned by name.

was arranged so that she and her patients could be transferred to the main hospital, farther from the scene of action. Neilly wrote of the two sisters: 'These ladies were the heroines of the siege.'[1]

It was getting dark. 'Through the grating of the windows,' Hamilton wrote, 'we could see them scurrying and scrambling to defend the points against which the firing was heaviest; we saw the limping figures of the wounded; on one occasion the door opened suddenly and three wounded Boers precipitated themselves violently into the room. The inside of the building was pitch dark by now, and lighted only by the fitful flashes of the rifles'.

At about 6.0 p.m. Eloff, accepting that he had been betrayed, went to Hore and offered him his surrender. The astonished Hore, who had very little idea of the general situation in the town, had difficulty in communicating the surrender to those outside. Eventually he flung open the door and bellowed the order to cease fire.

The Boers had lost their first real chance of taking the town twelve hours earlier, when their attack, so successful at first, had not been pressed home. 'I must confess,' wrote Neilly, 'that Eloff and his comrades carried out their work brilliantly, and if they had been supported Mafeking must have fallen after a good deal of bloodshed.' Their casualties were 59 killed and wounded and 108 prisoners, according to Baden-Powell; 36 killed and wounded according to the *Times History,* drawing on Boer sources (Baden-Powell's figure included 30 casualties whom he said were taken back by the Boers).[2] The prisoners were the first that had been taken during the entire investment, which that day was exactly seven months old. British casualties were four killed and ten wounded, and African casualties were eighteen; the half-starved Africans had taken a prominent part throughout.

---

[1] They were both mentioned in dispatches.
[2] A *General Order* posted that night, and signed by Cecil, gave the Boer prisoners as 25; a *General Order* the following day, after an opportunity for a proper count, gave prisoners as 108 and killed as 50. The *Mafeking Mail* gave a full and accurate account of the whole affair, and was banned in its entirety by Baden-Powell; it was eventually issued when Baden-Powell left the town in June. The *Mafeking Mail* gave the Boer losses as 10 known killed, 19 known wounded, with others being taken away by the Boers: about 50 altogether. At least 17 French were captured.

The defenders were jubilant. The prisoners, on being marched to the jail and the Masonic Hall, were assailed by groans and hootings from a mob of whites and blacks. 'Rule, Britannia!' and the National Anthem were sung all around the defences. In the hospital, the patients sat up and cheered and clapped. Baillie wrote that night : 'It is a good thing to be an Englishman. These foreigners start too quick and finish quicker. They are good men, but we are better, and have proved so for several hundred years. I had always wanted to see the Englishman fight in a tight hole, and I know what he is worth now. He can outstay the other chap.'

Eloff and his officers were invited to dinner by Baden-Powell and the staff. A pleasant evening was spent. Baron von Weiss spoke to Baden-Powell about a pressing personal problem : he was on leave from the German Army, and his leave was shortly up; he was apprehensive that if he was late back to his unit he might get into serious trouble. Baden-Powell indicated an understandable lack of interest. After dinner the Boer officers were escorted to Weil's house, the best in Mafeking, where they breakfasted with Lady Sarah the following morning. The Frenchmen said that they had enjoyed the fight, but they objected to the food which they were being served. Eloff himself is reported to have washed his hands in 'siege porridge', mistaking it for soap and water.[1] Baden-Powell offered to accept food from the Boer camp for the prisoners. An idea occured to him for getting 'The Boy' McLaren into Mafeking at last; he told Snyman that if 'The Boy' accompanied the supplies he could guarantee that they would be taken straight to Eloff.[2] Snyman was not anxious to comply, no doubt in the belief that Eloff would contribute better to an end of the affair by eating the Englishmen's almost magically extended rations than by fighting in their lines.

Throughout the day Baden-Powell had been cool and calm, even during the early hours of confusion. But the successful ending of the Boer resistance was due to the intelligent measures employed by Godley.

Baden-Powell had sent his usual daily letter out to 'The Boy'

---

[1] *The Last of the Gentlemen's Wars*, J. F. C. Fuller (Faber, 1937), p. 69.
[2] Letter to Snyman, 15 May 1900. *Weil Papers*.

McLaren in the thick of the fighting. He claimed that this was one of his ploys to confuse and discourage the Boers. He declared that after reading it the Boers waiting outside the town returned 'sullenly to their camps'. In the letter he said he hoped the wounded McLaren had not been too disturbed by the heavy firing during the night, but that a Boer attack had completely failed ('scuppered the lot', as he said, which was not perhaps the easiest way of communicating with Boers who did not speak colloquial English), and not forgetting to ask whether he required books or clean pyjamas.

The next day (apparently before a full count of prisoners) Baden-Powell wrote to Snyman, his most regular correspondent: 'I have the honour to inform you that in the fight yesterday a number of your burghers were killed and wounded, and that I have ninety prisoners . . . In conclusion, I should like to record my admiration of the gallant way in which your burghers fought yesterday.' It was, indeed, the last of the gentlemen's wars.

On 14 May the *Mafeking Mail* stated in its editorial: 'Today we start on the eighth month of siege. The time . . . does not seem to have passed so badly, although the awful monotony was sometimes irksome in the extreme.'

It seemed impossible that the Boers would now mount another assault on the town. The defenders of Mafeking slept with more happy contentment than they had known since the war had begun. The relief could not be far away, and soon all would be over. 'It gives a pleasant finish to the siege,' wrote Baillie of Eloff's raid, mindful of the long months of unwarlike inactivity. 'It wanted just a finishing touch to make it satisfactory.'

14. The Relief of Mafeking

At dawn on 16 May, 1900, the combined relief column rose, fed, struck camp and moved off to do battle for the relief of Mafeking. All were filled with excitement and with a sense of occasion.

The force was under the command of Mahon, whose colonelcy was senior to that of Plumer. Lieutenant-Colonel A. H. M. Edwards took over command of the 'flying column' from Barkly West.[1] Mahon was hampered by the convoy of wagons, which had enabled the 'flying column' to reach its present position with such speed. He did not have sufficient men to protect it and to execute a turning movement and a feint. He therefore wisely decided to approach the town straight up the river, from the west, from the same direction as Eloff had penetrated Baden-Powell's defences.

After dispatching a pigeon to Baden-Powell (which does not seem to have reached its destination), Mahon ordered the advance. His force was astride the river, with at first more on the north bank than the south. The way was over a succession of ridges, at right angles to the river; each had to be reconnoitred and then taken. At first there was no opposition. Behind the force, moving forward in line, the wagons that had not been left at Massibi's crashed their way over the trackless bush, followed by the herds of livestock driven on by Africans.

Snyman had recently lost such authority as he had ever had. Nevertheless it had been decided that an attempt would be made to beat off the relief column, a decision that was only explicable through wounded Boer pride; news of Eloff's bold failure was now general knowledge among the Boers. Commandant de la Rey had about two thousand men around Mafeking; nearly all these were preparing

---

[1] Later Major-General Sir Alfred Edwards.

to face Mahon, having come from the main Boer camps on the other, eastern, side of the town—thus leaving that area open.[1] De la Rey, who already had a considerable reputation, had, in fact, placed almost his entire force, with its artillery, between Mahon and Baden-Powell, who together outnumbered him. This could only indicate rashness bordering on irresponsibility, an incorrect assessment of the state of the defenders of Mafeking which could hardly have been borne out by the resistance recently shown to Eloff, or contempt for the offensive spirit of Baden-Powell. He spread his force out in a semi-circle, with his strength on either wing

After moving slowly but steadily forward for six hours, Mahon's force halted for water and a meal. It was at this time that, from certain high positions, Mafeking was first sighted. Young recorded that someone shouted : ' "There's Mafeking!" There was a rush for the coign of vantage and a great levelling of glasses. There it lay, sure enough, the little town that we had come so far to see—a tiny cluster of white near the eastward horizon, glistening amid the yellowish-brown of the flats. We looked at it for a few moments in silence, and then Colonel Mahon said : "Well, let's be getting on." '

Plumer's column became heavily engaged at a farm which was held by Boer riflemen, artillery and a machine-gun. He suffered casualties and was held up for some time. Eventually the place was taken by a rush on foot.

The crucial point of the advance was reached when de la Rey, who had all the while been fanning out his wings, struck inwards in order to encircle Mahon's entire force, at the same time putting down a heavy shrapnel, shell and rifle fire on both Mahon's flanks. It was the almost inevitable Boer tactic, and Mahon had been expecting it. He had kept some of his best troops, the Kimberley Mounted Corps, under Lieutenant-Colonel Peakman, as a rearguard. Thus when the Boers came pouring round the back of the British column, many of them even reaching the Molopo, they were met with such heavy and ferocious fire that they soon dispersed and made off. All the way from Barkly West Mahon had hardly made a mistake. He wrote in his dispatch : 'As I had to strengthen both my flank and rear guards at the same time I continued my advance on Mafeking

---

[1] Mahon's *Report* to Roberts, 23 May 1900, P.R.O.

slowly, the Boers retiring from our front and keeping up with us on the flanks . . . I attribute the smallness of our casualties to our very wide front and loose formation.'

Despite de la Rey's presence, the Boer attempt at encirclement had been 'far from venturesome',[1] and during the entire course of the action the British force kept on the move. Towards the end of the afternoon Edwards gained control of high ground commanding the Boer flank and gave chase to the enemy. The Boers disappeared from the field.

It appeared that the way was open to Mafeking. But the 'Mahout', conscious of the eyes of the world being fixed upon him, and with his reputation at stake, had no intention of rushing blindly forward. He was about to demonstrate the kind of commander he was. He collected his force together seven miles from Mafeking and ordered a rest till dawn. At the same time he sent out patrols, in the dusk, to reconnoitre the road into the town.

*

In Mafeking itself there had been a day of ill-concealed expectation. Since mid-day the rooftops had been crowded with sightseers watching the shell-bursts over the hills. Higher than anyone else was the Colonel Commanding himself, on a lookout which had been especially constructed on the roof of the railway sheds—the highest rooftop in Mafeking—which was reached by a climb up a long ladder. When nothing had happened, many people had gone away for lunch, or to see the final of the billiards tournament.

About 4.0 p.m. a heliograph had been seen flickering through the bright light and spelling out: *'How are you getting on?'* From the town went out the answer: *'Welcome.'*

Baden-Powell had prepared a 'Field Force' with one gun, under Walford. It was to be ready to take part in the action, and to assist Mahon's advance. Baden-Powell's handling of this force was not vigorous. He had ordered it to parade at 1.0 p.m., having seen the Boers moving towards the Molopo; 'But as there seemed no result from the Boer activity I let them fall out.' But, first, a carefully-posed

---

[1] *Official History*, p. 183.

group photograph was taken. From about 3.0 p.m. Baden-Powell had been able to see the fight going on from his lookout. 'The fight gradually moved towards Mafeking so, calling up the field force, I took it out . . and sent a few shells in the enemy's direction to create some sort of diversion.'[1] In his dispatch after the siege, Vere Stent wrote : 'One or two persons in the town thought he was not doing as much as he might to hurry on the relief.' Unlike some of Hamilton's critical comments, this one—from Reuters' man—appeared in *The Times,* no doubt because press censorship was relaxed after the siege.

The horses of the Protectorate Regiment that had not gone into the cooking pot were in good condition. The Army veterinary surgeon attached to the regiment had reported their health as 'satisfactory' in April, and of their forage he said : 'Quality good. Compressed hay very satisfactory ration.'[2] Had Baden-Powell thought it wise, therefore, two or three squadrons of the Protectorate Regiment could have gone out to attack de la Rey in the rear, and perhaps have inflicted a major defeat. (In his important interview afterwards, Churchill questioned Baden-Powell on this point : 'He said he tried to organize a field force to help the relieving column to come in, but the men could scarcely walk; still, they went out and fired off their guns in the enemy's rear, which, though not within range, perhaps disconcerted them.')

That evening a messenger arrived from Mahon to say he was camping outside and that he would attempt to enter the town the following morning.

One of Mahon's patrols, under 'Karri' Davies, the hero of the Jameson Raid, finding no opposition, decided to go on. It entered the town at about 7.0 p.m. that night, and the first people it met took little notice of it. But when Davies and his ten men of the Imperial Light Horse arrived before Baden-Powell's headquarters a small crowd of twenty or so people assembled around them and provided an exuberant welcome. The fact that men of the same regiment had been the first into Ladysmith was considered very apt. Davies and his patrol, standing holding their horses, joined in the singing of 'Rule, Britannia!'

---

[1] *Staff Diary,* 16 May 1900.
[2] Report of Lieutenant Dunlop-Smith, Army Veterinary Department, *Weil Papers.*

After this Baden-Powell went to bed.

*

At 11.0 p.m. Mahon ordered his force to be roused. At 12.30 a.m. in bright moonlight, it was on the move again. Its orders : to march on Mafeking.

Peakman, who had so ably protected the rear the previous afternoon, now had the honour of leading the column. Among the correspondents there was a race to get into the town first, but the troops themselves, weary and surprised, moved forward in good order. They began arriving in the town at 3.30 a.m.. They gathered at the polo ground and set up camp.

Baden-Powell's arrangements for sentries and patrols do not appear to have been good at this time He was awoken by a shake on the shoulder from one of the relief force itself : his brother. He thereupon leapt out of bed and joined Mahon and Plumer on the defences of the town in time for a cup of hot cocoa.

*

When the sun rose that morning the Boer outposts to the east of the town, where the main Boer force had retired, were astounded to find the relief force encamped within the defences. Snyman had sent a message to Pretoria at 9.30 that night saying that the relief column had been checked.

General Orders of that morning, 17 May, announced : 'Colonel Baden-Powell assumes command today of the forces assembled in Mafeking.' There followed generous praise to both Mahon and Plumer. Mahon appears to have given up interest in the proceedings on having successfully completed his mission. Baden-Powell, asserting his authority, got Godley to mount a bombardment on the Boer camps and positions with all available artillery. Having just been relieved, it would not be good to be invested again. Among the batteries which went out that fine, sunny morning were the apparently inexhaustible Canadians. It was later said that their entire performance would 'remain one of the proudest traditions of Canadian arms'.[1] Baden-Powell had ordered the relief column to

---

[1] *The Canadian Contingents and Canadian Imperialism*, W. S. Evans.

parade at 8.30 a.m. to help in chasing off the Boer force, but then changed his mind 'as the Boer was so quiet I presumed he meant to stay for the day'.[1] But seeing the Boers beginning to move off after all, he once again changed his orders and called out the confused troops. Few of them were needed as the Boers were already on their way, and once the shelling began they 'made off for the Transvaal as hard as they could go'. The armoured train went out, and at last was able to 'take' Game Tree Fort, where the Union Jack was raised.

As the Boers disappeared in a great cloud of risen dust, Baden-Powell decided not to give chase; his own men were listless, the relief force was tired. Not one British soldier followed the Boers into the Transvaal.

In the town there was considerable and natural excitement and emotion, with people walking about and talking gaily in small groups.

Two other brothers who met were the Godleys. Dick had been badly wounded in Mahon's advance the previous day, and his brother found him lying on a wagon. He had him brought to his dug-out, and later to the convent, where beds had been prepared for the relief column's casualties. Dick Godley's first meal in the town was 'siege bread', minced horsemeat and brandy and soda. In the afternoon most of the civilian population went over to the Boer lines, where a great deal of debris had been left behind, including some welcome food supplies; civilians and troops rummaged among the litter for souvenirs. Baden-Powell had a happy reunion with 'The Boy' Mc-Laren, whom the Boers had left with one other prisoner.

What most affected those who had been invested was the sight, after seven months, of completely strange faces and new listeners to talk to. What fascinated the new arrivals most was the impressive scope and sophistication of the defence-works and diggings, the amount of damage to houses and buildings by shell-fire as compared to the small number of casualties from the same source, and the evident absence of starvation among the Europeans. It was not at all what any of them had expected. Feelings of anticlimax, even of irritation, began to be felt. The afternoon and evening were spent in

---

[1] *Staff Diary*, 17 May 1900.

relaxation and, as Neilly put it, in the search 'for the wherewithal to fittingly celebrate the occasion'.

Two hundred and seventeen days : it had been the longest and most stultifying bore that any of the garrison and citizens of Mafeking could conceive of.

*

Next day the relief force was officially received in the town. It marched into Mafeking, proud and emotional, to stirring and patriotic music from the band. Every man, woman and child, white and black, formed up in the street to cheer. The Town Guard lined the route.

Baden-Powell was not on the stand to receive the column, for he, with Mahon, was riding proudly at its head. It was received by the Mayor, Mr Whiteley, who read an address.

There was a Thanksgiving Service, with the troops parading on three sides of a square on open ground beside the cemetery. The Last Post was sounded and three shots fired over the graves of the fallen—a salute which had not been given before in order to avoid unnecessarily alarming the Boers or the garrison. Hamilton described the scene : 'As the Colonel stood before us—the man who reaped the glory of the siege—we wondered whether beneath the calmness of his demeanour there lurked any feeling of regret, any half-cherished desire to express aloud to those who stood around him the potency of his sorrows. To him it was but the simple ceremony, and one, more-over, to be got through quickly, and indeed there was but little in the service. Occasionally the breeze which sighed so tremulously through the hedge of trees that fringe the graveyard wafted to us snatches of prayer . . . The Colonel Commanding reviewed the remnants of his force, unbending in so much that he addressed to each unit a few words of appreciation and of thanks.'

One observer remarked on the shabby appearance of Plumer's Rhodesia Regiment, its men in ragged and assorted articles of uniform. They were to depart almost immediately to help in establishing the rail link to Bulawayo. This caused some discontent, for Plumer's troops considered that if anyone needed a rest it was they. They had been unimpressed by the condition of the garrison, who seemed well-fed enough, as compared to their own; like the defenders of Mafeking, they had been on continuous active service since the start of the war, but they had experienced much greater rigours. After giving this order, which was not well received, Baden-Powell issued, on the 24th, an effusive congratulatory statement (he had already made one) on the performance of Plumer's men.[1] This does not seem to have had the required effect. With some asperity, Montmorency wrote: 'For seven months I had pigged it in the veld and the sensation of eating at a table and drinking out of a glass once more was joy ... To me the whole affair of the siege was at the time, and has always been, an enigma: what in the world was the use of defending this wretched railway-siding and these tin shanties? To burrow underground on the very first shot being fired in a campaign, and to commence eating his horses, seemed to me the strangest role ever played by a cavalry leader with his regiment of mounted men; by so doing, the action was fettered of useful troops which, had their mobility been preserved, might have been better employed, as Plumer's force had been, in patrolling frontiers, in making raids into the Transvaal and in harassing the enemy. The defence of Mafeking also imposed on the commander-in-chief of the forces in South Africa the necessity for detaching a column, hazarding it in a dangerous march—"up in the air", as the strategists say—exposed to flank attacks for the best part of two hundred and fifty miles, all for the purpose of avoiding the loss of prestige to our flag which the surrender of this not very important garrison might have involved.'

On arrival, the relief force had been—rather to its surprise—supplied by the town.[2] There were, in fact, sufficient supplies for several weeks. Although horsemeat (the greatest hardship) had been much used towards the end, beef had also been issued to whites about thrice a week, and fresh vegetables, tinned milk, 'siege bread', sugar, brawn, coffee and cocoa had all been available, although rationed. A huge stock of tinned beef had been kept in reserve and was still largely untouched. Since the departure of many Africans, their plight, too, had been partly eased. Mahon soon brought into town his five wagon-loads of provisions and stores, plus seventeen bags of flour

[1] Rhodes was pleased about the recognition of Rhodesian men and supplies by 'Powell' (Milner Papers, 26 May 1900).
[2] Life of an Irish Soldier, Sir A. Godley, p. 83.

and eighty-one head of cattle which were captured on the march, and 200 cattle and 1,000 sheep came up from Vryburg[1]. Thirteen wagons of supplies had been left by Plumer at Massibi's, and these were now brought in. But before they arrived Plumer and his force had already left the town, two days after its arrival. They were in bitter mood. 'I have never known,' wrote Montmorency, 'men so sulky or march with such bad grace.' Perhaps the sorest point of all was that it was known that a large quantity of mail was on its way to Mafeking, having been accumulated in recent weeks until the relief. For Plumer's force there was no mail.

On the way to Ramathlabama, Plumer's column came across the skeleton of Frank Milligan, the county cricketer who had been presumed killed in the sortie from Sefetili to Ramathlabama. A hand was uplifted, as though to shield the eyes from the sun . . . On 20 May Plumer's column, dispirited but proud, took the important Transvaal post of Zeerust. On 25 May they moved to Ramathlabama.

News of the relief had spread first to those closely concerned, as to wildlife before a forest fire. Frank Rhodes had informed Milner : 'Relieved Mafeking. Husbands safe.' The husbands in question were Lord Edward Cecil and Lord Charles Cavendish-Bentinck, whose wives still passed the days at Rhodes's mansion near Cape Town. Lady Violet Cecil's reaction was untypical. 'I was so upset by the news, good news being unusual, that I went to bed with a headache.' Milner, her great friend throughout the months of siege, hardly permitted himself to believe the news : 'It would be grand, grand, grand . . . There is nothing at all that I can say to you. I think you know what I should like to say. God ever bless you and give you all good and don't write. It is not a day for writing. Yours affectionately. A.M.'[2]

While Milner and Roberts waited for the news to be definitely confirmed, the newspapermen were blocking the cable lines with news that had set alight the western world.

*

In Britain, what had begun on Friday 18 May as an expression of

---

[1] Mahon's *Report*, 23 May 1900. Mahon's remaining 47 wagons were presumably left at Massibi's.
[2] *Milner Papers*, 18 May 1900.

relief from an anxiety which few had even been able to express became, as the week ended, a great national spree: the first occasion
on which the mass of the population had ever broken free from the
bonds of Victorian respectability. For some years those bonds had
been becoming increasingly loose, and in private they frequently had
been broken; now they had burst asunder. The legend—beloved by
themselves—that the British were a race of laconic, level-headed, stiff-
upper-lipped people not given to emotion, typified by the Duke of
Wellington, was about to be badly damaged. It seemed that reticence
had only been a characteristic of the upper class, and it was from that
class that the discontent at the continuation of Friday's orgy of emotion first came, although there was to be discontent among sections of
the working classes, too, but for different reasons. Meanwhile the
majority of the population made it clear that they had a great deal
more cheering and exulting to do; and as they realized that nothing
untoward was to happen to them for their lack of discipline, so their
confidence increased. On Saturday the crowd began to taste power.

Few, if any, firms had declared a holiday for Saturday, and there
was no official guide whatever. The Government, indeed, had still
not announced that Mafeking had been relieved. *The Times* reported
that 'by common consent a public holiday had arranged itself'.
Throughout the nation, factory gates opened but few people passed
through them. Offices remained closed. One bemused Financial
Correspondent in London wrote, in a tone of some reproof, 'hardly
any attempt was made to do business of any kind today in the City,
which was filled with an enthusiastic crowd, cheering and waving
flags and blowing horns . . . In the Stock Exchange both members
and clerks appeared quite unable to bring their minds down to business, and they accordingly gave themselves up to all kinds of hilarity.
Members shook hands, sang patriotic songs and, finally, all uncover-
ing, sang with much fervour the National Anthem.'[1]

The hard core of the crowd had not dispersed during the night,
and it was joined by a mass of commuters from the suburbs, many
of whom had travelled up much earlier than usual. By 10.0 a.m.
all traffic was again at a halt in the centre of the City, and there was
little traffic moving in the West End. Buildings were decorated in

[1] *The Times*, 21 May 1900.

banners and bunting of red, white and blue. Young women sat on the roofs of hansom cabs waving flags. Large pictures of Baden-Powell, cut from magazines, were pasted to windows. Even nature seemed to be rejoicing: suddenly it was warm with bright sunshine everywhere.

The Times that morning said: 'From a patriotic point of view, the spectacle presented by seven months of suffering and struggle has fired the spirit of the nation beyond all former precedent. The demonstration in London was unparalleled in recent times. There has been nothing like the defence of Mafeking in modern history.'

Of the scene in central London on Saturday, an eye-witness wrote:

White-haired old ladies were to be seen carrying a large Union Jack in each hand, and young women had colours pinned across from shoulder to shoulder. Sober-looking young men in spectacles stood at street corners blowing tin trumpets with all their might. In the city and the suburbs scenes were witnessed which have never been seen before in the history of this country. Well-dressed young women of usually proper demeanour traversed the roadways, arm-in-arm, six abreast, carrying flags and occasionally bursting into song. There was a singular absence of any official stimulus. Whitehall displayed never a flag . . . The American flag was frequently to be seen, in carriages in the Park, in Piccadilly, and at every American establishment that one noticed. In Fleet Street a gentleman of slim build and matter-of-fact demeanour, evidently from the United States, having burdened himself with more star-spangled banners than he could attach to his hat, shoulders, coat and trousers, unfolded a large umbrella and fastened to it the remainder of his stock . . . and walked thus up the street with perfect composure in a great halo of colour.[1]

A banner was hung across the house of Baden-Powell's mother near Hyde Park Corner. On it was written just one word—MAFEKING. A large portrait of Baden-Powell was also displayed, and on each side of it a bill-poster of a newspaper of the previous evening: 'Three Cheers For Baden-Powell'.

---

[1] *The Times*, 21 May 1900.

In the Victoria and Albert Docks there was only one foreign ship, a French vessel. Dockers threatened not to return to work on it unless it, like all others, was beflagged. The ship's captain complied. There was a remarkable scene in the Great Hall of Euston Station. The entire clerical staff of the London and North-Western Railway at Euston appeared on the gallery and descended into the magnificent and famous hall singing the National Anthem. Upwards of a thousand people were assembled, and the excitement was tremendous. At St. Paul's Cathedral there was a special Service of Thanksgiving. In his sermon the Dean said: 'It has been proved once again that the breed of Englishmen is what it used to be, in its traditional tenacity, its stubborn pluck, and its refusal to know when it is beaten.' He commented on the courageous, uncomplaining tone of Baden-Powell's communiqués. At the close of the sermon the hymn 'Now thank we all our God' was sung, and after the Benediction had been pronounced the congregation joined in singing the National Anthem.

A poem by the Poet Laureate, Alfred Austin, in honour of the event, was published that morning. It was written after the style of Drayton's 'The Battle of Agincourt', first published in 1627:

> Hemmed in for half a year,
> Still with no succour near,
> Nor word of hope to cheer
>   Wounded and dying.
> Fevered, and foiled of sleep,
> By the fierce cannons leap
> They still, still vowed to keep
>   England's Flag flying . . .

As the day went on the heat of patriotism here and there flared into something else. In Wales there was alarm when miners took the day off and marched up and down the valleys defiantly singing; in Abergele one man died of excitement. Elsewhere there was violence and intolerance. At Harlesden an attack was made by a large body of youths on the shop of a local greengrocer 'said to have pro-Boer sympathies'. Windows were smashed, 'and there was a great disturbance. Police were summoned and they charged the crowd amid a shower of rotten eggs'; several arrests were made and 'further disturbances were expected'. In Birmingham crowds did not show signs of dispersing from the streets from Friday night until well into Sunday morning. The Chief Constable of Birmingham published a request through the newspapers that the public should keep their festivities within reasonable bounds. At Dover there was serious rioting which started at the house of a certain Mr Brown, who was believed to have Boer sympathies. It lasted until nearly 2.0 a.m. on Sunday morning, and at length several hundred troops were called out from Dover Castle to restore order. For the most part, however, 'the police, with admirable good-temper and discretion, adapted their procedure to the occasion'. At many places effigies of Kruger, President of the Transvaal, were ceremoniously burned.

At Hatfield House, home of the Prime Minister, the scenes of rejoicing had an added incentive, because of Lord Edward Cecil having been at the siege. The Prime Minister's daughter wrote in a letter:

There has never been anything like it in our memory . . . The contrast of this exuberant intoxication of delight and the stiff-lipped silence while the strain lasted is very striking . . . Informal crowds came up to the house here on Friday, and they had a great elaborate demonstration yesterday . . . the result was wonderful, even my father was impressed. Several scores of the inhabitants of Hatfield dressed themselves up as soldiers, sailors, nurses, heaven knows what, arranged in symbolical groups with horses and cars and properties of all kinds, and marched through the Parish by night with torches, flags, and bands playing . . . with the mass of torches in front of the old house, and the shouting, cheering crowd it was really quite thrilling![1]

There had been a good deal of criticism of the war as a whole, as well as of the military commanders' conduct of it. Among politicians who had been critical of it were Sir Henry Campbell-Bannerman, Sir William Harcourt (who had denounced the war as 'unjust and engineered'), John Morley and a fiery young man named Lloyd George. But this was no time for criticism or doubts. Nevertheless, here and there, small but determined voices of dissent insisted on

---

[1] 25 May 1900, Viscountess Milner, p. 195.

being heard. Some brave socialists of Aberdeen held a 'Stop The War' meeting at a public hall. For four hours there was rioting outside, with those present in the hall unable to get away. The Gordon Highlanders were marched from Castle Hill Barracks to restore order.

The Times, which for years had considered itself the national recorder for posterity of all events, found these affairs too much for its traditional detachment. There was an unusually frivolous air in some of its reports, puzzlement in others. In its editorials it struggled to make sense of it all. For two days, Saturday and Monday, the top leader, or editorial, of comment was devoted to the subject—an almost unprecedented distinction for a military event; on Monday the second leader was also about the subject; on the fourth day the subject was dropped to the second leader alone.

No news in recent times has caused more intense excitement . . . it is instinctively felt that in Mafeking we have the common-man of the Empire, the fundamental stuff of which it is built, with his back to the wall, fighting an apparently hopeless battle without ever losing hope, facing overwhelming odds without a thought of surrender, bearing the extremity of privation without complaint, holding his courage high in spite of deadly physical weakness and disease, and at the long last coming out proud, tenacious, unconquered, and unconquerable . . . We have here the demonstration of the fundamental grit of the breed, the unanalysable qualities that have made the Empire, in spite of foolish politicians and blundering generals and the secular ineptitude of officials . . . With the aid of his brave subordinates Baden-Powell has saved the isolated British station, which the folly, the neglect, and the ignorance of others had endangered.

This last was a reference to a recent controversy about the preparations for the defence. According to the press it seemed that the military authorities in the Cape had given little if any encouragement to the intrepid colonel in his initial efforts to secure the town. There was a feeling that a grave scandal had been hushed up in case Mafeking had fallen. In any event, however, it was clear that without the determination of Baden-Powell the authorities would have had much to answer for. But lost somewhere among all the many hundreds of words of comment and praise in the most respected newspaper in the world was one remarkable sentence : 'From the point of view of military strategy it was probably a gross blunder to defend Mafeking at all.' This, as could be mistaken by no reader that day, was a reference to the 'blundering generals', not to anyone else. But still . . .

On Saturday night Baden-Powell's mother, and some close relatives, chose to visit the Alhambra Theatre. They sat in a decorated box and were the cause of a near-riot. Mrs Baden-Powell graciously acknowledged the applause and salutes of the audience, who repeatedly disrupted the performance to sing and cheer. At the Hippodrome, where there was 'An Entertainment of an Unprecedented Type : a Rising and Sinking Arena and Stage : Illumination of 100,000 Gallons of Water : 21 Fully-grown Forest-bred Lions'—several thousand copies of Baden-Powell's picture were distributed. At the Hotel Metropole, the guests for dinner were presented with Mafeking menus, printed on khaki paper with a photograph of Colonel Baden-Powell. On sale, and obviously long-prepared, were 'New National Medals to commemorate the heroic defence. Fine portrait of the gallant Colonel. Silver. 2s. 6d.'

On Saturday the Queen went on a visit to Wellington College. The little grey figure was greeted on the road by 'immense' crowds. The Queen noted in her diary that her people ran 'quite close to the carriage, cheered loudly, and finally sang "God Save the Queen". Flags were hung up and pictures of General Baden-Powell exhibited in honour of the relief. The people are quite mad with delight, and London is said to be indescribable'. A huge arch had been put over the road, with the words 'Welcome to the Queen of Mafeking'.

More and more in the later years of the century the British people had come to associate the many good fortunes that had befallen them since her reign had begun with the matronly mother-Empress herself.

The great Queen sent a telegram to Baden-Powell : 'I and my whole Empire greatly rejoice at the relief of Mafeking after the splendid defence made by you through all these months. I heartily congratulate you and all under you, military and civil, British and native, for the heroism and devotion you have shown——VICTORIA REGINA ET IMPERATRIX.' ('Drafted by herself at the dinner-table,' Baden-Powell later said.)

At Windsor that night the Queen and the Court witnessed a torchlight procession and demonstration in the quadrangle of Windsor Castle. The procession wound its way through the streets of Windsor and Eton, preceded by the Mayor in a motor-car, with the band of the 1st Life Guards, a number of other bands, and the drums and fifes of the 1st Grenadier Guards. The largest local crowds in memory lined the streets and church bells rang. Two thousand torch-bearing troops and borough officials passed under the entrance to the castle as the Life Guards played 'Soldiers of the Queen'. A newspaper reporter wrote: 'The scene at that moment was extremely picturesque, the numerous torches lighting up the castle precincts while the sky above the town was reddened by fire. When the last strains of the National Anthem had died away, the Mayor of Windsor stood forth and called for three cheers for the Queen. The response was most enthusiastic, the applause being continued for several minutes. The Queen subsequently sent for the Mayor, who was introduced by Lord Edward Pelham-Clinton. Her Majesty thanked the Mayor for the display and said that it was very pretty, and that she was glad it was such a fine night.' The rejoicings in Windsor town continued till dawn.

The Queen had sent a note of congratulations to the Prime Minister and his family. Lord Salisbury replied:

It is, indeed, a most blessed termination of a long and wearying anxiety. No news has yet arrived giving any intelligence of the state of health in which the besieged were found. The strain of their long hardships and exertions must have been very severe.[1]

On Monday news of the relief was confirmed in a telegram to the Colonial Office from Sir Alfred Milner, High Commissioner in South Africa. It said, tersely: 'Mafeking relieved May 17.' And, somewhat later, the Army too was at last able to announce the news after a telegram had been received at the War Office from the Commander-in-Chief, Lord Roberts. Some may have thought it was strange how little enthusiasm the Army seemed to be showing. Official announcements were made in the House of Lords by the

---

[1] 22 May 1900, *Letters of Queen Victoria*, Vol. III.

Marquis of Lansdowne and in the House of Commons by Mr Balfour.

Monday evening saw a resurgence of the festivities, especially in provincial cities, the official announcements being printed that day in the evening newspapers. On Tuesday the country refused to settle down, and Wednesday, being the Queen's eighty-first birthday, brought yet another renewal of crowds and patriotic fervour, with military parades, London traffic again at a standstill, and the centres of the great cities illuminated. It was not until Thursday that there was a general return to work and the flags began to be put away.

The scenes in London and elsewhere on Mafeking Night brought into coinage a word for use on all riotous or festive occasions with large crowds. It was a word the use of which was almost entirely confined to the needs of journalism; within a few years it appears seldom if ever to have been used except in its own celebration.[1]

The crowds and rejoicing at the Relief of Mafeking were never to be forgotten by those who witnessed them.

*

The effects of this sudden and tremendous escape of pent-up emotion, like compressed energy from some giant boiler, were not long in reaching Mafeking, remote and far away as it was. Enormous quantities of post began to pour into the town : first from South Africa, and then, as the mail-boats began to arrive, from all parts of the world. On one morning Lady Sarah Wilson received 100 letters. Many people received letters and telegrams from total strangers, from places in Britain of which they had never heard; others were from relatives and long-forgotten friends. All had the same theme : effusive congratulations and almost inexpressible gratitude for not giving in, before the eyes of the world, to the Boer hordes. On the opening of the telegraph line over 500 telegrams went into Mafeking before a halt was called by the exhausted operators. (One of them was the above message from the Queen herself to Baden-Powell.) Then another arrived, promoting Baden-Powell to Major-General : a promotion he had naturally coveted, and one which made him the youngest General

---

[1] *O.E.D.*, Vol. VI.

officer, at forty-three, in the British Army[1]. Letters by the thousand arrived for Baden-Powell, many of them addressed merely to 'The Hero of Mafeking' or to 'B.-P.' Baden-Powell's brother took over the job of handling this personal mail, which arrived by the mail-bag-full on every train; he organized a group of volunteers for opening and sorting the letters. (At his home in London, his mother and sister were devoting every day to a similar task: receiving letters, poems, presents, busts of the hero, trinkets with his portrait, china mugs and loving-cups, vases, solid gold medals, 'brooches innumerable' . . .)

Within a week of the relief, Mafeking was in an embarrassment of plenty. More herds of cattle had been sent in by Plumer, and had also been sent up from the south by men of the Kimberley Mounted Corps. Supplies came down the line from Gaberones on 22 May. And on 24 May the first real supply train arrived from the north, its trucks camouflaged with foliage and laden with supplies of all kinds. It rolled into the station with a tremendous scream from a special whistle that informed the town and the whole district of its arrival. 'Today the actual relief of the place has been completed,' said Baden-Powell in *General Orders*, no doubt to the surprise of Mahon's 'flying column'. On the same day the Queen's birthday parade was held, but only about thirty per cent of the total force in Mafeking attended and the ranks were, therefore, somewhat thin. That evening Baden-Powell gave a dinner for about fifty of the senior officers and staff, for which Plumer came down the line (which was now open, but which Baden-Powell wanted protected). Almost the only thing lacking was champagne: whisky-and-water was used as a substitute. 'And there were many of the company,' wrote Pollock of *The Times*, 'who had for some time been unaccustomed to even so moderate a luxury.' Two nights later the correspondents with the relief column gave a dinner at a hotel for Baden-Powell and his staff: celery soup, oyster patties, chicken cutlets and asparagus, roast duck and green peas, roast sirloin of beef and horseradish, game, strawberry tartlets, eggs on toast—eight courses in all, and washed down

---

[1] This had been suggested by Wolseley on the day before the relief, and had since had the formal acceptance of the Queen. Wolseley wrote to his star protégé: 'You now have the ball at your feet and, barring accidents, greatness is in front of you.'

with Léoville 1887, Pommery and Greno 1889, and Crème de Noyaux.

Baden-Powell had been fully occupied preparing his remarkable Report for Lord Roberts, which was naturally of considerable length. As if anticipating criticism, he set out nine 'points gained' at Mafeking : 8,000 Boers being 'contained' at the beginning, and 'prevented' from joining with the Boers near Tuli or Kimberley (a very typical Baden-Powell way of looking at things); 2,000 to 3,000 Boers being 'employed' later; expenditure of enemy in ammunition and casualties; large stores protected; railway plant and stock 'saved'; asylum given to British refugees from the Transvaal; 'most' of the local tribes remained loyal; loss of prestige to Cronje's force; Eloff and 108 Boers and foreigners taken prisoners-of-war. Beneath this list, Baden-Powell gave four 'points gained' by Plumer : preventing invasion of Rhodesia via Tuli; holding the railway 200 miles south of Rhodesia; protecting the natives; repairing the railway to within forty miles of Mafeking, establishing a secure base for the escaping natives from Mafeking and collecting supplies for relief of Mafeking (all one 'point'). Beneath this, Nicholson's force was dismissed in two-and-a-half lines; Holdsworth was not mentioned in the entire Report, and Llewellyn only once. Neither did the prevention of the fall of Mafeking as a signal for a Boer rebellion in the Cape appear among the points gained by the defence. In the Report Baden-Powell stated that 20,000 shells had been fired by the enemy—an average of well over a hundred rounds a day; it is known that on many days there was no firing at all, that some of the Boer guns did not fire for weeks on end, and that 'the enemy used to fire three or four shells every night, no more'.[1] The printer put '2,000', but Baden-Powell changed it back again to '20,000'.

Even in his moment of triumph Baden-Powell did not forget, in his Report, to pay off old scores. Those who had, wrongly, questioned his early defence arrangements, and the journalists who had complained of the treatment of the Africans, were criticized and slapped down. The Report ended with a long list of recommendations, including the name of nearly every officer who had been in Mafeking. Such recommendations were normal practice in the writing of dispatches, but what was not normal was Baden-Powell's private letter

---

[1] Churchill interview, *Morning Post*, 28 June 1900.

to G.H.Q. which followed, pouring cold water on some of his own recommendations ('Cecil did his best but was not much use' etc., although the Cadets in fact proved so successful that in April they had been increased to a total of forty).[1] Thus he contrived to satisfy both himself and his officers.

The old naval gun and the railway-workshops gun were lined up in the main square as proud relics of the defence. With all this going on. few people had noticed the two British soldiers who had arrived in the town on 23 May. They had escaped from the prisoner-of-war compound at Pretoria, 180 miles away, and had walked all the way. 'The men were almost as interesting as the guns,' wrote Hamilton icily, busy composing his final dispatch to *The Times*.

The Town Guard had been disbanded, and now all energies were being expended on dismantling the shelters, clearing away the barricades and repairing the buildings. 'The garrison itself,' wrote Hamilton, 'has mainly rested, taking itself idly and participating in the few last deft touches with which Colonel Baden-Powell has adorned the siege.' There were a great many group photographs of those who had been in Mafeking during the investment: all units, with officers and men, and just officers; Hussar officers, past and present; Lancer officers; Freemasons; fourteen Germans; ex-Naval men; twenty-three Australians . . .

The irritation that had afflicted Plumer's men was now felt among Mahon's. Young wrote: 'Life [in Mafeking] was dull beyond words . . . I tried hard to fancy that the people of the garrison bore in their faces or manners some sign of the strain which they had undergone. But the months seemed to have left no traces except on the buildings and on the cemetery . . . They took less interest in their food than did we, their deliverers.'

Colonel Frank Rhodes, on the other hand, was enjoying himself. He had been completely overcome by the sight of the dapper hero himself. 'I should say [he is] the best man the country has produced. He is plucky, very quick, very slim . . .'[2]

On 28 May Mahon was ordered south to join up with Hunter. His column left Mafeking in a very different spirit to that in which

---

[1] *Roberts Papers.*
[2] *Milner Papers*, 1 June 1900.

it had arrived. One of those who met them was Lieutenant-Colonel E. H. H. Allenby,[1] who wrote: 'Met one or two of Mahon's people who relieved Mafeking. They had a sharp fight before they got there, and they are a little sore as they say that Baden-Powell thinks he did it all himself.'

*

During the defence Baden-Powell's command had spent £123,251 of public money (of which over £50,000 went to the Weils, not counting the debt owed to them by Cecil for supplies in excess, never made public, which was eventually paid off by the authorities). In receipts it had made £9,300 (not including about £6,000 which Baden-Powell made for the Government by his bank-notes being kept as souvenirs instead of being cashed in, but including the £3,242 from the proceeds of the soup kitchens, nearly all of which came from the inhabitants of the African village). Compensation for shell damage was assessed at £16,462.

The casualties incurred during the siege were described in the *Official History* as 'small losses'; this may have been so in comparison with, for instance, the campaign in Natal, but it hardly does justice to the losses suffered in particular by the Protectorate Regiment during October 1899, and at Game Tree Fort, and of the British South Africa Police at Cannon Kopje and elsewhere. There are two main sets of figures: Baden-Powell's in his official report, and the returns filed in the volume kept at the War Office, based on the nominal rolls of all the units, regular and irregular, engaged in the war. Baden-Powell's figure for troops killed, wounded and missing is 212: that of the War Office file, 197.[2] This discrepancy must be accounted for by the non-appearance of the Railway Volunteers in the War Office figures. Out of 44 officers in the garrison, 4 were killed and 22 wounded or missing. These figures included the category of 'slightly

---

[1] Later Lord Allenby. *Allenby Papers*, 29 June 1900 (family).
[2] *War Office Papers*, P.R.O. Including four Bechuanaland Police casualties. A later set of War Office figures deals with the statistics of specific actions. Fatal casualties in the first twelve months of the war on all fronts were 10,698 including those from disease.

wounded', but did not include the Cape Boys or coloured irregulars, who had fought stubbornly at the brickfields and elsewhere.

The figure given in Baden-Powell's official biography, of a total of 326 casualties (including Cape Boys, etc.) out of 1,019 combatants, is incorrect: it was from a total which included 116 Railway Volunteers and 68 Cape Boys (these latter must have been augmented during the defence as their casualties were given by Baden-Powell as 93), who were not included in the figure of 1,019. Baden-Powell's grand total of 316 included a heading *Died* (in addition to *Killed and died of wounds*) 16, and *Accidents* 5. He gave a figure of 329 Africans killed in action or died of wounds, as compared to 71 Europeans.

Boer casualties during the defence were given as 'about 300' by one source, and as 1,000 by Baden-Powell in his Report.[1]

Only four white civilians were killed during the seven months.

Plumer's battle casualties, during much the same period, were 153: these did not include those who died from disease or accidents. Of the regular officers with Plumer, 4 were killed, 2 crippled by wounds, and 2 others badly wounded. Of the 450 men of the Rhodesia Regiment, 106 were casualties by 31 March, before most of Plumer's major engagements.[2] Plumer submitted no final official report, as technically he was part of Baden-Powell's force. In his Official Report of 30 pages, Baden-Powell devoted less than half a page to Plumer's force, and gave no casualty figures.

Casualties in the relief column were 37 according to Baden-Powell, and 25 according to final War Office figures.[3]

Had the defence been a success? Baden-Powell could hardly be expected to think otherwise. He wrote that it 'in the end succeeded in its object'.[4] But what was its object? Over the years Baden-Powell gave more than a dozen, of which certainly not all were successful.

The *Official History*, in as fine an example of double-talk as has

---

[1] *Times History*, p. 597. Baden-Powell gave 'about 600' as the Boer casualties in the first four weeks of the siege. De la Rey gave total casualties of his commando group from the start of the war till December 1901 as 550: *Dispatches of de la Rey, Smuts, etc.—Extracts* (Munich, 1902), B.M.

[2] *Frontier Patrols*, C. Harding, 11 October 1899 to 24 May 1900; *Times History*, p. 209; Pollock, 249 n.

[3] *Siege Diary*, 17 May 1900, and *War Office Papers*.

[4] *Lessons from the 'Varsity of Life*, p. 203.

ever appeared in an official publication, declared: 'If the siege of Mafeking had not been able to absorb sufficient numbers of the enemy to retard seriously the course of the main Federal Campaign, it had yet detained many, and had, in short, justified every reason which had induced Baden-Powell . . .'[1] If the object of the defence was to hold the enemy to it, and if to an ever-decreasing extent the Boers had accepted the bait, it was more due to their own lack of military vigour and consideration than to the efforts of Baden-Powell, who remained supine for months at a time while the Boers trickled away to face Plumer and to tend to their farms. The main characteristic of the defence was its passivity—a fact which has been ignored by historians and biographers. In six months only two actions were initiated on the British side, the first of them being both fiasco and disaster. If Baden-Powell, with 1,500 or so men available to him at the start, and over 2,000 at the end, had threatened Cronje's communications and the weak northern side of the Transvaal what glory might have been his? But it is certain that no glory could have been greater than what he had, and was to receive. Major-General R. S. S. Baden-Powell was the greatest English hero since Wellington, and the most popular since Nelson. If fame had been his ambition, he must surely have reflected in the succeeding months that his desire had been granted with excessive, preposterous and even deranged generosity.

[1] *Official History*, p. 184.

15. Epilogue

The reaction of many people was to get away from Mafeking as fast as they possibly could. Weil made haste for Kimberley. Baillie, who had got himself into financial difficulties through gambling, handed over to a relief from the *Morning Post* and begged a lift on Weil's wagon. Hamilton returned immediately to London, preparing his book while on the journey. Within two weeks of his return he was sent off by *The Times* to China, where the Boxer uprising was threatening the foreign legations in Peking; he embarked for the East nine weeks after being relieved at Mafeking. Neilly busied himself with his book, in which he was to write : 'Frankly, our defenders' pluck did not save Mafeking, great and heroic though that pluck was. The cowardice of the enemy saved us.'

The rail link south was being repaired by a party of Royal Engineers but Lady Sarah, who had a great desire to board a boat at Cape Town for England, could not wait. With Mrs Godley, who arrived in the town from Bulawayo, she decided to go to Pretoria in a cart drawn by a pair of handsome white horses. The rail connection to Cape Town from Pretoria, which Roberts entered on 5 June, was believed to be intact. So confident was Lady Sarah of both herself and Lord Roberts that she departed from Mafeking on 4 June. She was completely overcome at 'the wonderful feeling of relief and freedom at being able to drive at will over the very road which once had been covered by Boer wagons'.

Baden-Powell, whose force was ready to move off after two weeks, was ordered to advance on the town of Rustenburg. He left Mafeking on 3 June. Plumer took a northern route and Baden-Powell and Edwards a southern; altogether Baden-Powell had about 1,100 men. Nearly all those who had survived the investment, except for Cecil, who was given administrative duties in the Transvaal, rode out with

Baden-Powell : Fitzclarence, Godley, Hanbury-Tracy, Gordon Wilson . . . Two hundred men and two guns were left, to garrison Mafeking.

Baden-Powell's mission was to help clear the territory between Mafeking and Pretoria of the enemy, who were still roaming around in commandos under de la Rey and Grobelaar. Snyman had been ousted and had lost all authority, his commandos having attached themselves to de la Rey or gone off on their own. Since the collapse of the Orange Free State and the flight of President Kruger from Pretoria, following the Boer failure to seize their chance early in the war, the Boer forces had become more disintegrated than ever; some people even believed the war was virtually over and were leaving for home. Many Boer leaders thought differently; they saw no reason to give in because they had lost a few names on the map.

Roberts entered Pretoria. Solitary on his horse, leading a huge parade in the main square, he saluted as the silk flag made by Lady Roberts was raised over the city.

Baden-Powell reached Rustenburg, where he found Piet Kruger, the President's son, who had tried unsuccessfully to organize the burghers into opposition.

The telegraphic lines from Rustenburg to Pretoria had been cut, and Baden-Powell decided to go to Roberts himself for further instructions. With Godley, Wilson and a few others, he rode to the capital of the Transvaal. He was flabbergasted at the reception he received : an escort to meet him, thousands cheering his progress in the streets, Roberts himself greeting him on the steps of the Residency, accommodation in a luxurious house 'belonging to some local millionaire'. Roberts, submitting Baden-Powell's report to thhe War Office, praised him and the defence, and declared : 'The distinction which Major-General Baden-Powell has earned must be shared by his gallant soldiers. No episode in the present war seems more praiseworthy . . .'[1] Seems? Roberts offered no resistance to the general demand for Baden-Powell as the hero of the war.

In Pretoria, at the same time, was Lady Sarah Wilson. They did not meet, although Lady Sarah had a glimpse of Baden-Powell in a procession: 'An imposing sight, preceeded by a company of

---

[1] Lord Roberts to Secretary of State for War, 21 June 1900, P.R.O.

turbaned Indians.' Lady Sarah and Mrs Godley had arrived in Pretoria in less than two weeks, having negotiated the territory in their cart before British troops had been able to do so. They had succeeded in driving the 230 miles from Mafeking without being molested by anyone—'a strange contrast between the powerful column, seeing an enemy behind every bush, and the sprightly young ladies (well known in the fox-hunting world), caring nothing at all for all the Boers in Christendom.'[1] Roberts, seeing two English ladies on the sidewalk, stopped in surprise. He had last seen Mrs Godley hunting in Meath. 'I shall never,' wrote Lady Sarah, 'forget the inexpressible sadness of his face . . . the man who at an advanced age, and already covered in so many laurels, had, in spite of a crushing bereavement, stepped forward to help his country.'

Lady Sarah had experienced some difficulty in finding accommodation. At length the manager of the Grand Hotel had taken her to a room which was shortly to be vacated. In it a young man was discovered packing away clothes, papers and 'campaigning kit'. The manager was startled to see the young man turn and affectionately embrace the lady. The man was Winston Churchill, and before leaving he was able to escort his aunt around the scene of his famous escape. But Churchill was in a hurry: a general election was on hand at home, and at such a time Pretoria was not the place in which to be, although, unlike many others, he had no illusions about the war being nearly over.[2]

Churchill, it is perhaps needless to say, had been one of the first to enter Pretoria. With the Duke of Marlborough, he had gone straight to the prisoner-of-war compound to relieve the inmates. ('I raised my hat and cheered. The cry was instantly answered from within.')

Churchill had just completed his latest dispatch to the *Morning Post*. It was the first important interview with Baden-Powell since the relief; it was by the man who had until then been himself the hero of the war; and it was about the man who had taken over that mantle. It had, in the public's mind, therefore, a particular flavour to it. Spread over three days in the *Morning Post,* it was unlike any

[1] *Story of The Imperial Light Horse.*
[2] Interviewed on his return, Churchill told the press: 'It would be quite a mistake to think that the war has come to an end.' *Morning Post*, 23 July 1900.

other dispatch Churchill sent from South Africa. He was usually more than free with his opinions, but on this occasion there were none. It was an almost verbatim interview, with hardly a comment, except at the end, when there was a reference to the Boers themselves being involved in the adulation of the Hero of Mafeking; Churchill concluded: 'Apparently Boers and British have something in common.' The only flattering notice from the author of the articles was a reference to Baden-Powell's high-pitched laugh: 'He laughed in a way that showed that months of anxiety had, after all, made some impression even on his unyielding spirit.' Baden-Powell insisted that, 'We are all astonished to find so much interest taken in the defence of Mafeking,' although such astonishment must have been tempered by the very full accounts of the interest which he had received from home before being relieved. Churchill took the precaution of showing his report to Baden-Powell before dispatching it; the latter's only comment was: 'Talking to you is like talking to a phonograph.' Churchill commented: 'I was rather pleased with it, too.'

The authors of the books on Baden-Powell which shortly appeared were more forthcoming than Churchill; their admiration was unbounded. In a biography, which appeared within hours of the news of the relief, Harold Begbie wrote:

If you find yourself in a few months' time drifting into conversation with a good-looking, bronzed stranger, this side of fifty, who puts rather pointed questions to you, after having studied your thumbs, boots and whiskers intently . . . it would, of course, be Baden-Powell. It is when Baden-Powell puts his frock coat into a drawer, pops his shiny tall hat into a box and slips exultingly into a flannel shirt that the life of a scout seems to him the infinitely best in the world . . . However soundly he sleeps, if anyone comes within ten yards of him, tread he never so softly, B.-P. wakes up without fail, and with a brain cleared for action . . . Once, after two months of wandering, he got into an hotel and, after dinner, into a bed. But it would not do, he says; in a twinkling he had whipped the blankets off the bed and was lying outside on mother earth, with the rain beating upon his face, and deep in refreshing slumber . . . The best-tempered fellow in the world, and blessed with the keenest humour, he can be as uncompromising a martinet as the

sternest fire-eater of old days—*when there is a real necessity for it,*
. . . On his wanderings over the face of the earth Baden-Powell
has had many narrow escapes of death . . . We see him walking
through the streets of Mafeking, now glaring with hard, steely
eye into the forts which throw their coward shells into the women's
camp, now turning to give an order with clenched hands and
locked jaws, and now stooping down to lift a child into his arms
and caress away its little fears. Be sure that never a thought of
adding to his own reputation enters the mind of Baden-Powell
in little Mafeking.

Bremner Smith, in another book soon on sale, wrote :

Wherever he goes his mind is at work, and it is almost as difficult
for him to look at a man and not know all about him as it was
for Sherlock Holmes . . . His astounding pluck in the endurance
of severe physical strain . . . He is the beau ideal of a soldier.

Baden-Powell, it seemed, was the utter perfection of an Englishman, an almost god-like figure, who possessed in some miraculous
way every attribute admired by his age : mysterious like Holmes;
artistic like the characters of *Trilby* without being bohemian;
affecting languor in the heat of conflict like an insolent Guards
Officer in a Ouïda novel; with a splendid name like some character
of fiction; stern with the disobedient; upright and unflinching in the
face of enemies who were cowardly and villainous and unworthy
of him; as comfortable sleeping rough in his flannel shirt as leaving
Claridges in his silk top hat; the author of military textbooks and
sporting ones as well; above all a man who could show the world
what it meant to be an Englishman, a Soldier of the Queen, who sent
gay and plucky messages while on the very brink of death from
starvation and while holding out day after day with thinning ranks
around his tattered Union Flag against vast hordes of the foe . . .

It was so perfect that it was almost as if they had made him themselves for their own satisfaction and pride.

*

Meanwhile the short, sensitive, frail-looking man, with a uniform which always seemed totally immaculate even when campaigning, who was worrying about his balding head, with the light smile and the quick laugh, was beset with military problems.

Baden-Powell seems to have been impressed by the military advantages of holding a town as against the obvious risks of manœuvring for favourable position against the enemy in the open : in the latter context he had great respect for the Boers. Having got his force safely to Rustenburg, he was not easily persuaded to take it out again. Attempts to 'police' the area and clear it of the enemy were made by small columns which he sent out from the town. There seems to have been some confusion among Plumer's men. Montmorency wrote : 'Baden-Powell, being the senior, was actually in command, nevertheless a certain amount of misunderstanding reigned and the staff work was decidedly bad; we were constantly perplexed with orders and counter-orders. One day we would evacuate some key position in the Magaliesberg mountains, only to be ordered, twenty-four hours later, to recapture it at all costs.' In June there was little activity. During the first weeks of July the Boers were more active in the district, and Baden-Powell was ordered to concentrate his force on Rustenburg again. He had reported to Roberts that there were larger Boer forces in the area than had been thought; he was also worried about the security of his supply line from Mafeking. Carrington, still assembling his force, was hurried down from Rhodesia with all the troopers he could muster, to garrison Mafeking and to protect Baden-Powell's supply line. Methuen was sent up with a column from the south.

The Boers were all around Baden-Powell once again, and Methuen had to force his way to him through an enemy force under Commandant Lemmer. He broke through near Rustenburg on 21 July, at one end of a pass known as Olifants Nek, but, as the *Times History* points out, 'the success of the movement was marred by Baden-Powell's inability to cut off the Boer retreat . . . in spite of the fact that he had previously reconnoitred the [pass], he was unprepared for [their] method of escape.'[1] Baden-Powell had been informed twice

---

[1] *Times History*, p. 356. A cousin of the Godleys was killed with Methuen in this action; an indication of the contribution many families were making to the war through the introduction of large bodies of volunteers.

by Methuen as to the time of his arrival, and Roberts himself, 'to make sure that there could be no mistake', had also telegraphed the exact date of Methuen's arrival; but when Baden-Powell's force, under Plumer, arrived at the far end of the pass the Boers were already streaming through and could not be cut off. The escape of the Boer force at Olifants Nek was a grave disappointment to all British troops in the Western Transvaal.

It had been planned by Roberts that once Methuen and Baden-Powell had joined up, their combined force should move to Pretoria. Events, however, prevented this; and Methuen was called away without entering Rustenburg. After replenishing Methuen's force, Baden-Powell, careful as always of his supplies, still had provisions for sixteen days. He did not move. He wrote plaintively in the *Staff Diary*: 'Pointed out to Lord Methuen that I am left as helpless as before.'

Carrington was ordered to move up from Mafeking to join with Baden-Powell at Rustenburg.[1] Roberts also decided to move the comparatively large force of Lieutenant-General Ian Hamilton, which included Mahon's column, into the Rustenburg area from Pretoria. One of his main tasks would be to extricate Baden-Powell from Rustenburg and 'bring away'[2] his force to Pretoria. Hamilton became heavily engaged by Boer commandos, threatening his flanks and supply lines. That was not his only problem, however, for Baden-Powell had no desire to leave Rustenburg, in which his force of nearly 1,500 men had been for over a month apart from the sorties and the sad episode of Olifants Nek.

For weeks Baden-Powell had been preparing for siege at Rustenburg. But the Boers had seemed less anxious to invest than Baden-Powell was to be invested. Since the end of June he had been sending out messages beginning 'All well here . . . .' During early July a system of alarms, defensive earthworks, water supplies, rationing and other arrangements for siege were made. Dummy mines were laid. On 11

---

[1] The *Official History*, p. 336, writes of Carrington being ordered to 'relieve' Baden-Powell at Rustenburg.
[2] *Times History*, p. 360. Hillcourt says (p. 214) 'to bring Baden-Powell and his men safely back'. The German *Official History* states that Baden-Powell was 'taken out of Rustenburg' by Hamilton.

July Baden-Powell wrote in the *Staff Diary* that two courses were open to him: to vacate Rustenburg and 'probably join Roberts', or to 'sit tight where we are and if necessary undergo investment for a time—as it will draw off a large number from Lord Roberts'. It was clear which course Baden-Powell preferred. But if the latter were to be the course followed, then he did not want another section of his force—four miles away—in the town with him: 'They should rather get away to open country than fall back on the town. We shall not want their help here—they would be more men and horses to feed—and on the other hand they would be of real value if free to patrol the country elsewhere and could eventually join Lord Roberts.' He told Roberts that he had one month's supplies at Rustenburg, 'and for moral effect am preparing to hang on here.' Next day he wrote reassuringly in *General Orders*: 'It is our business to sit tight at Rustenburg . . . if a force of enemy comes to invest us here, it will cause us no harm and will reduce the numbers opposing Lord Roberts.' On 13 July, Baden-Powell declared in *General Orders*: 'So long as the defenders of a position have taken a good cover, and stuck to it, they cannot be turned out by the Boers.'[1]

The Boers hovered around the town; helio messages flickered across the hilltops to Pretoria till sunset each day; and Baden-Powell—ruled by his military philosophy of 'sit tight'—waited.

At length, the Boers obliged. From 22 July to 4 August, Baden-Powell was invested once more. On 24 July he reported that he had supplies till 10 August. On 27 July Roberts asked him what he was doing in Rustenburg. Baden-Powell said that if Roberts would send some infantry to garrison the town, then he would be glad to be doing 'some more actively useful work, instead of keeping this mounted force bottled up here'. But Roberts pointed out that he did not want Rustenburg garrisoned at all. On 28 July Baden-Powell wrote again to Roberts saying that he wanted to stay where he was. Two days later came Roberts's reply, disapproving of the investment, and saying that he preferred 'mounted columns on the move'. He asked whether Baden-Powell was still in Rustenburg, and if so what he proposed to do about leaving it. As the correspondence continued the numbers of Boers around Rustenburg—according to Baden-

---

[1] *Staff Diary*, July 1900; *General Orders*, July 1900.

Powell—increased steadily: 2,000 on the 20th, 2,000 to 3,000 on the 25th, 3,000 on the 29th, 3,200 on the 31st. On 30 July Roberts told Baden-Powell to leave Rustenburg as soon as the 'relieving force' of Hamilton arrived. He pointed out that Baden-Powell's force was urgently required elsewhere. Baden-Powell immediately sent out a runner, asking the Commander-in-Chief to reconsider. He said that he now had three weeks' food supplies. On 31 July he sent a letter and a heliogram, 'urging moral value of retention of Rustenburg'.[1]

In the correspondence that took place between Field-Marshal Lord Roberts and Major-General R. S. S. Baden-Powell, the former treated the latter with all the respect due to the greatest figure of the war so far. He explained that he wanted Baden-Powell out of Rustenburg for 'strategical gain'. Baden-Powell explained that he wanted to stay there 'for moral effect, to give sanctuary to peacefully disposed Boers and to provide a base of supply for mobile columns'. When Hamilton arrived, he still declined to go. He wrote 'insistently' on the subject. Ian Hamilton forwarded his views to the Commander-in-Chief. Baden-Powell said he would be glad to hold the place with only four guns and less than 1,000 men; having long been aware of the capabilities of the Boers in assault and investing, he was able to do so with every confidence. Roberts said that he wanted his forces 'employed in beating the enemy in the field'. He again ordered Baden-Powell to get out: 'despite the temporary loss of prestige'.[2]

It is interesting to note that in this exchange Baden-Powell used many arguments that he used for the defence of Mafeking. Writing to Baden-Powell later, Roberts carefully explained his problems. He said that if, at the time, he had not been using a large force to supply Baden-Powell at Rustenburg, he would have been able practically to surround the main Orange Free State force still in the field, under Assistant Commandant-General Christian de Wet: 'all troops are required for what I venture to think is more important duty'.[3]

Before reluctantly setting out for Pretoria, Baden-Powell was obliged to co-operate in the rescue of the hapless Hore, who, while guarding Baden-Powell's supply line between Mafeking and

---

[1] *Staff Diary*, 24 July 1900 to 31 July 1900; and *Roberts Papers*.
[2] *Official History*, pp. 335, 338, 339.
[3] *Official History*, p. 336.

Rustenburg, had been besieged at Brakfontein on the Elands River. Hore had over 300 men, mostly Queenslanders. He was surrounded by de la Rey. Baden-Powell's last order to him had been to 'make himself snug in case of shell fire, till big column, which will shortly arrive, chases enemy away'. Now Baden-Powell was expected to do something about Hore himself. But when heavy firing was heard from Elands River, fading into the distance, it was assumed—without waiting for the report of the two scouts that Baden-Powell had sent out—that Hore had been relieved by Carrington from Mafeking. Baden-Powell moved away. Carrington had, however, been beaten off. Hore was still besieged, desperately short of ammunition and suffering severe casualties. According to those who experienced both, two days at Brakfontein were worse than seven months at Mafeking. Most of the column and its transport were crammed into a space of only three and half acres. Forty-nine soldiers, two civilians and twenty-four Africans were killed: 431 horses were killed by shell-fire or had to be destroyed. 'The camp presented a horrible scene of carnage at the close of the siege.'[1]

Of this episode, a historian of the war notes Baden-Powell's 'culpable failure to exercise elementary boy-scout care to help Colonel Hore'.[2]

On his way to Pretoria, Baden-Powell became involved in efforts to capture the columns of de Wet and Grobelaar. He found the Boer force, but instead of blocking the two passes available to the Boers for escape, he set up camp. In a message to Roberts that night, he said: 'I have closed the passage to the enemy and was shelling his convoy just before sundown.'[3] This was dramatic news, as de Wet had too often escaped before, and President Steyn of the Orange Free State was believed to be with him. Baden-Powell's column slept: in the morning both passes were found to be held by the Boers. Before attacking, Baden-Powell decided to wait for rations to be brought up. Roberts urged him to 'press hard': de Wet could be taken. Ian Hamilton and Major-General A. H. Paget were also getting into

---

[1] *The Queenslanders at Elands River* (Privately, 1900), B.M. Hore was relieved by Kitchener. Forty years later Godley gave an entirely different version of the whole affair.

[2] Kruger, p. 452.

[3] 22 August 1900, *Roberts Papers*, P.R.O.

position. The Boers left. Baden-Powell pressed on. On the morning of 26 August he occupied Nylstroom, thereby placing himself between de Wet and Grobelaar. He sent off a messenger to Grobelaar, suggesting that they might negotiate. The Boer commandant 'showed no astonishment when he was gravely advised to surrender by a commander who was himself between two lines of fire'.[1] Fortunately, the Boers had no use for prisoners. Paget telegraphed Roberts: 'In accordance with your instructions I have sent runner to recall Baden-Powell at once.'[2] On his retirement it was entirely typical of Baden-Powell that he should send a demand for surrender also to de Wet.

He sent back to Roberts a long report on the escape of de Wet, in which he held Paget responsible.

Only the most sycophantic of his biographers have claimed that Baden-Powell's three months in the Western Transvaal were an entire success. Little was heard at home of the investment of Rustenburg. The *Times History* attributes the escape of de Wet, in which Baden-Powell played a not unimportant part, 'very largely to the absence of any organized system of scouting'.

Baden-Powell was ordered to retire on Warmbad. He reached it on 27 August. At this point Roberts reacted with unusual speed. He called for Baden-Powell, suggesting he take immediate leave. Within two days, Baden-Powell had handed over his command to Plumer (Godley taking Plumer's command).

For some time Milner had been trying to get Roberts and the War Office to agree to a new police force, which would eventually control the territory taken from the Boers in the Orange Free State and the Transvaal. For three months Milner had been suggesting such a course. Roberts had recently agreed, and he had written to Milner, earnestly asking him to accept Baden-Powell as the leader of the police. Milner had been delighted at the suggestion of such a famous figure taking the appointment, and within hours Baden-Powell was on his way to Cape Town.

*

---

[1] *Official History*, p. 368.
[2] 26 August 1900, *Roberts Papers*.

At Cape Town, Baden-Powell was greeted by officials on the station platform shouting 'Hurrah!' He was carried out on their shoulders to the vast, roaring crowd waiting outside. It was the start for Baden-Powell of a new life. It was the sort of thing which was to happen to him, more or less, for the remainder of his days: Baden-Powell's generation never forgot their gratitude to him.

Baden-Powell had sent home, by H. J. Whigham of the *Daily Mail,* a statement to the public, which appeared in most of the newspapers. Written in the jolly, making-light-of-it-all style which had so endeared him to millions, he thanked the thousands of anonymous correspondents; he wrote from 'out here in the veldt', and said: 'I hear that mail-bags are following me with still more . . . it more than repays us for any inconveniences we may have suffered in doing what was no more than our duty to our Queen and to the prestige of our own countrymen.' With the modest reference to 'any inconveniences' and the unconquerable patriotism, admiration turned to adoration.

The composers of light music were at work, and soon thousands of copies of sheet music were coming from the presses: 'The Mafeking Waltz', 'The Mafeking Grand March', 'Our Hero B.-P.', 'The Hero of Mafeking Waltz', 'The Baden-Powell Schottische', 'Major-General British Pluck.' ('All alone, alone, 900 miles from Cape Town, Baden-Powell took his stand, with a small heroic band.') Baden-Powell accepted all the hero-worship with modesty and an air of slightly bemused surprise.

One of the first things he did for the South African Constabulary was to design its uniform from his own sketches. It was a fine affair, with stetson hats especially imported from America and fitted with feather plumes dyed green; the uniforms had green-and-yellow piping. There was naturally a special and quite splendid uniform for the commander of the force, which had affinities to the uniforms of an admiral, general and chief constable. As his chief of staff Baden-Powell was fortunate to have the admirable Nicholson, the same man who had managed to keep Plumer supplied throughout the months of investment. Command of one of the four divisions was given to Colonel Sam Steel of the North-West Mounted Police, who was able to provide much useful advice. This period saw Baden-Powell's best official work. On his first return to England, where he went straight to the home of 'The Boy' McLaren, he felt obliged to travel incognito in a carriage tacked on to a non-passenger train. He assumed the name of Colonel Nicholson. Fame was one thing: mobs were another.

The relief of Mafeking had enjoyed some political influence as well as public acclaim. Two by-elections followed it at a short interval. In the Isle of Wight, Captain J. E. B. Seeley[1] (Conservative), who was serving with the Yeomanry in South Africa, stood against a local landowner of great popularity. Seeley more than doubled the previous Conservative majority. South Manchester had been held by the Liberals at the General Election with a majority of 78: it now went to the Conservatives, who had promoted the war, with a majority of over 2,000.

Roberts, the victor of the Boers, or so it seemed, replaced Wolseley as Commander-in-Chief of the Army. Tired and frail, 'Bobs' survived till 1914, when he died, appropriately enough, not far from battle.

In January 1901, Queen Victoria died. The Relief of Mafeking had thus been the last great event of her remarkable reign.

*

Eloff and the Mafeking prisoners were transported to St. Helena, from where they were released on the conclusion of peace: Lieutenant Murchison to prison on the Isle of Wight.

Lady Sarah Wilson worked in London for the Mafeking Relief Fund, £7,500 of which had been cabled to Baden-Powell immediately on relief and 'placed at your disposal and discretion'. The Fund had been started by her sister in a letter to *The Times* ('starvation in the immediate future lies before them . . . Loyalty was their cry, and freedom and justice their household gods. Have not their courage and endurance thrilled the whole world?') By 1909 only £29,267 had been raised, a small figure in comparison to other Boer War appeals, but it was gratefully received in Mafeking; after distribution over £3,000 remained, and this was formed into a Fund for

---

[1] Later Lord Mottistone, and War Minister, 1912–14. For political influence of Mafeking *q.v.*, *Annual Register*, 1900.

occasional grants in future years to those who had been in the town during its defence.

Lord Edward Cecil, in due course, died prematurely, and Lady Violet, predictably, married Viscount Milner, thus crowning a relationship that had begun at the time of Mafeking, which had itself—with the Baden-Powell brothers, the three Godleys, the Wilsons, the Cecils, the Fitzclarences—always had the elements of a great family party.

Plumer's Rhodesia Regiment was disbanded in October, 1901. Plumer cultivated his Army career as best he could, and was little known outside the Army. He continued to be handicapped by his short sight; in 1903 he became Quartermaster-General. After the war he was presented by the British South Africa Company, on behalf of the people of Rhodesia, with a sword of honour, in a quiet ceremony at the company's offices at St. Swithins Lane, London. The Duke of Abercorn said that Plumer had combined bravery and duty with a sense of diplomacy; no general in the field had performed such gallant service under such trying conditions. 'The Board is fully sensible of the fact that it was mainly owing to the presence of your force on the southern borders of Rhodesia, and to the masterly operations directed by you, that the Boers were forced to abandon all ideas of invading the country.'

Plumer took his sword and left. He was friendly with Baden-Powell all his life. But not all Baden-Powell's contemporaries were well-disposed towards him. Baden-Powell's war decoration was the c.b., which went to nearly every regular colonel sent to the war. Kitchener was not his greatest admirer. Years later General Sir Beauvoir de Lisle was to write that Plumer never received recognition for his work in South Africa, which was 'more wonderful work' than the defence of Mafeking.[1] But Baden-Powell's critics kept their views out of print; and, although many military reputations never recovered from the Boer War, Baden-Powell's could hardly be damaged, so great was his renown. Early in 1903, when his fame as a great fighting commander was still at its zenith, he was brought back from South Africa and made Inspector-General of Cavalry—an unusually popular appointment with the public. His tour of duty

---

[1] *Reminiscences of Sport and War* (Eyre & Spottiswoode, 1939).

in that important post was not inspired. No Inspector-General before or after spent so much time away from England, or paid such attention to his responsibilities abroad. Thus the pattern seemed to be set for his constant travelling on behalf of the scouting movement in later years. He relied heavily on the practical advice and opinions of Douglas Haig, a dedicated soldier with more push and more determination, who was his opposite number in India. In a remarkable moment of self-appreciation, Baden-Powell once admitted: 'I was entirely unfitted, both physically and intellectually, for the position of I.G. of Cavalry.'[1]

When the First World War began, Baden-Powell—who had retired early—offered his services; but Kitchener told him, with some relish, that he was more useful to the nation leading the Boy Scouts. Baden-Powell had revealed (as a result of his 'spying') that the Germans planned to invade the Yorkshire coast, 'rush' over an army of 90,000 and expel every man, woman and child from Yorkshire and Lancashire: within a few hours some fourteen million people would be starving. Unable to take part in the war, Baden-Powell published a book in which he recounted some 'spying episodes', including the German invasion of the north of England which he had obtained from 'certain gentry', his travels in Dalmatia long before with butterfly nets, and with advice on disguises, sketching the enemy's position, etc.[2] A sad little book, written as all his books, in a racy, simple style beloved of children, it ended—'one recognizes that it may have invaluable results for one's country in time of war . . . knows in his heart of hearts that he has done as bravely for his country as his comrade who falls in battle.' In that year Plumer was the most respected general in the British Army, and Mahon was Commander-in-Chief at Salonika. Rumours insisted that Baden-Powell was in Germany on Secret Service work.

Over the years Baden-Powell wrote many books; more and more aware, perhaps, of the shaky foundations on which his great reputation was built, he tried to disclaim the heroic nature of the defence which he at the same time recounted with relish. Again and again

---

[1] *Lessons from the 'Varsity of Life*, p. 260.
[2] *My Adventures As a Spy* (Pearson, 1915).

he wrote of the tricks he had played on the Boers, of the fighting in the brickfields, of the home-made gun, named 'Wolf' after him. It was a part he was expected to play, and it was one he clearly enjoyed; besides, the books sold deservedly well and the proceeds were always needed by the scouting movement. In 1907, in the midst of action-filled anecdotes about 'the siege' and surrounded by his own extremely dramatic sketches, he wrote : 'the so-called siege has from various causes been given an exaggerated reputation when it was in reality an investment—of rather a domestic kind at that.'[1] In another book he paid generous tribute to Plumer. It has been said that self-deception is the greatest vice of the English, and certainly there was far less of it in Baden-Powell than there was in the British public at large, which insisted on its hero.

Baden-Powell lived all his life with the knowledge that his great fame was based partly on a misconception. It would have taken exceptional strength of character to have put the matter right in the strongest possible terms, perhaps in a public statement; but there was no need to, for Baden-Powell must have realized at some time that he had fulfilled a public need. Nevertheless, his strange position may have explained his touchiness about the stamps and other matters. When Churchill published an extremely flattering essay on him, in which he this time praised the defence but mentioned in passing that Baden-Powell's 'bright fruition of fortune' at Mafeking had brought upon him 'a chilly fog' from his Army contemporaries, Baden-Powell responded with an extremely tart retort in his next book.

Histories of the campaign all tended to place the importance of the investment—among the many reasons that Baden-Powell himself gave for it from time to time—on the numbers of Boers that it had detained from other fronts. Baden-Powell never claimed to have attracted Boers to himself after the departure of Cronje, but in stating his figures of the numbers of Boers engaged he often omitted to make it clear that the numbers he gave referred to the beginning of

---

[1] *Sketches in Mafeking and East Africa*. But he headed his report to Roberts, 'The Siege', and described it as such throughout and in all his later books ('the long and trying siege', etc.). He wrote one other important retraction, again surrounded by contrary material: 'Mafeking was, as an actual feat of arms, a very minor operation which was given an exaggerated importance.' (*Adventures and Accidents*).

the war, and rather than the later period, when Roberts's campaign
had begun. The relevance of the investment to the campaign, and its
importance, if any, does depend to some extent on the number of the
Boers engaged there; this figure is therefore important. Without
producing further evidence Baden-Powell's version of it escalated
steadily over the years:

General Orders, 13 October, 1899 .... 5,000 to 6,000
Report to Lord Roberts, May, 1900 8,000
Interview with Churchill, June, 1900 .... nearly 9,000
Sketches in Mafeking and East Africa, 1907 .... up to 9,000
Adventures From the 'Varsity of Life, 1933 .... over 10,000

Then, in 1937, he published an account of a leisurely trip around
Africa, visiting the various Boy Scout centres, entitled, very typically,
African Adventures. In it he wrote: '12,000 Boers came up and surrounded the place, and shelled us and made various attacks, but we
were able to hold them off for seven months.'

*

Baden-Powell resigned from the Army in order to devote his time
to the Boy Scouts, at the suggestion, he said, of Edward VII. This
great movement needed his whole-time support as well as his enthusiasm. He had formed the Boy Scout movement after the success of his
scouting books, which had proved more popular when presented to
boys than to soldiers.[1] Baden-Powell's prestige was tremendous; he
could have entered politics,[2] or many other walks of life, but he
chose to dedicate himself to young people, and it was a singularly

---

[1] The vast success of the scouts publications was partly due to the acumen of
their publisher, Arthur Pearson, a newspaper proprietor of classic mould described in the D.N.B. as 'alarming . . . intellectually he was unfitted to guide,
much less to form, public opinion . . . His opinions were the caprice of his un-
criticized intuitions, and he was resentful of opposition, impatient of argument.'
Baden-Powell enlisted Pearson's support in 1907, and the latter's organization
boosted the movement, for Pearson had vision as well as caprice.
[2] On being asked about this, Baden-Powell ended speculation by his characteristic reply: 'Delighted—which side?'

happy choice for all concerned. Once again the uniform was designed by the founder, and no one could have done so better. Chief administrator of the movement was 'The Boy' and when the two of them took some boys to the first camp, on Brownsea Island, it was the Union Jack of Mafeking which flapped above them. In 1912 Baden-Powell, aged fifty-five, finally married: and the scouting movement became stronger and more widespread still, with a firm international base. Its influence remained with many all their lives.[1] His sister established the Girl Guides; his brother Warrington wrote for the Sea Scouts; his wife was Chief Guide. Baden-Powell dedicated the remainder of his life to the movement. He enjoyed it quite as much as did any boy. He became the hero of virtually every middle-class boy, and many of the girls, in the nation and far beyond it. He travelled and worked ceaselessly on behalf of this great youth movement, and attended enormous gatherings where thousands and thousands of boys, all dressed in a uniform composite of his own scouting outfit and that of the South African Constabulary, greeted him, the great hero. The motto of the Scouts, like that of the South African Constabulary, was *Be Prepared*, derived from Baden-Powell's initials.[2]

It was a movement which kept many children from the hooliganism and waywardness in which some would no doubt otherwise have taken part, and which, by making young people more aware, broadened many lives; even though all boys want to be men, and only some men want always to be boys. It became the most successful and useful youth movement the world has known, and made Mafeking worth while in a way that at the time even Baden-Powell himself could never have imagined.

In 1938 Baden-Powell went to Kenya, where he died in 1941. He had become not only a hero, but also one of the best-loved men in the world; humorous, friendly, and gentle; a very familiar figure with

---

[1] General Keith Johnson, U.S. Army Chief of Staff, 1966, keeps his old *Boy Scout Handbook* with his Bible in his office.

[2] Baden-Powell later insisted that this had nothing to do with him. The constabulary had chosen the motto 'for themselves partly because it spoke to their readiness to take on any kind of duty at any time, and also because it brought in my initials'. But in a fourth edition of *The Matebele Campaign* he wrote when describing a letter addressed simply to 'B.–P.' 'for me it has been a hidden meaning—Be Prepared' (20 January 1901).

his fleshy knees, his avuncular moustache, his long short-trousers, and his inevitable stetson hat. He was buried in view of Mount Kenya. Over thirty years before, in a quiet village in Tipperary, almost alone, forgotten and comparatively unnoticed, had died the man who had said that it was best for South Africa to have both Dutch and British territories and that to mix the two would one day end in disaster : Lieutenant-General Sir William Butler, who also had done his duty as he saw it.

Bibliography

A. <u>Mafeking (Diaries, Papers, primary material)</u>

African Adventures, Baden-Powell (Pearson, 1937)
Adventures and Accidents, Baden-Powell (Methuen, 1934)
Lessons From the 'Varsity of Life, Baden-Powell (Pearson, 1933)
Sketches in Mafeking and East Africa, Baden-Powell (Smith, Elder, 1907)
Staff Diary, dates in Sept., Nov., Dec., 1899, May, 1900 (Boy Scouts of America, New Brunswick, N.J.)
Mafeking: A Diary of the Siege. F. D. Baillie (Constable, 1900)
Diary (M.S.), G. H. Bell (Rhodes University, South Africa)
Diary, A. M. Craufurd (Crampton's Magazine, 1900)
Life of an Irish Soldier, Sir A. Godley (Murray, 1939)
The Siege of Mafeking, J. A. Hamilton (Methuen, 1900)
Besieged With B.-P., J. E. Neilly (Pearson, 1900)
South African Memories, Lady S. Wilson (Arnold, 1904)
Private Papers (M.S.), B. Weil (B.M.)
General Orders, Mafeking, 1899–1900 : *Order Book* (N.A.M.) : another copy in *Weil Papers*
Report on Operation & Siege to Royal Commission, Baden-Powell (N.A.M.)
Report to Lord Roberts on Siege, Baden-Powell (P.R.O. : W.O. 32,861) : another copy with Boy Scouts of America
Standing Orders, Rhodesian Frontier Force (N.A.M.)
Roberts Papers (P.R.O. : W.O.105.7 and W.O.105.15)
  Correspondence with Baden-Powell, Plumer, etc
  Dispatches of Baden-Powell, Plumer, Mahon, Nicholson, etc
Mafeking Mail, Oct. 1899–June 1900 (B.M.)
Morning Post, 1899–1900
The Times, 1899–1900

Chief Engineer's Report on Siege of Mafeking, C. B. Vyvyan (P.R.O.: W.O. 108.77)

B. Other Primary Material

Report of the Royal Commission on the War in South Africa (1903)
Other *War Office Papers* (P.R.O.):
Minutes Prior to the Outbreak of War, Lord Wolseley (W.O.32.269)
Correspondence on South African War, Lord Roberts (W.O.108.74)
Staff Appointments in South African War (W.O.32.239)
Messages to G.O.C. from Plumer and Nicholson (W.O.32.861)
Recommendations for Victoria Cross (W.O.32.861)
Correspondence on Trophies of Mafeking (W.O.32.561)
Actions in South Africa Deserving or not Deserving of Record in Officers' War Services (W.O.108.3)
Casualty Lists, South African War (W.O.108.2)
Staff Diary, 19 May 1900—31 July 1900 (N.A.M.)
Rhodes Papers, 1899–1900 (Rhodes House Library, Oxford)
Official Transvaal Dispatches (Translated) 23 October 1899–12 March 1900 (N.A.M.)

C. The Relief and Plumer's Column

The Canadian Contingents and Canadian Imperialism, W. S. Evans (Unwin, 1901)
Khaki and Blue, R. S. Godley (Lovat Dickson, 1935)
Frontier Patrols, History of the B.S.A. Police, C. Harding (Bell, 1937)
Plumer of Messines, Sir C. Harrington (Murray, 1935)
M.S., H. P. de Montmorency (P.R.O.: W.O.108.29)
With Seven Generals in the Boer War, A. W. A. Pollock (Skeffington, 1900)
The Colonials in South Africa, J. Stirling (Blackwood, 1907)
The Relief of Mafeking, F. Young (Methuen, 1900)

D. Histories

> *The Official History of the War in South Africa,* Vol. III (Hurst
> & Blackett, 1908)
> *The Times History of the War in South Africa,* Vol. IV, L. S.
> Amery and B. Williams (Sampson Low, 1906)
> *The Cambridge History of the British Empire,* Vol. VIII, ed.
> E. A. Walker (Cambridge, 1963)
> *German Official History of the War in South Africa,* 2 Vols.
> (Murray, 1904, 1906)
> *South Africa and the Transvaal War,* L. Creswicke (Jack, Edin-
> burgh, 1900)
> *The Great Boer War,* Sir A. Conan Doyle (Smith Elder, 1902)
> *Death of the Last Republic,* P. Gibbs (Muller, 1957)
> *The Boer War,* E. Holt (Putnam, 1958)
> *Good-bye Dolly Gray,* R. Kruger (Cassell, 1959)
> *History of Southern Africa,* E. A. Walker (Longmans, 2nd. ed.,
> 1959)
> *With the Flag to Pretoria,* Vol I, Vol. II, H. W. Wilson (Harms-
> worth, 1901)

E. History of the Investment

> *Baden-Powell at Mafeking,* D. Grinnell-Milne (Bodley Head,
> 1957)

F. Biographies : Baden-Powell

i *Baden-Powell: The Two Lives of a Hero,* W. Hillcourt with
> Olave, Lady Baden-Powell (Heinemann, 1964)
> *Baden-Powell,* E. E. Reynolds (Oxford, 1942)
> *The Piper of Pax,* E. K. Wade (Pearson, 1924)

ii *The Wolf That Never Sleeps,* H. Begbie (Richards, 1900)
> *Col. R. S. S. Baden-Powell,* R. J. Bremner Smith (London, 1900)
> *Baden-Powell of Mafeking,* J. S. Fletcher (Methuen, 1900)
> *Baden-Powell,* R. H. Kiernan (Harrap. 1939)

G. Biographies : other

Autobiography, Sir W. F. Butler (Constable, 1911)
The Life of Joseph Chamberlain, Vol. III, J. L. Garvin (Macmillan, 1934)
My Early Life, W. S. Churchill (Butterworth, 1930)
Great Contemporaries, W. S. Churchill (Butterworth, 1939 ed.)
Kitchener, Sir P. Magnus (Murray, 1958)
Memoirs, P. Kruger (Unwin, 1902)
The Milner Papers, Vol. II, ed. C. Headlam (Cassell, 1933)
My Picture Gallery, Viscountess Milner (Murray, 1951)
Rhodes, J. G. Lockhart and the Hon. C. M. Woodhouse (Hodder & Stoughton, 1963)
Lord Roberts, D. James (Hollis & Carter, 1954)
The Life of Lord Roberts, Sir G. W. Forrest (Cassell, 1914)
The Letters of Queen Victoria, Vol. III (Murray, 1932)

H. Background

Annual Register (Longmans, 1899, 1900)
The Anglo-Boer War, T. C. Caldwell (Heath, Boston, 1965)
The War in South Africa: Its Causes and Effects, J. A. Hobson (Nisbet, 1900)
The Fall of Kruger's Republic, J. S. Marais (Oxford, 1961)
England in the Nineteenth Century and After, D. Thomson (Penguin, 1950)
British History in the Nineteenth Century, G. M. Trevelyan (Longmans, 1937)
British Documents on the Origin of the War, 1898–1914, G. P. Gooch and H. Temperley. Vol. I, (H.M.S.O., 1927)

Index

'B-P' *means* Colonel (*later* Major-General) Robert S. S. Baden-Powell

Index © Cassell & Co, 1966